University

Reference Only

# THIS BOOK MUST NOT BE REMOVED
# FROM THE LIBRARY

# MANUAL OF ARCHIVAL DESCRIPTION
## Third Edition

# Manual of Archival Description

## Third Edition

**Margaret Procter and Michael Cook**

Gower

British Library R&D Report 5965
© British Library Board 2000

SIG 786
ISSN 1366-8218

Published by
Gower Publishing Limited          Gower
Gower House                        131 Main Street
Croft Road                        Burlington
Aldershot                         Vermont 05401
Hampshire GU11 3HR                USA
England


Margaret Procter and Michael Cook have asserted their right under the Copyright, Designs
and Patents Act 1988 to be identified as the authors of this work.

British Library Cataloguing in Publication Data
Procter, Margaret, 1959–
    Manual of archival description.   –   3rd ed.
    1. Cataloging of archival material    2. Descriptive cataloging
    I. Title    II. Cook, Michael, 1931–
    025.1´714

    ISBN 0 566 08258 6          776814
                                   y


Library of Congress Cataloging-in-Publication Data
Procter, Margaret, 1959–
    Manual of archival description / Margaret Procter and Michael Cook. – 3rd ed.
        p. cm.
    Rev. ed. of: Manual of archival description / Michael Cook. 2nd ed. c1989.
    Includes bibliographical references (p.  ) and index.
    ISBN 0-566-08258-6
      1. Cataloging of archival material–Handbooks, manuals, etc. 2. Cataloging of archival
    material–Great Britain–Handbooks, manuals, etc. 3. Cataloging of archival
    material–English-speaking countries–Handbooks, manuals, etc. I. Cook, Michael,
    1931– II. Cook, Michael, 1931- Manual of archival description. III. Title.

Z695.2 .C67 2000
025.3´414–dc21                                                          00-021004


Typeset by IML Typographers, Chester and printed in Great Britain by
MPG Books Limited, Bodmin

# Contents

v

# List of figures

**List of figures**

# Introduction

In the 11 years which have elapsed since the publication of the second edition of this manual, there have been substantial developments and innovations affecting the ways in which archivists describe their holdings, and in which they deliver the results of their work to a wider audience. Many of these developments appear in some form or other in *MAD2* – the levels and hierarchies of *ISAD(G)* are very familiar to anyone who has worked with *MAD*; SGML, mentioned as having potential for the control of archival description, has come into its own with the development of EAD; while other initiatives and developments, which seemed to hold promise as suitable archival tools, have disappeared, if not without trace, then certainly without having the impact which was once expected – MARC(AMC), for example, does not appear in this edition of *MAD*, nor do the Common Communications Format or Museum Documentation Association standards. This is not to say that the related environments from which these schemes sprang have become irrelevant – indeed, technological developments are enhancing the possibilities of resource discovery across the whole cultural spectrum. The harbinger of such new ways of access to information is of course the Internet, whose possibilities were undreamt of a decade ago. We can now look for information about archival holdings from Abingdon to Adelaide. But it remains axiomatic that the speed of the delivery of the information does not necessarily bear any relation to the quality of that information.

*MAD2* sought to provide rules for ensuring that descriptions of archival entities were of a consistent and appropriate quality. To facilitate discussion of archival description and the application of the rules themselves, it further sought to provide a taxonomy for archival descriptions. The appearance of a third edition would suggest that this approach has been successful, and it is certainly true that a standardized vocabulary of archival description has come into general use. Speaking of 'levels of description', for example, will not produce the blank expressions which it might have done a decade or so ago. The adoption of the manual as a textbook, or at least as a reference book, by the majority of the British archive training schools has of course done much to introduce new generations of archivists to a formal, standardized approach to description, while the increasing, although by no means universal, adoption of automated systems for cataloguing has forced repositories to review and revise existing house practice in a more structured way. The ready adoption of *ISAD(G)* by the professional organizations demonstrated a willingness on the part of British archivists to take standards on board, and this willingness was at least in part engendered by the community's generally successful adoption of the concept (if not always the finer detail) of *MAD2*. Initiatives such as the National Council on Archives' *Rules for the construction of personal, place and corporate names* have added to the archivists' armoury of standards at a time when funding agencies are increasingly requiring adherence to these as a prerequisite for the allocation of resources.

The first two editions of *MAD* appeared as a result of research funding from the Research and Development Department of the British Library, which led to the establishment of the Archival Description Project. The funding of such professional research has also been an area which has seen shifting fortunes in the past 11 years. Ideally the Archival Description Project team (informally reconvened) would have liked to have conducted a thorough review of national and international developments in the field of archival description and delivery methods associated with archival description, setting out best practice and thoroughly revising the rules and recommendations of *MAD2*. It proved impossible in 1998 to identify funding opportunities for this type of comprehensive revision; the alternative, proposed by the publishers, was a 'light revision' of the existing text, and it was on that basis that the current authors started work. They were gratified by the high level of interest and response to the new edition from the archive community; interestingly, the majority of respondents were those who had actively contributed to the development of *MAD2*. The consultation process was carried out almost entirely electronically, leaving the authors to wonder how they managed before the advent of e-mail.

Not surprisingly it proved difficult to stay inside the limits suggested by the phrase 'light revision', and although the organization of *MAD3* remains the same as that of *MAD2* there are many changes within the text, and in some places these are substantial. The routine application of *MAD* within repositories has in itself made revision much easier – the vocabulary has been assimilated, problems have been confronted and solved by individuals, and compromises have been suggested. On a more global level, *MAD3* has assimilated the structure and terminology of *ISAD(G)* (although the influence of *MAD* is clearly evident in *ISAD(G)* itself). An obvious example of this is *MAD3*'s adoption of 'series', rather than 'class' as the Level 3 descriptor.

The inclusion of special formats in *MAD2* presented the opportunity of dealing with the reality of descriptive practice in the generalist repository. In revision, the authors were pleasantly surprised to find that, on the whole, archivists regarded these sections as authoritative or at least found them helpful. In this edition, some of the chapters, notably those for film and video archives and sound archives, have been substantially revised while others, such as the chapter on photographic archives, have been enhanced. The chapter on electronic records must, again, necessarily remain a work in progress. Virtually rewritten, the authors would encourage the profession to take up the challenge of producing the full-length text on the subject so urgently needed.

In terms of presentation, *MAD3* includes a wider range of examples to illustrate the formats and individual data elements; these examples draw not only on hard copy formats, but on finding aids made available electronically (particularly over the Internet). The availability of these electronic metadata has served to reinforce the point, made strongly in earlier editions, that it is the quality of the content which is important – without appropriate descriptive standards the communications format, however sophisticated, can do nothing to deliver a meaningful response.

Margaret Procter and Michael Cook
University of Liverpool

# Organization of the manual

The manual is divided into five parts.

## PART I

Part I lays down general principles about the nature of archival descriptions and the problems involved in writing them. One of the most obvious things about archival descriptions is that they will not easily submit to any standard of uniformity, in the sense of laying down rigid norms. The aim of this part of the manual is to encourage compatibility between different traditions of archival description by stating general basic principles and setting down a central core of common practice. This part will be mainly useful in the context of first-entry training, but all first-time users are recommended to begin by reading it.

## PART II

Part II contains a table of the data elements occurring in archival descriptions. The 89 individual data elements are divided into two sectors, seven areas and 26 sub-areas, thus allowing the data elements to be used in connected groups.

In designing the table of elements, and in particular in allocating technical terms to its parts, the authors pay regard to earlier traditions of descriptive work, including that embodied in *AACR2*. *MAD2* attempted to assimilate terminology and points of practice derived from the traditions of sister bodies in the information professions, wherever these seemed appropriate. Accordingly, the seven areas of the data elements table may be compared with the 11 areas of *AACR2*.

## PART III

In Part III we show how the data elements, grouped into their areas and sub-areas, may be put together to make archival descriptions. Models are provided which are appropriate to descriptions at the various principal levels of management group (Level 1), group and subgroup (Level 2), series (Level 3), item (Level 4) and piece (Level 5). This is followed by guidance on how to combine descriptions in various ways. Part III concludes with standard listing conventions.

## PART IV

Part IV consists of a typology of archival descriptions, in which the rules and recommendations of *MAD3* are illustrated. Examples from actual practice are used wherever possible. The principal models for description, and the main ways in which these are combined with each other, are illustrated in this part. It is recognized, though, that in real life many different situations will occur. Procedures to meet these will have to be devised by the archivists working on the task, using the general rules and the principles which underlie these specific models.

## PART V

Part V contains the special formats. These are models for writing descriptions of archival materials which have a special character. They are designed primarily for use in general archival repositories and not in specialized repositories devoted to specific media. The specialist manuals which exist for these specific media will therefore still be required for specialized work.

There are two kinds of special formats. The first consists of material which is traditional in form (that is, mainly paper based), and is special only in that it exists in very large quantities in many large repositories and can be listed or described in ways specific to itself. The two formats of this kind in *MAD* are title deeds, and letters and correspondence. In drawing up standard formats for these, the authors have again had regard to the considerable amount of earlier work done by major repositories and cataloguing pioneers.

The second kind of special format is of archival materials which are quite different in technical ways, or in their physical make-up, from traditional paper-based material. This category includes photographs, cartographic material, architectural and other plans, sound recordings, film and video material and electronic records.

## APPENDIXES

### 1   Dictionary of technical terms

One of the purposes of the original Archival Description Project was to establish an agreed vocabulary for archival description. It was difficult to find agreement among professionals and between published glossaries and dictionaries. The dictionary of technical terms that appears at the end of *MAD3* represents the result of careful consideration of the terminology in light of the philosophy and analysis of the manual, but it has benefited substantially from the continuing work within the international archives community to establish a common vocabulary.

*Note:*   These technical terms appear in italic when first mentioned in the book. This enables the reader to cross-refer to Appendix 1.

### 2   Brief bibliography

This has been limited to works directly referred to in *MAD3*, or which are specifically relevant to questions of descriptive standards.

### 3   *ISAD(G)*

The *General International Standard Archival Description* has become a widely recognized and adopted standard within the British archival community. *MAD3* has assimilated, or made correspondences with, many of its rules, and it is reproduced here for reference. The standard is currently (1999) under review.

### 4   *ISAD(G)*/EAD/*MAD3* mapping

This is included as a reference source to help with preparation for retroconversion, data exchange and similar automated projects.

# Acknowledgements

## ACKNOWLEDGEMENTS TO *MAD2* (1989)

A work such as this depends on the labour and cooperation of many people, acting together and singly. The project team is very conscious that it is not possible to thank or to acknowledge everyone who deserves it, and hopes that any friend and colleague whose name is wrongly omitted here will overlook the fault. We would like to record our special thanks to those whose names are given below, and we would like to acknowledge and thank the following institutions for permission to use their material:

Adam Green and the Berkshire Record Office; Birmingham Library, Archives Department; Jacqueline Kavanagh and the BBC Written Archives; J.P. Hudson and the British Library Department of Manuscripts; Ian Dunn, Caroline Williams and the Cheshire Record Office; Jeannine Alton and the National Cataloguing Unit for the Archives of Contemporary Scientists, University of Bath; Marcia Taylor and Bridget Winstanley and the ESRC Data Archive, University of Essex; Jackie Cox and Clare Clubb and the Guildhall Library Manuscripts Department, Corporation of London; Gareth Williams and the Gwynedd Archives Service; Nicholas Kingsley and the Gloucestershire Record Office; Hertfordshire Record Office; Hull City Archives; India Office Library and Records; Ken Hall and the Lancashire Record Office; Liverpool City Record Office; Alistair Tough and Richard Storey and the Modern Records Centre, University of Warwick; National Museums and Galleries on Merseyside; Nottinghamshire Archives; Sheila Kurtesz and the Sir John Cass Foundation Archives; Debbie Vernon and the archives service of RTZ plc; Sheffield Record Office; David Robinson and the staff of the Surrey Record Office; Michael Roper, Mandy Banton and John Post and the Public Record

Office; Ruth Vyse and the Barnsley Archives Service; Kath Rolph and the Tyne and Wear Archives Service; Keith Sweetmore and the West Yorkshire Archives Service, and the Public Record Office of Northern Ireland. Much of the detailed work has been built up in seminar and workshop sessions, and we would like to thank once again the organizers and participants in those.

The sections on international standards have been much assisted by Hugo Stibbe (Office for Archival Descriptive Standards, National Archives of Canada); Jane Thacker (Secretary of ISO/TC9/SC9), and Ben R. Tucker (Office for Descriptive Cataloging Policy, Library of Congress).

Michael Cook and Margaret Procter
University of Liverpool
June 1989.

## ACKNOWLEDGEMENTS TO *MAD3*

The authors are delighted to have the opportunity to thank again the many people listed above who contributed to *MAD2*. In some cases the latter have been able to contribute to the development of *MAD3* in the light of applying *MAD2* principles in practice during the intervening 11 years. The authors are happy to record their thanks for a second time, and in addition to thank those other individuals and institutions who have responded so readily to requests for advice and help and willingly given their permission for their material to be used:

Anne Venables and Anglesey County Record Office; Jonathan Pepler and Cheshire Record Office; Kevin Matthias and Denbighshire Record Office; Pat Whately and the University of Dundee; Gareth Williams, Gwynedd Archives Service; Chris Kitching and Dick Sargent, Historic Manuscripts Commission; International Council on Archives; Caroline Williams, Liverpool University Centre for Archive Studies; Christine Woodland and the Modern Record Centre, University of Warwick; Ishbel Barnes, George Mackenzie, National Archives of Scotland; Caroline Dalton, and the Warden and Fellows of New College, Oxford; Sarah Tyacke and the Public Record Office; Society of American Archivists; Geoff Yeo, Royal College of Physicians of London; Walsall Local History Centre; Paul Watry, University of Liverpool Library.

Further acknowledgements for work relating to special formats appear in Chapter 17.

Margaret Procter and Michael Cook,
University of Liverpool

# PART I
# THE NATURE OF AN ARCHIVAL DESCRIPTION

# 1

# What are archives?

**1.1**   There has been much discussion of this question, particularly on the point as to whether there is a significant difference between archives and collections of manuscripts. The view taken in this manual is that there *is* a distinction between these, but that it is significant for descriptive purposes only in extreme cases. The extremes are represented by the following two models:

**1.1A**   The *Public Archives Service*. This is typified in Britain by the Public Record Office. In this tradition archives are managed by a department of the organization which created the records. Few or no materials other than those created by the governing organization are taken into the system, and the main effort of the archives' staff is to manage the accrual of new material coming into existing classes, or into new classes created by the originating departments. An important part of the service's retrieval of information or of documents may be for officials in the employing body, who require the data or materials for administrative reference.

**1.1B**   The *Historical Manuscripts Library*. In Britain this is typified by the British Library Manuscript Collections. Here the materials are acquired by purchase, gift or bequest from sources external to the library. The materials acquired are appraised, in order to ensure that they deal with appropriate subjects, but do not otherwise have any common history. In many cases the materials accepted are likely to be individual items (such as parchments or volumes) without an organic relationship with any generative system. Users of these materials are mainly members of the public, whose purpose is to conduct research.

**1.2**   In practice, most archives services combine these traditions to some extent. A common situation is one where accruals of archives are received from several sources. These include the employing organization, but archives (sometimes with periodic accruals) are also received from outside organizations (archival responsibilities being delegated); the archives of defunct bodies are conserved; and manuscripts which are of relevance to the repository's interests are collected. The local authority record offices in Britain generally follow this mixed tradition.

**1.3**   The practices and traditions of the two extreme cases are brought closer together by two factors. First, both models are concerned with the acquisition, conservation and exploitation of materials important to particular fields of study. Both the public archives services and the manuscripts departments of national libraries and museums are necessary parts of the overall information resources of the nation. Each is complementary to the other, and to other collections of archives or manuscripts held in non-national, local or private institutions.

**1.4**   The second factor which brings the two extreme cases together is the fact, empirically observed, that the materials held in each of the two kinds of institution are rarely entirely without some of the characteristics of materials sought for by the other. In a public archives service, for instance, many of the materials received will have some of the characteristics of collections of manuscripts. Archives received as accruals from a record-generating department may be technical reports (capable of being described under bibliographical rules), or even collected manuscript materials.

**1.5**   In the same way, manuscript collections acquired by a library may display archival characteristics: the papers generated by an individual or by an organization may be acquired as a whole by the library. Such materials have the most important characteristic of archives in that they have been generated by a single system, and were transferred to the archives service as a whole in order that they should be conserved and used within a self-explanatory context. Even though the nature of this transfer may be by loan, purchase, gift or rescue, one may still say that archival responsibilities have been delegated to the new custodian.

**1.6**   Because there is likely in practice to be no very clear-cut distinction between the two traditions, the view of this manual is that a standard for describing archives should begin by seeking to cover the needs of public archives services, but also go as far as possible towards covering those of

4

manuscript libraries. Where the recommendations of this manual cease to be applicable, it should be possible to apply the rules of bibliographical description.

**1.7** In-house manuals of instruction may still be necessary, to ensure that the principles and models indicated in *MAD3* are successfully applied to meet the needs and specific practices of particular archives services.

# 2

# Archival arrangement

**2.1**    The arrangement of archives is an essential feature of their management. This is true of the physical arrangement of materials on the shelves, but it is also true that arrangement is an important part of the intellectual management of the information contained in the materials. It is this intellectual management, or control, with which archival description is mainly concerned.

**2.2**    It is an important professional duty of an archivist to provide for what Sir Hilary Jenkinson called the 'moral defence' of the archives. This means that the arrangement of an archival accumulation should be based upon an analysis of the structure and methods of the originating organization and should display an understanding of the functions of different parts of the accumulation, in their relation to each other.

**2.3**    This understanding is achieved by studying and recording the original system by which the archives were generated. The archival materials may then be arranged, as far as possible, so as to preserve the original system. Beyond this brief statement, this manual does not deal with the subject area of archival arrangement (except in a brief discussion about classification schemes which lie outside the scope of this manual – see Section 9.9), but it is necessary to remember that this process of analysis and reconstruction is also an essential part of the final system for retrieval of information and exploitation of the archive. The arrangement of archives is an essential preliminary to their description.

# 3

# The function of a finding aids system

**3.1**   The theory of finding aids can be simply stated. The original materials can themselves only be arranged physically in one particular order, and this should normally be the order which demonstrates or preserves the system which brought them into being. However, users who wish to gain access to the information held in the materials need to have some way of assessing how that information might relate to the subject of their enquiries. The finding aids which help them to do this in effect allow the archives to be scanned in different and various alternative orders. They also provide access points which allow users to find the best place at which to start their search. These tools are the more necessary since users cannot normally scan the original materials themselves, which are boxed and shelved in closed storage.

**3.2**   Archival description, therefore, is aimed at setting out the various possible arrangements of the materials, as well as the original structural order. By writing down essential descriptive facts about the originals, the archivist is able to create a set of representations, which can in a sense stand in for the originals, and can be set out, arranged and classified in any number of different ways. In information theory, these descriptive substitutes are known collectively as the representation file or files. In real life, representation files in an archival repository are components of a complex finding aids system, in which the individual finding aids take the form of catalogues, lists, inventories, calendars or guides. These are backed up and linked together by retrieval aids such as indexes.

**3.3**   In effect the creation of one or more representation files enables the material to be arranged in an equivalent number of different ways.

However, if descriptions are really going to act as substitutes for the originals, then it is important to ensure that they are effective representations. Moreover, different representations are needed for different purposes. There is a general rule, therefore, that an archival description should contain, as far as possible, just those elements of information which are required for the purposes of a particular representation, and should omit data which is not needed in that particular context, thus avoiding redundancy or confusion.

**3.4**   The main skill in writing archival descriptions lies therefore in determining the nature and identifying the function of the representation file(s), and then in applying the planned system successfully to the special character of the archives in question, addressing the needs of the users and of the archives service itself.

**3.5**   Different types of representation files are needed to carry out different functions. Some are to provide administrative control of the material, some to provide intellectual control of the information based in them. Consequently, there may be many representation files used by an archives service. Ideally, they should be combined in a single finding aids system, which may be defined as a set of different representation files designed to control the management and use of an archival accumulation. The general principle is that within one archives service there should normally be a finding aids system which consists of the following:

- *web pages* providing at least general information about the repository;
- a *principal representation file* containing descriptions in structural order (that is, a list of any set of archives in an order which demonstrates the original system);
- *secondary representation files* for administrative control and repository management (for example, accession registers, shelf lists);
- *secondary representation files* in subject order (for example, a repository guide);
- *retrieval aids* (for example, 'instructions to users', indexes);
- *specialized representation files* to control processing in specific areas and to describe technically distinct materials (for example, conservation log);
- *authority files*.

Rules and recommendations for the design of finding aids systems, and for fitting together different types of finding aid, are given in Chapters 5–8.

8

**3.6**  The principal representation file, then, should ordinarily be in a structural form; that is, it should demonstrate the archival relationships between the components of the archive: this provides moral defence for the archive. (See Section 2.2 for moral defence.)

It is not easy to define clearly the phrase 'archival relationships', although it is one in constant use among archivists. Archival relationships are those links between components of an accumulation of archives which demonstrate either the original system under which the documents were generated, or an arrangement which was imposed upon them by subsequent administrative or business use. The term suggests that there is a distinction between this (archival) arrangement and any other, arbitrary, one (such as alphabetical or chronological order) which might be imposed by a librarian or user at some later stage. A finding aid in structural form and covering the contents of a complete archival accumulation should in principle be written at more than one level to provide the necessary contextual information. In addition, it is recognized that it is vital to maintain the original structural order in order to preserve and present evidential and informational values as demonstrated in the original created order.

The main representation file may take other forms. An assembly of higher level (defined in Chapter 5) descriptions (usually, but not necessarily, of group, subgroup, series) may be put together to form a guide to the contents of a repository. Such a guide may also be a structural description, based on the archival relationships of the originals.

**3.7**  Other representations, usually containing simpler descriptions, may be arranged and used as management tools for the control of the archives considered as physical objects forming the stock of the archives service.

**3.8**  Secondary or additional representation files, as well as other retrieval aids, may be arranged and presented in ways that promote subject access. These may be termed subject-based, as opposed to structural, finding aids.

Further examination of the objectives and function of finding aids appears in Section 9.4.

**3.9**  Indexes are retrieval aids which provide access points into the representation files, so that users can find out where to begin their search for information. Normally any representation file which contains free text should be indexed. In addition, automated systems may provide specialist fields for index data.

Indexes to different files may sometimes be merged into a union index, but there are many difficulties in achieving this, and it is difficult to recommend it without qualification. Merged indexes may be an important element in an integrated finding aids system. Indexing is a complex activity on which there is a considerable literature. This manual does not deal with the principles and problems involved.

Further consideration of indexing appears in Sections 9.5 and 9.8. See also the rule of representation, Section 8.4.

# 4

# Levels of archival description

**4.1**  Archival material must always be managed, and therefore described, at more than one level (the multi-level rule: see Chapter 5). This is not necessarily true of library collections of manuscript material, so that this feature of archival description is one which causes the most misunderstanding between archivists, museum curators and librarians.

**4.2**  It follows from this that the units of description, where archives are concerned, are usually collectivities. The cataloguing units analogous to books in libraries are groups, subgroups or series (all of which are collectivities), as well as items or pieces (which are unitary).

**4.3**  There may be many levels of archival arrangement, and hence of description. There must always be a minimum of two. Four levels are normally needed to provide satisfactory finding aids to the holdings of a repository, and there is a strong possibility that at least two more will be needed in some cases. There is no limit, in principle, to the number of levels which may be used. Figure 4.1 illustrates some possible levels of arrangement.

**4.4**  On the other hand, the physical extent of the archives is not a criterion for establishing levels of archival arrangement. Consequently, although the higher levels, such as groups, normally represent very large accumulations of material, there are also cases where groups are very small. At the extreme, a group can sometimes consist of only one item.

**4.5**  To establish the nomenclature of these levels, a definition of the terms used is given in this section. In practice, it is often less confusing to

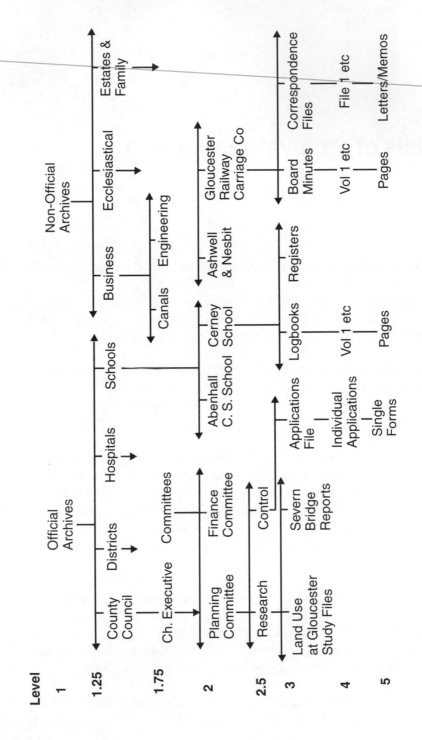

**Figure 4.1  Levels of arrangement and description**
[*Source:* Gloucestershire Record Office]

use numbers to denote levels than to use terminology which may seem over-complex. The numeration of the main levels is intended to be standard, so that descriptions may be readily compared and accessed.

## 4.6 THE LEVELS OF DESCRIPTION

### 4.6A Level 0: Repository

The highest level is that of the *repository*. Any system of multi-repository finding aids, or national registration, or simply data exchange, must provide for a repository identification and the repository code allocated by the National Register of Archives should be used in this context. When international access to descriptive records is envisaged, the appropriate country code of ISO 3166 (*Codes for the representation of names of countries*) should be used in addition.

Comparable cooperative finding aids are also in use among museums and libraries. However, in the following analysis the repository level is treated separately since, although it should appear in the heading of archival descriptions, there is no need to take decisions about it in relation to sets of archives being arranged or described within the repository.

This level is numbered 0.

### 4. 6B Level 1: Management group

Within the repository, the number and structure of the levels to be used in the case of any particular archive may be decided in the light of the nature of the materials being processed, together with management needs. Repositories frequently divide their holdings into groups that have some common characteristic or relationship. These categories of holdings are usually treated as divisions of archival level: for example, county record offices often divide their holdings into Official, Private and Ecclesiastical archives. These and similar divisions then constitute the broadest level for management and description purposes: the application of this is most often seen in guides to repositories.

Groupings of this kind may be termed *management levels*. The use of the term 'record group' in the USA may be compared.

Management levels are numbered 1.

Management levels may have subordinate sublevels, numbered as 1.nn (1 + decimal fraction).

Divisions of the holdings of a repository below Level 1 may be considered 'real' (as opposed to conceptual), because they are based on actual physical accumulations of archive material, and not upon some perceived likeness between the creating agencies, or upon management convenience.

Figure 4.1 illustrates the use of management levels in a repository.

### 4.6C   Level 2: Group
*ISAD(G)   Fonds*

**4.6C1**   The *group* is the largest entity of organizationally related records established on the basis of provenance: the archives of a distinct organization, body or individual.

Group levels are numbered 2.

**4.6C2**   In manuscript libraries, and in archives services which receive significant quantities of material from exterior sources by purchase or on deposit, the term *collection* has in the past been used for a similar body of archives. 'Collection' should be restricted to cases where there is an artificial gathering together of manuscripts from diverse sources, which are to be treated as a group.

**4.6C3**   The term 'group' does not imply any specific size or bulk in the archive holding concerned. In most archive services, groups may be large or small. The essential point is that a group is an assembly of archival entities which belong together because they were generated by a body with a distinct character and a certain degree of autonomy.

Notwithstanding any levels established for repository management (Level 1), the group is the principal level of archival description, and is the basic entity for purposes of management and description.

**4.6C4**   Descriptions of the groups held by a repository may be regarded as forming a separate file from descriptions at lower levels. This is because frequent changes in the administrative structure of creating organizations have loosened the connection between groups and series. The file of group/subgroup descriptions may then be regarded as a type of authority file governing elements in the descriptions of series and below. If this separation between group and series level is effected, the repository must make sure that adequate cross-reference exists.

The *International Standard Archival Authority Record for Corporate Bodies, Persons and Families – ISAAR(CPF)* – sets out the types of information to be included in an archival authority record and should be used in the creation of any such authority records such as those to be included in the proposed National Name Authority File.[1]

**4.6C5**   Repositories should have a rule about how to establish group levels within the context of the totality of their holdings. It is important that when all arrangement has been done, descriptions of the archives of all distinct record-creating entities should be set at Level 2. This allocation of level refers to (a) the distinctness or autonomy of the body which created the archives; and (b) the presence of these archives, or a part of them, within the repository. It does not relate to political or administrative hierarchies or levels of dependency among outside bodies.

This can be illustrated by examining pre-1974 English local government. Urban District Councils exercised fewer powers, and might in some circumstances be subjected to oversight by the county councils, but despite this administrative dependence UDCs rank as groups (Level 2) in their own right, as indeed would County Boroughs or Parish Councils. Thus these record-producing organizations can be numbered as follows:

| | | |
|---|---|---|
| Level | 2 | Essex County Council |
| | 2.5 | Essex County Council Education Department |
| Level | 2 | Churchtown UDC |
| | 2.5 | Churchtown UDC Cleansing Department |
| Level | 2 | Chapeltown UDC |
| | 2.5 | Chapeltown UDC Cleansing Department |
| Level | 2 | County Borough of Burnley |
| Level | 2 | Habergham Eaves Parish Council |

## 4.6D   Level 2.5: Subgroup

*ISAD(G)   Sub-fonds*

**4.6D1**   The *subgroup* is a body of related records within a group, usually consisting of the records of a subordinate administrative unit, or of a functional division within the creating organization, or simply of a function distinguishable from others represented in the material.

**4.6D2**   Subgroups are numbered by using decimals to indicate values between 2.001 and 2.999. This device allows a virtually indefinite number of levels of subgroups (subgroups of subgroups, in effect) to be inserted at

---

[1]   For information see *British Library Research and Innovation Report 91: National name authority file: report to the National Council on Archives* by Peter Gillman, 1998, available at:
http://www.hmc.gov.uk/pubs/pubs.htm [viewed 10 February 2000].

levels below that of the group. Since subgroups are always dependent on the group they belong to, any access to data (for example, through automated databases) should occur at Level 2, with the descriptions appropriate to decimals of 2 appended.

**4.6D3** Subgroups are in principle natural divisions within groups. Groups may also be divided into subgroups for purposes of repository management. Where this is done, the subgroups are subdivisions of a group, established by archivists as a result of analysis, enabling the group to be broken up into manageable smaller units. Subgroups therefore should serve this purpose, that is, they should be convenient in size wherever possible. However, ideally subgroups are 'natural': they should represent the archives of distinct organizational divisions of the originating organization, or distinct functions which can be distinguished in the materials.

**4.6D4** Where administrative subdivisions did not exist in the originating body, an analysis may reveal that different functions can still be identified. This is particularly useful in the case of the archives of a private individual. An individual might very probably have had functions or activities in several different spheres of life, or in connection with different projects: these may be made the basis of subgroups in arranging that individual's papers.

**4.6D5** It is sometimes possible to confuse subgroups and series (Level 3), especially in the case of smaller archival accumulations. The principle is that subgroups are based upon an analysis of the originating organization (or the various aspects of the life of a person) and the different functions documented in the archive; whereas series are based upon a physical likeness or character, derived from the way they were created and used in the originating system.

In past practice, subgroups and series have often been merged, especially where a particular group has been managed at less than four levels. This is not good practice. If difficult cases arise, it is better to leave the subgroup level unused, and use series as the main description level.

**4.6D6** The group and subgroup levels are intimately linked, since the functions represented in subgroups are interlinked in the activities of the originator. Since the analysis of original structures is of the essence of archival description, it is suggested that subgroups should generally be picked out in the text of group descriptions, with their own headings or side-headings. In some cases subgroup descriptions are present but are buried within the text of group descriptions, without separate headings.

## 4.6E   Level 3: Series[2]

**4.6E1**   The *series* is a set of documents which result from the same original compiling or filing process, are of broadly similar physical shape and informational content, and are referred to collectively by a specific title (for example, invoices, series attendance registers, out-letter books).

Series level descriptions are numbered 3.

**4.6E2**   In manuscript libraries, for practical purposes, a moderately sized assembly of items gathered together because they are of a common character may be taken as a series.

**4.6E3**   More generally, there are occasions where composite series may be permitted. This is where a group or subgroup consists mainly of individual items or very small series without strong distinguishing characteristics. In this kind of case, it may be convenient to divide the items into composite series, each consisting of items of reasonably like character. (A typical example might be 'Memorabilia'.) The practice is not encouraged, but is permitted where otherwise it would be difficult to find an intermediate grouping for the materials which would assist management. Notwithstanding this provision, it is always permissible to leave the series level empty if the original material lacks it.

**4.6E4**   Series may be divided into subseries if the physical character of the series, as determined by the original system, suggests it. An example might be the case where a filing system has developed a specialized subsystem based on a single set of files, especially where this subsystem appears at a particular date and is reabsorbed into the parent series at another date.

Figure IV.15 (see pages 147–8) illustrates a subseries description.

## 4.6F   Level 4: Item
*ISAD(G)   File*
**4.6F1**   The *item* is the basic physical unit which is used in the handling, storage and retrieval of archives.

**4.6F2**   Normally, an item has an easily recognizable physical integrity. For example, bundles, files, volumes or rolls are clearly items because they

---

[2]   In previous editions of *MAD* the term 'class' was used at Level 3. This has changed in line with common national practice (including PRO usage) and international practice (*ISAD(G)*).

are physically appropriate for handling. A practical definition might be that items are the units which are produced for reference in the searchroom. A records management service may typically deal with a box at this level. Items are often divided further into individual documents – these can be described at Level 5 (see Section 4.6G).

**4.6F3** There may be some difficulty in determining whether to set descriptions at Level 4 or at Level 5. Sometimes item-level descriptions are determined by repository practice, as when a decision has been made to take the physical unit such as the box, bundle or container as the basis for listing within a group.

In other cases, item descriptions may be used to represent an intermediate stage in the levels. If this is done, item descriptions will form headnotes to piece descriptions. Alternatively, Level 4 may be omitted. There should be agreement on policy in this regard, since access to data at Levels 4 and 5 may be significant in inter-repository on-line networks.

**4.6F4** Where a series consists only of individual documents, and the box or bundle is not used as a unit of description, it will not be necessary to use Level 4.

### 4.6G   Level 5: Piece
*ISAD(G)   Item*
**4.6G1** *Pieces* are the indivisible individual documents which make up an item. Level 5 descriptions are only possible where Level 4 is used.

**4.6G2**  When pieces are components of items, it may be useful or necessary to describe these separately. Thus a volume contains separate folios, gatherings or pages; a file contains separate sheets or pages; a box (where this is the item) contains many files, bundles or loose papers, and so on. Some of these may themselves contain individual components: a box may hold a set of booklets or folders, each containing papers or pages.

Pieces within pieces are theoretically subpieces, but this ugly term may perhaps be avoided in practice by using appropriate traditional terms such as page, folio, folder, and so on.

# 5

# The multi-level rule
## *ISAD(G) §1 and §2*

**5.1**  Archival descriptions should normally be written at two or more levels, a higher level and a lower level.[1] These can also be described as governing and subordinate levels.

**5.2**  *Higher level descriptions* govern related lower level descriptions, by giving information on background, context and provenance, together with information which applies to the whole of the governed materials. *Lower level descriptions* provide information specific to the material. Planning decisions must therefore be made to decide which levels should be used, how they should be distinguished, and how they should be combined in the final finding aid.

**5.3**  When completed, a finding aid must contain higher level and lower level components. Either of these may contain more than one level. Generally, higher level descriptions are at group, subgroup or series level, and lower level descriptions are at item or piece level. However, whether a description may be seen as higher level or lower level is entirely relative: an item description may act as the higher level component of a finding aid comprising mainly piece descriptions, for example. Similarly, sets of group or series descriptions are lower level in relation to management group or group descriptions.

---

[1]  The terms 'higher' and 'lower' replace the terms 'macro' and 'micro' which were used in *MAD2*.

## 5.4 Higher level descriptions
*ISAD(G) §2.1*
Higher level descriptions have the following characteristics:

- they describe the archival entity as a whole, and do not deal with it on a one-by-one basis;
- they include all common or overall information relating to the entity covered;
- they provide one of the instruments for the management of the archives within the repository;
- they allow users to isolate relevant groups, subgroups or series within which items or pieces may be searched for;
- they may often be suitable for inclusion in authority files.

## 5.5 Common and relevant information
*ISAD(G) §2.2*
Information which is common to the different parts of an archive should be given at the highest possible level of description (the higher level description), and not repeated in each successive lower level description.

If this rule is neglected, redundancy usually results *(ISAD(G) §2.4)*.

For example, use:

| D19/3/ | Diaries 1901–1907 |
|--------|-------------------|
| 1 | 1901 |
| 2 | 1902 |
| 3 | 1903 |
| 4 | 1904 |

And not:

| D19/3/ | Diaries 1901–1907 |
|--------|-------------------|
| D19/3/1 | Diary 1901 |
| D19/3/2 | Diary 1902 |
| D19/3/3 | Diary 1903 |
| D19/3/4 | Diary 1904 |

## 5.6 Lower level descriptions
Lower level descriptions deal with those components of the archival entity which are governed by a higher level description, on a one-after-another basis. They may serve to identify specific items or pieces for production to users, or to direct users to the whereabouts of specific finding aids.

## 5.7 Combining descriptions

*ISAD(G) §2.3*

Descriptions of related archives at different levels are frequently combined in one catalogue, but each level should always be distinguished from others. This can be done in the preliminary listing stage by writing the appropriate level numbers in the left or right margin, or, where the list is being prepared for public searching, by consistent use of typeface styles or sizes at the different levels, providing a visual aid to level analysis. In an automated system it is of course easy to include the level number in a dedicated field where it can be shown or suppressed as required.

**5.8** Common information in the higher level description may be set out for the direction of the user in a headnote, explaining the structure of the descriptions which follow. Alternatively, higher level descriptions may appear as title pages to lower level descriptions which follow (Chapter 6) or in a separate linked file such as those provided as authority files.

**5.9** Large and complex archival accumulations will tend to require description at four or more levels. Most commonly these are group, sub-group, series and item and/or piece levels, but other combinations are possible. Additional levels may be inserted below each of these. Where this is done, level numbers using decimals can be used to distinguish one from another.

**5.10** Small and simple archival entities will normally need description at two or more levels. Even an archival entity consisting of only one document needs a two-level description. In this case, the higher level description would treat the document as a series or as a group. The lower level description would deal with it as an item or piece and would contain more detailed information. The higher level description may be set out as a title page before the lower level description, or as a headnote above it, or in a separate linked file.

**5.11** However, it is sometimes permissible to omit the lower level descriptions, and to give only the higher level ones, where it is desired to give users a broad overview of holdings, without a detailed or specific aspect. In principle, it is never acceptable to provide lower level descriptions without appropriate higher level descriptions to govern them. This is because the higher level descriptions provide information on background, context and provenance which is required for the moral defence of the archives. Although in practice many users appear to be satisfied with discrete lower level (usually item) descriptions, archivists must nevertheless supply the related higher level descriptions somewhere in the finding aids system, in order to maintain the integrity of the information provided. This rule particularly operates where the finding aids system is automated, since in these systems users can call up items without first consulting the higher level descriptions.

**5.12** Multi-level descriptions of the same archival entity, or parts thereof, should be cross-referred where necessary. However, good organization of the material will reduce the need for many cross-references. It is preferable that cross-references should not be inserted into text in great numbers; they may be placed in separate fields or spaces on the page. Cross-references may also be made by the use of information in headnotes. Multi-level descriptions may share an index.

An assembly of descriptions of different archives at the same level, or range of levels, may need cross-references to the appropriate lower level descriptions. These descriptions too may share an index.

# 6

# Fitting levels together: headnotes, title pages and linked files

**6.1**  Finding aids systems are made up by combining sets of descriptions at different levels, with links between them. The different format of each level may make this difficult in some cases, and certainly introduces an important difficulty when automation is in view. Indexes should be provided to give additional access points.

**6.2**  Group, subgroup and series descriptions relating to the same archive accumulation are usually closely related to each other. A normal arrangement of these descriptions is:

Level
   2    Group
   2.5  Subgroups at end of main text
   3    Series in structural order

This would be a customary arrangement in a *guide* to the holdings of an archives service where sets of descriptions at Levels 2 and 3 are combined horizontally (see Figure IV.6, p. 143). The whole gives an overview of the general holdings of the repository, or of a significant part of it.

**6.3**  Similarly a *catalogue* is a set of descriptions which relate to a single area of the holdings of a repository, usually a group/collection with its components, but also often the contents of a management group (Level 1). The catalogue brings together related descriptions at levels down from the group as far as the item or piece, again with an index to bring it together. This is a vertical combination.

**6.4** Descriptions may be combined by cross-referring between separate files. If this treatment is decided on, higher level descriptions form authority files. National and international standards exist for the creation of these authority files, that is, NCA *Rules* and *ISAAR(CPF)*.[1]

**6.5** Alternatively, descriptions may be combined within the same finding aid using the relevant higher level description as a *headnote*. Thus a group description may serve as the headnote to a series of series descriptions. More usually, a series description may be used as the headnote to an item description. In fact, since any description must have a reference heading which places it in context, some sort of headnote of this kind is normally essential.

**6.6** It is possible – indeed usual – for more than two levels of description to appear on the same page. Where this happens, the headnote to the lowest level may be an entry within a sequence which is itself governed by a higher level description. Thus there might be a sequence of descriptions like this:

Level 2.5    Subgroup description
Level 3      Series within the subgroup
Level 4      Item within the series
Level 3      Another series
Level 4      Item within the series
             etc.

There are models for headnotes at any level. (For rules and examples see Section 15.11.)

**6.7** Another way of linking higher level and lower level descriptions is by means of a *title page* or *title page section*.
    The principal function of a title page is to display the identity statement (usually the title) of an archival entity, together with other useful information. This may amount to the whole of a higher level description, thus forming a reasoned introduction to the lower level descriptions which form the bulk of the data. Title page sections are expanded title pages, where extensive textual entries follow the higher level title.
    A title page section may be followed by a list of contents of the descriptions which follow.

---

[1]    See Appendix 2: Brief Bibliography for details.

# 7

# The two modes of archival description

**7.1** Archival descriptions fall into two broad types, based upon the way in which they are laid out. The two different styles of layout are called *modes*. Descriptions at any level may belong either to the *paragraph mode* or to the *list mode*. *Paragraph mode descriptions* are those in which most textual entries are lengthy and are set out like text in a book; *list mode descriptions* are tabulated.

Guidelines for constructing paragraph and list mode descriptions are given in Section 15, and examples of the various modes described here are given in Part IV.

**7.2** Finding aids in *list mode* consist of tabulated columns, in which the entries for any individual level appear arranged under the field heading in columns, each entry occupying column spaces horizontally across the page. This mode can only usefully be employed when the main text entry or entries (typically in central columns) is relatively short. There is no formal limit to the length of textual entries in list mode fields, but the need to limit tabulated margins to left and right will determine the practical limitations of this mode.

List mode descriptions may include entries at different levels, the higher levels governing the lower levels. Where this is done, level distinctions are indicated by setting the left and right margins: the higher level descriptions will have narrower margins than the lower level descriptions which depend on them.

**7.3** Finding aids in *paragraph mode* consist mainly of free text entries written out consecutively down the page, like numbered paragraphs in a book or report. This style is clearly to be preferred wherever text of several lines is to be entered for any field.

Although paragraph mode is quite normal for group descriptions, it can be used also for any level. The important consideration is the presence of long text or the desire to use the whole width of the page.

**7.4**   The mode which is chosen for any particular finding aid should remain constant throughout. To change from one mode to another within one finding aid is not recommended, although it is permissible to use a paragraph-mode higher level description as a headnote to cover a list-mode lower level set of descriptions.

**7.5**   Very commonly, descriptions at group, subgroup and series levels are set out in paragraph mode.

Description at group level is customarily based upon a free text administrative and custodial history, together with a content and structure note. Subgroups may be defined within this administrative and custodial history, but may have a secondary free text history of their own, which gives some general description of the physical nature of the materials.

Series are normally described in a free text summary: this is the Content and Structure Area, in which the bulkiest element is the abstract. This may be accompanied by specific information (size of holding, physical format, dates) in dedicated fields which figure somewhat more prominently.

**7.6**   In the same way, descriptions at item or piece level are commonly set out in list mode. In particular, items or pieces are often described in tabulated lists containing three or more fields (typically reference, title, span dates).

**7.7**   Despite these common patterns, finding aids which employ list mode for group, subgroup or series descriptions and paragraph mode for item or piece descriptions are to be found. The mode chosen should correspond to the objective of the finding aid and the quantity of free text to be entered, and is not determined by the level of description being used.

**7.8**   The kinds of information used in descriptions at each level are described in more detail in Chapter 15.

# 8

# Depth of description

**8.1**  Repositories are responsible for controlling the quality of their archival descriptions. An important factor in this is consistency in depth of description. In deciding this amount of detail regard must be had to the several factors noted in this chapter.

**8.2**  Depth of description must be determined, in the first place, by the aims of the office's finding aids system, or the objective of the listing work in hand. The next most important factor is the type of documentary material that is to be dealt with (special formats demand appropriate treatment). After this, the main determining factor is that of the resources available: resources of space, staff, time and skill. Since these, and the relative pressure of work waiting to be done, must always vary, the depth of description for the same type of records may vary between record offices; however, at the highest levels standards must be consistent in terms of content.

In terms of international exchange of information, *ISAD(G)* specifies the minimum information required in its Section I.5 (see p. 265).

## 8.3   Preliminary or bulk listing

Repositories which use a system of double listing (an initial preliminary list, followed in due course by a final description) may aim to produce a brief summary list based upon a rapid initial analysis. *MAD* does not offer models for preliminary listing, but recommends none the less that analysis into levels be carried out, and level numbers written in the margin against the first line of the entry in any particular description. It should be possible to see to which levels preliminary (or bulk) lists are intended to belong.

# RULES GOVERNING DEPTH OF DESCRIPTION

## 8.4    The rule of representation:

*Every description should be able to serve its purpose as a representation of the original it refers to.*

**8.4A**    Descriptions are representations of the original documents, or sets of documents, on which they are based. These representations have been made in order to carry out some purpose for which the original was not available. See the principle of the representation file, Chapter 3.

**8.4B**    In most cases, archival descriptions are 'general purpose' representations which have been created in order to facilitate access to the materials for undifferentiated series of users. In other cases, they can be specialized finding aids. These will include a means of accessing all the material relevant to a specialist purpose and are directed to a special series of users (for example, lists of maps, or photographs, or material relating to trams, where each discrete description is drawn from the finding aid of a different group). At the same time they will contain some explanation as to how the particular finding aids relate to the general finding aids system.

**8.4C**    The representation should always be adequate for its purpose; that is, users should be able to identify which material they wish to see, by reading the finding aid.

**8.4D**    Various refinements of this purpose are possible. Users at a distance, who are not able to order up the originals, may be able to use published representations for some of their purposes. Very full representations, in the form of calendars or transcripts, may be able to replace their originals – in this case the representation file is a surrogate file. The exact fullness of the representation required is a matter of repository planning.

**8.4E**    Other purposes may be administrative. For example, repository management may demand that there should be a shelf list, or location register, in order that a stock check can be done, or particular materials found. A shelf list should probably only contain such data elements as reference code, title, size/bulk and location. This information is enough to provide a representation which is adequate for its purpose, and more detail would only get in the way.

## 8.5    The rule of information retrieval:

*Descriptions should contain in their text all the keywords needed in order to pro-vide retrieval in the circumstances envisaged for this representation.*

**8.5A**    Keywords, in this sense, are the terms which could be used in a search, either manual or by automatic means. Keywords may be written into narrative text fields (for example, within an administrative and custodial history) or they may appear in dedicated fields provided for them in the finding aids design. When they are given as headings in dedicated fields they are usually called access points. See Section 9.5.

**8.5B**    The range and accuracy of searches possible may be improved if an index vocabulary or thesaurus has been provided.

## 8.6    The rule against bias:

*Descriptions should accurately reflect the actual content, meaning or signifi-cance of the original they represent.*

**8.6A**    It is possible for a description to misrepresent the original it refers to. This is sometimes because old and inappropriate finding aids are still in use, but there are also examples where a bias has been introduced as a result of poor planning of recent finding aids.

**8.6B**    The possibility of bias arising from inappropriate description must always exist. Representations cannot normally be full replicas of the original, but must be designed to contain only the data most relevant to the immediate purpose of the representation file (Section 8.4A). Even though they may suit the immediate purposes of the control or retrieval system, representations can only be partial portraits of the original. If the features selected for inclusion are an accurate reflection of the original in the circumstances, the portrait is in effect a good one. In other cases, the data elements highlighted may correspond to currently fashionable topics. In any case, however good the likeness is, it is effective only in the context it was designed for.

**8.6C**    Bias may be introduced because the description offered is too brief, or because it is too full. Description may be made at an inappropriate level, or at an insufficient number of levels. In particular, details appropriate to lower level descriptions may introduce a bias when put into higher level descriptions, because they will generate keywords for index or search which overweigh terms relating to what are genuinely the dominant subjects.

**8.6D**   Bias may also be the result of inappropriate data elements being selected for inclusion. It may be possible to use the headnote to explain policy on choice of data items, particularly where a particular kind of user is in mind.

Writing in place-names which are appendant to personal names in title deeds, for example, might result in clogging the place-name index. Similarly, to write in the places of domicile of witnesses in title deeds might give a bias to descriptions or retrieval aids based on topographical holdings.

Again, in Quarter Sessions rolls, more index entries might be made for cases of riot than for other events. Without a covering explanation, this might give a bias to the final description, by suggesting that questions of riot occupied the business of the court in some special way or that the county was continually in uproar.

**8.6E**   Bias may also be the result of a lack of uniformity in the description of different parts of the repository's holdings. If there has been a variation in the depth of description accorded to later accessions, because of lack of resources, then users may not be certain what reliance to place on the finding aids, or they may give a misplaced reliance on them. Repositories should seek to introduce quality control processes which will enable depth of description to be standardized at appropriate levels.

# 9

# Other aspects of archival description

**9.0**   As well as level and depth, other aspects of description should be considered when designing a finding aids system:

9.1   The variety and uniqueness of archival materials.
9.2   The size and complexity of the originating organization.
9.3   The accrual of new material to existing classes.
9.4   The purpose and design of finding aids systems.
9.5   Access points into the finding aids system.
9.6   Retrieval strategies by users.
9.7   The variety of terminology used.
9.8   Indexing.
9.9   Classification schemes.
9.10  Reference coding.
9.11  National and international standards and formats applicable to archival description.

## 9.1   The variety and uniqueness of archival materials
**9.1A**   It is axiomatic that each archive accumulation has a character of its own, and that this character impresses itself on the form and content of its finding aids. Archivists are often advised to allow the archive to speak for itself in shaping the descriptive material.

**9.1B**   At the same time, the describer's independence in allowing this self-expression of the archive may be circumscribed in two directions. Even where the guidelines set out in *MAD* have been applied, a repository may also try to lay down a house style which determines at least the general appearance of the resulting lists, and the examples in Part IV show that in practice most archive accumulations are particular instances of broad groups or categories of archive types. Even where there has been no guidance from house styles, archivists have usually tried to follow pre-established patterns or classification schemes wherever possible.

**9.1C** *MAD* guidelines still allow an archive accumulation to impose its own special character upon the descriptions based on it, and at the same time, also, to:

- conform to house styles and standards; and
- conform to appropriate general models.

**9.1D** *MAD* standards aim to provide a model which, while remaining sufficiently flexible to allow a proper response to the needs of specific archives, allows for the interrogation of comparable data within different repositories with a minimum of adjustment on the part of researcher or archivist.

## 9.2    The size and complexity of the originating organization

**9.2A**    The size and complexity of the originating organization is an important factor in the design of finding aids. A large and complex organiz-ation produces archives which will need to be arranged in several levels. These levels have to be combined, and retrieval aids provided, to bring the components of the finding aids system together.

**9.2B**    Neither size nor complexity affects the analysis of a set of archives into levels of arrangement. It is possible to meet groups which consist of few items, or even of only one. Subject to the multi-level rule (Chapter 5), any appropriate level of description may be used or omitted in any particu-lar case.

**9.2C**    The design of databases, and of rules for house styles, must allow for this diversity of structure – *MAD* gives models for different circum-stances, but it will often be necessary to adapt these to local and specific conditions. Due attention should always be paid to the possibility that information sharing or remote access may be available, and there should be consistency in the construction of descriptions appropriate to the *MAD* levels. A 'class' in one repository may be a 'series' elsewhere, but both of them are Level 3 and the descriptions appropriate to them should be comparable.

**9.2D**   Changes in the administrative structure of the creating agency may affect the way in which accruals are managed: see Section 9.3.

## 9.3   The accrual of new material to existing series
**9.3A**   The ability to manage accruals to existing series is central to archive administration.

It is of course a question mainly for archives services which manage materials accruing from continuing bodies, such as government depart-ments, and can therefore best be illustrated by practice in large repositories attached directly to an administration. However, even manuscript libraries can experience the phenomenon of an archive accumulation which arrives in two or more successive deposits, and sometimes in a series of deposits which are likely to recur an indefinite number of times.

**9.3B**   Some archival entities have received accruals in the past which have affected their structure, but further accruals are not expected. In general it is good practice to retain the arrangement determined by the originating system, including the divisions which may have been intro-duced by deposit in two or more accruals. However, there may be cases in which this would create unnecessary anomalies, and where it would seem desirable to restore an underlying original arrangement.

**9.3C**   Administrative change over time causes problems in the manage-ment of later accruals. When an archive-generating function is transferred from one administrative department to another, the archives service must inevitably make a decision about how to deal with new accruals of archives relating to that function. Such accruals must either be added to the original series or they must be treated as a new series.

If the former choice is adopted, an anomaly will arise, for the later sections of the relevant series will appear to be in the 'wrong' group: archives will be listed under the general heading of a department which did not in fact have any responsibility for their creation. If the latter choice is taken, the continuing records of a particular function will be broken up into sections not necessarily readily understood by users, and divided among different groups.

The latter approach gained wide currency in the last few years, most notably through its development by the Australian archives community. Here, the 'wrong' group problem is solved by the separation of administra-tive histories from the series of records they (and their successors) produce. These administrative histories form an authority file which can be attached to the records according to the date the physical records were produced.

**9.3D**   It is recommended that in repositories where there are regular accruals to groups and/or series, descriptions at group, subgroup and series level should be processed and stored separately from descriptions at item and piece level (with suitable cross-references). The higher level descriptions may then be regarded as an authority file governing the lower level descriptions.

**9.3E**   Solutions to the problems of accruals belong mainly to the area of archival management rather than that of archival description, though obviously the solution adopted will have an effect on the finding aids and means of access. Successful assimilation of new accruals depends on the design of the levels of arrangement and description.

**9.3F**   A repeated sequence of new accruals to a series will tend to produce unnaturally long series, and therefore unwieldy finding aids (at least in terms of hard copy lists). Where there are frequent accruals, the resulting lists may have numerous amended sections.

The prospect of constant new additions will make it difficult to provide an accurate overview, or higher level description, and at item level some way will have to be found of incorporating new lists. Users may have to consult different annual sections or appendixes to the list. Cross-indexing will be made difficult, and complex referencing may be needed. Periodical reassessments, resulting in newly written higher level descriptions or revised authority files, should be made. This suggestion reinforces a general recommendation that all publicly available finding aids need to be revised from time to time.

**9.3G**   Where later accruals to a series have been restructured or re-referenced by an organization which has taken them over before their transfer to the archives, then, in general, it would be preferable to retain the later structure and references. (For example, two companies carrying out the same type of business may merge, and the filing system of one is merged into the filing system of the second, acquiring thereby a new reference. A full description of a whole series would include a note of the obsolete reference codes, as well as referring to the merger itself in the Administrative History Sub-area of the group or subgroup description.)

**9.3H**   If there are to be accruals to the archives of a superseded body, this body should be treated as a group or major subgroup. In all cases, the higher level description should make the accrual status clear to the searcher by entries in the Administrative and Custodial History Sub-areas.

**9.3I**   Where there are gaps in sequences of archives, reference codes indicating the missing entities should be provided in square brackets if possible.

**9.3J**   The interspersal of later accruals within a numbered sequence is problematic. The use of subnumber 4/57/1 for an accrual to 4/57 implies a hierarchical relationship which does not, in fact, exist. A solution is to give the accrual the next number in the sequence, but put the description itself in its correct place. For example:

| | |
|---|---|
| 4/56 | 1918–1919 |
| 4/57 | 1919–1920 |
| 4/108 (sic) | (Nov) 1920 – (June) 1921 |
| | This volume, missing until 1998, was purchased at auction. |
| 4/58 | 1921–1922 |

The reference is after all used primarily as a unique identifier for retrieval, a process which needs little or no contextual information.

Generally, the problem of referencing accruals will be mitigated if the reference codes are numbered in sequences which are confined to specific levels or sections. See Section 9.10 for reference codes generally.

## 9.4   The purpose and design of finding aids systems

**9.4A**   A finding aids system may contain both structural and subject-based finding aids. (Examples are given in Section 3.5.) Structural finding aids will always be regarded as primary by archivists, and will normally constitute the main representation file, because they provide for the moral defence of archives.

Structural lists, however, may not be regarded by users as the most immediately useful, and in extreme cases it may even be necessary to provide specific programmes of user education to make them intelligible. Subject-oriented finding aids do not give moral defence of the archives but may be more immediately usable to many readers.

With due regard to the principle of moral defence, in cases of doubt the requirements of users should be taken as the guiding principle in the planning of a finding aids system.

**9.4B**   The aim in establishing a finding aids system is to ensure that each finding aid has an objective complementary to the objectives of each of the other finding aids.

**9.4C**   There are two broad categories of finding aids. First, those whose objective is management or administrative control (the management of the physical processes, including retrieval). These are finding aids constructed mainly or entirely for the use of staff within the archives service (in-house finding aids: an example would be a location list or shelf register). Secondly are those finding aids concerned with intellectual control (the management of the information contained in the material), intended both for archives service staff and external readers.

**9.4D**   Finding aids intended for access by users should be regarded as published material. Wherever possible, this publication should be formal, making use of legal deposit and cataloguing-in-publication (CIP) facilities. Where this is not possible, *de facto* publication may be achieved by making the finding aids available to users in the searchroom, via the Internet, and by distributing copies to the National Register of Archives, and to appropriate reference points (such as public or academic libraries) elsewhere.

Finding aids intended only for in-house use are not subject to the requirement of publication. The degree of confidentiality to be accorded to in-house finding aids is of course a matter for decision by the repository itself.

**9.4E**   Recommendations and rules for combining sets of descriptions, given in Chapter 15, should be followed.

## 9.5   Access points into the finding aids system
*ISAD(G) §I.8*
**9.5A**   Every finding aids system has access points. These are the points at which any user, whether internal (repository staff or staff of the employing agency) or external (academic or member of the public), begins a search for relevant material. It is desirable that the finding aids system should be planned in such a way that suitable access points are presented to the user, and lead to successful retrieval outcomes.

In *AACR2*, access points are entries in dedicated fields which can be extracted in turn and used as a heading to a bibliographic description. The function of access points within an archival finding aid is somewhat different, since the single-level set of descriptions is not a practical model. Instead, access points should be regarded as entries within fields or within records at different levels, which can be identified for retrieval by some searching process, and which will lead the user from one level of description to another.

Access points should be subject to authority control.

**9.5B**  Initial entry to a finding aids system may be from the top or from the bottom of the finding aids system. Entry from the top occurs when users begin with the higher level descriptions and proceed to the lower level, or from the less detailed to the more detailed. For example, they may use a guide to find which groups are likely to be of interest, and from there go to series and item lists. (Higher and lower level descriptions are explained in Chapter 5.)

**9.5C**  Initial entry from the bottom is by means of an item or piece list, or by their indexes. There are certainly many common situations where this is the most appropriate method, although in principle it is not possible unless the user already has some background knowledge which will supply the most essential information about the structure or context of the archive. This information is normally obtainable from the higher level descriptions, although it may already be available to expert users from external sources. For example, family historians may be able to go direct to a particular parish register, but they will be drawing upon a store of pre-existing information about the historic boundaries of parishes, the nature of parish archives and the kind of information held in registers. In fact, a concealed initial entry always exists where a reader uses pre-existing knowledge to go straight to lower level descriptions.

**9.5D**  There may also be initial access by way of retrieval aids, such as 'advice to users' leaflets, or indexes.

**9.5E**  As a general principle, where on-line searching is not an option, finding aids which contain free text should also have an index to that text. (See Section 8.5.)

**9.5F**  In general, the question of appropriate access points should be considered when finding aids systems are designed. These planning decisions will have their effect on the shape of the lists and indexes produced.


## 9.6   Retrieval strategies by users

**9.6A**  There are three principal strategies employed by users (including staff users) to identify archival documents relevant to their enquiry. These are direct identification, browsing and scanning.

**9.6B**  *Direct identification* occurs when the user knows one or more of the identifying features of the documents sought (for example a specific name, date or reference code). These can be read off, and the document ordered.

In terms of the finding aids, the main requirement is that the data belonging to each entity should be clearly identifiable as belonging together. The reference code or other call number should be easily spotted and transcribed. For this to be clear, it may be necessary to repeat the full reference code for each entry.

**9.6C** When *browsing*, users read pages of the finding aid in order to pick up any information or ideas which strike them as useful. It is common to employ faster reading techniques, which usually involve focusing the eyes on an imaginary vertical line down the centre of the page. Keywords which appear in the text on either side of this line can be recognized in passing. A short line and clearly printed text are helpful.

In browsing, the user's immediate retrieval objective is often not clearly defined. This strategy is most usefully employed with free text descriptions such as those in the Administrative and Custodial History or the Content and Structure Areas.

**9.6D** When *scanning*, the user's retrieval objective is likely to be more or less clearly defined. The action of scanning is to identify specific keywords, names, character strings or references by running the eye over the finding aid until these appear. The user will rapidly identify the fields or spaces on the page on which targets are likely to appear. For this strategy, a strongly formatted page with dedicated fields will be best.

**9.6E** Since there is therefore some degree of conflict between the page layout and field structure most suitable for each mode of retrieval, it is important that finding aids should be formatted appropriately, so that information for scanning is separated from information for browsing. Sets of descriptions should normally be assembled on a well-designed page, in which blocks of text (for example the narrative descriptions) occupy the centre of the page, and data which can be put into dedicated fields (for example dates, reference numbers) will occupy their own spaces on the paper. Easy identification requires that each entity in the list should be clearly separate from any other.

**9.6F** List mode finding aids are generally more appropriate for scanning, while paragraph mode finding aids are more suitable for browsing. *MAD* formats are intended to be sufficiently flexible to allow a range of combinations, and all *MAD* layouts contain some structured areas as well as free text. (List and paragraph mode finding aids are explained in Chapter 7.)

## 9.7 The variety of terminology used

Although there is a good deal of broad agreement on the principal technical terms, there has been imprecision as to the names to be used for the different kinds of finding aid. *MAD* gives a standard definition for each term in 'Dictionary of technical terms' (see Appendix 1).

The ICA's *Dictionary of Archival Terminology* (revised), along with *ISAD(G)* Section 0 and *ISAAR(CPF)* Section 0 provide an international vocabulary for archival descriptions.

## 9.8 Indexing

**9.8A**   It was noted in Section 3.9 that indexes are an essential part of an archival description, and in Section 9.5D that they are necessary access points to a finding aids system. The importance of indexes in archival description (traditionally not great) has been increasing in recent years. Indexes should be planned, and should be a part of an integrated finding aids system.

**9.8B**   Users should have direct access to indexes.

**9.8C**   Indexes are secondary retrieval aids. This means that their aim is to lead users to descriptions in the finding aids system, rather than directly to original materials. It is recommended that indexes should refer to keywords within the finding aids and not to data in the originals which has not been described in the finding aids. Where the latter practice does occur, the indexes form one of the central components of the finding aids system, and are primary retrieval aids.

**9.8D**   Index references should be reference codes rather than page numbers. Usually this means that description sets at Levels 3–5 tend to be more suitable for using reference codes in the index (although the references to long textual fields in descriptions at group level may be best done by page number).

**9.8E**   It is possible to amalgamate or merge indexes in various combinations, either manually or by translating them to a computer format. This means that the indexes within a finding aids system should if possible have a common infrastructure and format. Indexing should be based upon a coherent philosophy and upon a controlled and structured vocabulary. If there is an appropriate list of terms, use it.

Distinctions of level should be maintained. In any case, it is probably not possible to devise or adapt a common vocabulary for the whole area of archival content from repository to item- or piece-level descriptions, although there have been several attempts to do so. The most successful thesauri are those constructed for defined in-house purposes, but the possibility of vocabularies/thesauri/classification schemes being developed to cover medium- or subject-specific areas cannot be discounted.

**9.8F**   The development of on-line search facilities may have weakened the case for investment in indexing structures but technology does not threaten the norms for standards of description, since the principle that free text descriptions should contain all the keywords necessary for searches is unaffected (Section 9.5).

### 9.9   Classification schemes

**9.9A**   The aim of classification schemes is to improve compatibility between descriptions, and to avoid the need for archivists to duplicate analysis and research. Non-archival classification schemes are not generally suitable because they are, in general, designed for secondary (that is, bibliographical) sources rather than primary sources.

**9.9B**   Archivists should consider using existing classification schemes if a satisfactory scheme exists. There will be very few cases where there is no useful precedent or pattern which will serve to direct archivists' arrangement of the material into levels, and their arrangement of the resulting descriptions. It is often necessary, however, to introduce local variations into any such scheme to accommodate unique features in the archive being described.

**9.9C**   It is important to distinguish between the different kinds of classification schemes in use. Some are based upon an analysis of functions in the originating organization, some upon the physical form of the archival materials, and some analyse certain elements in the origin or content of the archives (such as reference to manorial courts). Some classification schemes are a mixture of one or more of these elements. In some schemes different elements coincide.

Thus, in the classic scheme for Quarter Sessions archives, developed originally in the Essex and Bedford record offices, there are functional divisions: the Court in Session; Enrolment, Registration and Deposit, and so on. In other cases the divisions are based upon the form of the records (bundles or order books).

In another commonly used scheme, that for parish archives, categories based on function and those based on form clearly coincide – for example Registers.

**9.9D**   Classification schemes based upon subject are not suitable for the structural description of archives because they would override the arrangement derived from provenance, and introduce complications or dispersion where different subjects are dealt with in the same class. Classification schemes are only suitable for application to archives where:

- the classification scheme is based upon the administrative structure and functions of the originating organization, and not upon subject;
- the originating organization is one of several which have the same title, administrative structure or general character, each organization operating in a different territory or with some other individuating characteristic; and
- the archive is complex enough to demand the use of a classification scheme.

Thus archival description should follow the arrangement of the material, which in turn reflects the original system which generated it. However, classification schemes which are current in the library or museum communities could be used for structuring secondary finding aids, such as indexes.

**9.9E**   There are also conventions governing the format of finding aids (particularly published finding aids) which may be termed classification schemes. Thus it is customary to arrange the management groups and group descriptions in a guide so that the official archives groups come first, followed by groups from other areas of origin – for example, ecclesiastical, private. In general where a format convention is operating, it should be followed.

## 9.10   Reference coding

**9.10A**   Reference codes are the link between the original materials and the representations of them which are the finding aids. At the end of the process, each archival document must have a unique reference number which will identify it.

Archival description has no other direct interest in these reference codes, except that they should be in a form which is capable of entry into the descriptive format. This may be a problem in some cases when computerization occurs (because of difficulties in sorting to the appropriate hierarchical levels inherent in reference codes), and is always important when the format of archival descriptions affects the efficiency of retrieval.

**9.10B**   There are five possible objectives in designing a reference code, though it is difficult to achieve them all simultaneously:

1.  Reference codes identify physical items for *retrieval*, and therefore are included in a location index.

2.  They identify pieces in *citation*. Since it is impossible to keep track of all citations, this requirement means that reference codes should if at all possible be permanent.

3.  They indicate to readers the present custodian of archival materials and may suggest something of their *context*. Full codes should therefore carry an element to identify the repository: this should be the National Register of Archives repository code, and in an international context the ISO national code[1] (GBR).

4.  Reference codes may suggest a *relationship* with other groups, subgroups, series, items or pieces; they may also give an indication of which level the cited description is dealing with. This means that there should normally be a distinct parameter within the code corresponding to each level. (See Section 14.2.) However, where there is a large number of levels within a group, rigid adherence to this principle may lead to errors and undue complexity in citation, or in searchroom requisitions. Simplification is recommended in this case.

5.  They should act as a *security* check.

**9.10C**   In some repositories an additional feature of the reference codes (derived from the classification scheme used) is a subject element, designed to allow retrieval of relevant documents following certain kinds of subject enquiry.

For example, some systems will allow the retrieval of all documents which bear upon manorial rights, or which deal with estate management. Because of the possible confusion between structural and subject elements, this practice is not recommended.

**9.10D**   Description formats must be able to accommodate existing reference codes, even where these are lengthy or employ unusual alphanumeric combinations. Codes should appear on each page or section of the description.

**9.10E**   Accession numbers are often used for document identification, temporarily in many cases, permanently in some. This practice is not ideal, since it abandons several of the objectives listed in Section 9.10B, and may depend on subsequent relisting taking place (Section 8.3). On the other

---

[1]   ISO 3166:1997 *Codes for the representation of names of countries.*

hand, relisting may allow better analysis and a more rational permanent coding.

**9.10F**    The choice of letters in reference and classification codes is often based on the desire for a mnemonic system. This is only successful where there is a limited number of categories. As a system it was abandoned in the Public Record Office, and *MAD3* recommends that mnemonic systems should not normally be used.

**9.10G**    The problem of gaps in sequences of archival materials was discussed in the section on accrual (Section 9.3).

## 9.11    National and international standards and formats applicable to archival description

*MAD3* has been compiled while a number of standards and formats for archival description or data exchange are in use or are under development in some parts of the world.

The most important of these standards are as follows:

9.11A    *ISAD(G)    General International Standard Archival Description.*

9.11B    *ISAAR(CPF)    International Standard Archival Authority Record for Corporate Bodies, Persons and Families.*

9.11C    *AACR2R    Anglo-American Cataloguing Rules*, 2nd edition, revised.

9.11D    *APPM    Archives, Personal Papers and Manuscripts.*

9.11E    SGML/EAD    Standard Generalized Markup Language/ Encoded Archival Description, HTML and XML.

9.11F    MARC(AMC)    Machine Readable Cataloguing, Archives and Manuscripts Control.

9.11G    *RAD    Rules for Archival Description.*

9.11H    ANSI/NISO    Z39.50–1992 *Information Retrieval Service Definition and Protocol. Specification for Library Applications.*

9.11I    Dublin Core.

9.11J    National Council on Archives, *Rules for the construction of personal, place and corporate names*, 1997.

### 9.11A    *ISAD(G)    General International Standard Archival Description*

See Appendixes 3 and 4.

Adopted by the International Council on Archives in 1994. This standard sets out its aims (in Section I.1) as follows:

> This set of general rules for archival description is part of a process that will:
> a. ensure the creation of consistent, appropriate, and self explanatory descriptions;
> b. facilitate the retrieval and exchange of information about archival material;
> c. enable the sharing of authority data; and
> d. make possible the integration of descriptions from different repositories into a unified information system.

The standard is therefore intended primarily to enable the international exchange of descriptive data, and is not intended to serve directly as a national or in-house standard for general archival description. It underwent a revision process in 1999 but this looks unlikely to result in any substantive changes.

*MAD3* incorporates the *ISAD(G)* data structure.


### 9.11B   *ISAAR(CPF) International Standard Archival Authority Record for Corporate Bodies, Persons and Families*

Adopted by the International Council on Archives in 1996. This standard sets out its aims in Section I. The following extract from Section I.4 indicates their general scope:

> Where a number of repositories hold archival documents from a given source they can more easily share or link contextual information about [their provenance or origin] if it has been maintained in a standardized manner. Such standardization is of international concern when the sharing or linking of contextual information is likely to cross national boundaries...

Taken in conjunction with *ISAD(G)*, this standard therefore enables archivists to set up and maintain descriptive systems in which contextual information (about the creators of archives) is kept distinct from content information (about what the archives actually say). Contextual information can then be kept in structured files that enable exchange of information about creator bodies. Such files are visualized as being an authority system, with the following purpose (Section I.3):

> Such a practice enables the linking of [contextual information] to descriptions of archival documents from the same creator(s) that may be held by more than one repository, or separately held archival documents and library materials that have the same creator(s), or records that remain in the custody of their creator. Such links can facilitate historical research and improve records management practices.

*MAD3* incorporates the *ISAAR(CPF)* data structure.

44

**9.11C    *AACR2R    Anglo-American Cataloguing Rules*, 2nd edition, revised**

Issued by the Library Associations of Britain, USA and Canada, the most recent revision being that of 1998. In 1961 the International Federation of Library Associations and Institutions (IFLA) undertook a study of (library) cataloguing principles that resulted in an agreed statement (the Paris Principles). Subsequent work produced the International Standard Bibliographic Description (ISBD). The first edition of *AACR*, in 1967, was based upon this underlying standard.

*AACR* are now used in library systems and services in most English-speaking countries and have influenced many non-Anglophone standards. Revision work on it is continually in progress, and is especially important, given the rapid growth of electronic and centralized cataloguing agencies and information networks. *AACR* deals not only with printed material: it also covers cartographic materials, manuscripts, music, sound and film recordings, graphic materials, electronic datasets and three-dimensional artefacts, and there are many provisions in it that cover all types of bibliographic description. Interpretative manuals are available for many of the specialized chapters. Its general introduction states:

> These rules are designed for use in the construction of catalogues and other lists in general libraries of all sizes. They are not specifically intended for specialist and archival libraries, but it is recommended that such libraries use the rules as the basis of their cataloguing and augment their provisions as necessary.

The approach taken in *MAD3* is that archival description practice should follow the same standards and practices as bibliographic description wherever possible. The early chapters of *MAD3,* however, show that archival description is not based upon the same principles, and that library practice is rarely appropriate as a model. Wherever library and archival practice appear to coincide, *MAD3* has adopted the terminology of *AACR2* even where this has meant a movement away from previous custom among archivists.

In particular, *MAD3* uses the concept of functionally grouped data elements which is an important feature of *AACR2*, together with the associated terminology. In *MAD3*, data elements are grouped into seven areas, which may be contrasted with *AACR2*'s 11 areas. The content of the areas, however, is different, since most of the areas of *AACR2* are not relevant to archival materials.

Some of the main points of difference between the two standards are as follows:

1.  *Main entry. MAD3* accepts that archival entities, at all levels, must
    have titles. In archives, these titles are normally supplied by the
    archivist on the basis of an examination of the entity being described.
    In most circumstances the title will contain a reference to the creator.

2.  *Statement of responsibility.* Archival materials do not normally have
    an author in the same sense as published materials do. Contextual
    information takes the place of this data element.

3.  *Chief source of information.* The chief source of information (in the
    sense intended by *AACR2*) is the archive itself; alternative sources of
    information are any other sources available, including the results of
    functional analysis carried out by archivists on the creator body or
    bodies. It was not thought useful to use this concept since it was so
    general. [Note: in American practice, the chief source of information
    is pre-existing finding aids to the archives being described.]

4.  *Added entries, subject added entries.* Some highly formatted systems
    for archival description (particularly those using MARC) do provide
    fields for added entries: these are sortable headings replicating data
    given in free text in the context or content description (Administrative
    and Custodial History or Abstract in *MAD3*). It was thought that this
    was a specialized application that should not feature in the general
    description rules.

5.  *Uniform title.* There are some cases where this concept may be appli-
    cable to archives, but they are rare. Cases where groups may have
    been scattered among different repositories or custodians can be met
    by the use of *ISAAR(CPF)* rules.

6.  *Access points.* It is accepted that archivists can use the concept of
    access points, and that in principle access points should be governed
    by authority rules.

7.  *Personal and corporate names. AACR2* gives rules for the construc-
    tion of these names. Archivists are advised to use the rules of the
    National Council on Archives instead. The reasons why the NCA
    *Rules* did not adopt those of *AACR2* are given in the preface to those
    rules.[2]

---

[2]   Section 1.5.1.

**9.11D** *APPM* *Archives, Personal Papers and Manuscripts*, **2nd edition, 1989**

By Steve Hensen, Society of American Archivists, Chicago.

Based upon *AACR2*, *APPM* aims to provide cataloguing rules for archivists who are using library-based media, particularly on-line databases using the MARC format. These rules have been formally authorized for this purpose by the controlling authorities of RLIN and OCLC. *APPM* makes provision for multi-level linked descriptions, and for making descriptions of aggregated entities. Hensen's introduction examines the structure of an *AACR2* catalogue entry, and sets out the principles upon which archival description must be constructed. It is assumed that archivists will use *APPM* to structure entries within appropriate databases, and that therefore they will already have written finding aids for their materials. No models are given in *APPM* for these finding aids.

*APPM* gives rules for the construction of names, and for supplying titles.

**9.11E SGML/EAD Standard Generalized Markup Language/ Encoded Archival Description**

See Appendix 4.

SGML has been adopted as an international standard and is a generic coding language used for marking up texts, including electronic texts. It is intended for use with any type of document, and therefore contains a wide range of possible formats. Users of SGML proceed by analysing the structure of a document, identifying structural elements such as headings, subheadings, title pages, lists, and so on. They can then mark these features by inserting tags from the tag library offered by the standard.

In practice, most documents can be characterized as belonging to specific types or families. These types can be assigned to a particular Document Type Definition (DTD), for which a set of models are provided. Archival descriptions are recognized as one type of document for which a model is provided: this is EAD.

At the beginning of the development project, the following functional requirements were identified as necessary to making archival finding aids available to users of networks:[3]

● presentation of comprehensive and interrelated descriptive information;

---

[3] University of California's Berkeley EAD progress reports at
http://sunsite. berkeley.edu/FindingAids/EAD/history.html
[viewed on 13 January 2000].

47

- preservation of hierarchical relationships existing between levels of description;
- representation of descriptive information inherited from one level of description to another;
- navigation within a hierarchical information architecture; and
- element-specific indexing and retrieval.

The *Tag Library version 1.00* has been published by the Society of American Archivists[4] and on-line.[5] In the development stage it was claimed (1997) that

> the potential to revolutionize the world of finding aids by providing a single standardized encoding through which archival descriptions can be exchanged and used, [and by simplifying] the process of creating machine-readable finding aids in the future as the use of SGML tools becomes more widespread and better understood.[6]

### HTML and XML    HyperText Markup Language, Extensible Markup Language

Both HTML and XML are simplified versions of SGML that have been adapted to allow documents to be formatted in data exchange systems and especially in the World Wide Web (WWW). Each offers the user a set of tags by which structural elements can be identified, and a set of rules by which the tags can be used. Up to the present, HTML is the markup language normally used to format documents for the Internet, and its use is explained in the guidelines produced by the UK Archives and the Internet Group.[7]

### 9.11F    MARC(AMC)    Machine Readable Cataloguing, Archives and Manuscripts Control

MARC is a general format for data held in exchangeable bibliographic databases and in library catalogues. There are special variants for different types of bibliographic information, one of which is AMC. MARC is very widely used for all types of bibliographic processing and data exchange and is therefore relevant to archivists who wish to participate in these.

---

4   *Encoded Archival Description Tag Library, version 1.0,* Society of American Archivists, Chicago, 1998.
5   Library of Congress EAD official web site at http://lcweb.loc.gov/ead/eadtlweb.html [viewed 14 April 2000].
6   Library of Congress EAD official web site at http://www.loc.gov/ead/eadback.html
7   *Writing web pages: guidelines for archivists* produced by the Archives and the Internet Group, 1997. Available at http://www.hmc.gov.uk/archinternet/wwwguide.htm [viewed January 2000].

The AMC variant of the MARC format was issued in 1984 by the Society of American Archivists and other interested bodies in conjunction with the Library of Congress. It has now been fully integrated into USMARC and is subject to the overall control of MARBI, the managing authority for the format. At the time of writing, negotiations for the integration of USMARC and UKMARC are being held.

During the years 1993–97 the Information Technology Group of the Society of Archivists was developing a specific version of AMC for use with UKMARC. This development has now been halted, and British archivists are advised that if they wish to use MARC they should consider the following alternative procedures:

1. *Use of UKMARC*. The British National Bibliography department of the British Library has indicated that archivists may apply for the adoption of new fields within UKMARC. These will be adopted provided that they do not conflict with comparable fields in USMARC. A number of fields relevant to the needs of archivists have already been adopted in the format.

2. *Use of USMARC*. This is the recommended course, since there is already a considerable body of experience in North America and elsewhere in the use of the format and variant, backed by publications and on-line e-mail lists.

### 9.11G  *RAD   Rules for Archival Description*, **Bureau of Canadian Archivists 1990**

The official standard for archival description in Canada. Developed after wide consultation and experiment this is undoubtedly the best organized and most comprehensive standard in existence at present. It is widely used in Canada by official and private archives services. At the time of writing discussions are in progress for the production of a new version that will incorporate *APPM* and provide a general standard for North America.

Unlike *MAD3*, *RAD* took as an essential principle that archival descriptions should be standardized at input rather than at output stage. *RAD* therefore provides archivists with a standard set of data elements required for describing sets of archives at each recognized level of description (fonds, series, file, following the terminology of *ISAD(G)*). It specifies the punctuation for the outputs that follow, and establishes rules for the creation of multi-level descriptions, but does not prescribe how these should be handled in output from the descriptive system, nor does it prescribe the specific structure or content of the different types of finding aid.

*RAD* is available from the Bureau of Canadian Archivists, based at the National Archives of Canada, Ottawa.

## 9.11H ANSI/NISO Z39.50–1992 *Information Retrieval Service Definition and Protocol Specification for Library Applications*

Z39.50 is also an international standard: ISO 23950.

This standard forms part of a long list of related standards issued by the (US) National Information Standards Organization, in association with the Library of Congress. It is designed as an application within the Open Systems Interconnection (OSI) framework. It specifies the techniques needed for sending a search request from one technological system to another, for replying to this request with an intelligible message reporting the search result, and for implementing a request to receive bibliographic records in a readable form. It is not a data content standard (such as *MAD3* or *RAD*); it is not a data structure standard (such as MARC). It is a tool for allowing communication between different descriptive systems and technologies.

Technological standards of this type are needed where documents are published electronically through a variety of formats: this is always the case where material is made available through electronic channels. Experimental archival applications are at present in progress.

## 9.11I Dublin Core

A meeting held in Dublin, Ohio, in 1995 sought to identify the basic data elements required to provide a simple resource description that would allow users to find bibliographic information held in electronic databases, whatever their technical form. The original meeting was continued at another, held in Warwick University in 1996.

The resulting standard identifies 15 essential data elements:

- Title
- Author or creator
- Subject and keywords
- Publisher
- Other contributors
- Date
- Resource type
- Format
- Resource identifier
- Relation
- Source object

- Language
- Coverage
- Description (content)
- Rights management.

Descriptions using this framework of data elements may be seen as intermediate between the fully analysed data structure of MARC and the unformalized documents frequently found on the Internet. The object is to provide an interchange format for descriptive metadata, and set out a shape for documents that have structure and are made available for remote access. At the time of writing no specific application of this venture has been produced for archivists.[8]

### 9.11J   National Council on Archives, *Rules for the construction of personal, place and corporate names*, 1997

Prepared under the editorship of Dick Sargent (Historical Manuscripts Commission), 1990–97, and often referred to just as '*NCA Rules*'.

Section 1 outlines the scope and purpose of the *Rules*:

> Archivists commonly use proper names ... when describing, cataloguing and indexing their holdings. Most of them have some rules and means of ensuring consistency in the form and choice of these names, at least when using them as index headings... Such in-house consistency should now be extended to nationally agreed Rules.

The *Rules* are available on-line.[9] They should be used in conjunction with *MAD3* when access points using proper names are being set up. A similar authority system for subject terms is under investigation.

---

[8]   See http://purl.oclc.org/dc// [viewed January 2000].
[9]   See http://www.hmc.gov.uk/nca/title.htm [viewed January 2000].

# PART II
# THE DATA STRUCTURE OF AN
# ARCHIVAL DESCRIPTION

# 10

# The purpose of data structure in archival description

**10.1**  Archival descriptions are essentially structured. They are made by putting together a planned combination of recognized and labelled items of information. These items of information are *data elements*. The data elements which are to be used are selected from a list, which is given in Chapter 12. In the context of automated systems, data elements are termed fields.

**10.2**  The data elements selected are then fitted together in ways that con form to the patterns or models of archival descriptions given in Part III. These patterns provide a framework for information specific to the archival entity being described.

**10.3**  It is a basic principle of archival description that data element patterns should be constructed with a view to making searches as easy as possible.

A structured description which contains a set of data elements laid out in the form of one of the models for an archival description provides a useful basis for the management and retrieval of information from archives. This is because the data elements can be made to facilitate techniques for searching. This is true whether these techniques are manual (scanning, browsing), or automated (on-line search). Since particular data elements can be labelled by tags, or identified from their position on the page, searches can be concentrated on those sections of the description which are most likely to contain the information sought. Because of this, archival descriptions will normally contain an apparatus of some kind which enables each data element to be easily identified (Section 9.6).

**10.4**   Archival descriptions therefore are organized collections of data which are the values assigned to particular data elements. The data content in each element is given its character by the nature of the element concerned, and may therefore be strictly controlled by the rules for that element. Despite this, most or all archival descriptions necessarily contain free text, and this in whatever mode is selected for descriptions. It is an important principle that no field in an archival description should be arbitrarily limited in length. A parallel principle is that free text should contain all necessary keywords for retrieval of the materials or the information in them (Section 8.5).

# 11

# How the table of data elements is made up

**11.1**   The table of data elements which is given in Chapter 12 contains a list of what are considered to be all the data elements normally used in archival description. If additional data elements are needed in particular cases, these may be supplied in accordance with local practice. The reference in the left-hand column is to the section in Chapter 14 where each data element and its usage is described further.

**11.2**   The table of data elements is divided into two main sectors. The Archival Description Sector contains information which is primarily for the guidance of users, and data entered into it is in the public domain. Data elements in this section are cross-referenced to the corresponding section of ISAD(G). (See Appendix 3.)

The Management Information Sector contains information needed for the administrative control of the archival materials and of processes within the repository, and data entered into it is generally not in the public domain.

**11.3**   Within the sectors, data elements are grouped into *areas* and *sub-areas*. This is for the convenience of archivists carrying out the description process. It is assumed that when manual listing is being done, archivists will not subdivide the data they input into detailed data elements, but will write free text into the undivided areas of sub-areas, except in cases where there is special need for more detailed structuring. Automated descriptive systems may have distinct input fields corresponding to individual data elements or groups of data elements.

**11.4**  It is expected that in normal circumstances, archival descriptions will always contain entries into data elements in the Archival Description Sector. Entries within the Management Information Sector are only needed where the repository is using *MAD* standards to control internal management. The level at which the description is being set makes no difference to this principle.

**11.5**  If the archival entity being described is one of the special formats, different rules apply. For these, see Part V.

# 12

# Summary table of data elements

## ARCHIVAL DESCRIPTION SECTOR

| | | |
|---|---|---|
| **14.2** | **Identity Statement Area** | *ISAD(G) §3.1* |
| 14.2A | *Reference Code* | *ISAD(G) §3.1.1* |
| 14.2B | *Title*<br>Form, type or genre<br>Name | *ISAD(G) §3.1.2* |
| 14.2C | *Simple Span or Indicator Dates* | *ISAD(G) §3.1.3* |
| 14.2D | *Level Number* | *ISAD(G) §3.1.4* |
| 14.2E | *Extent and Physical Character* | *ISAD(G) §3.1.5* |
| **14.3** | **Administrative and Custodial History Area** | *ISAD(G) §3.2* |
| 14.3A | *Administrative or Biographical History*<br>Source of administrative authority<br>Office-holders/personal or corporate names<br>Place of origin<br>Previous administrative systems and identification codes<br>Significant dates | *ISAD(G) §3.2.1–3.2.3*<br>*ISAAR(CPF)§2.1–2.3* |

14.3B    *Custodial History*                      *ISAD(G) §3.2.4–3.2.5*
                Sequence of ownership changes
                Place(s) of custody
                Terms of transfer and access conditions
                Price, and source of funding
                Date of transfer to the archives
                Source references

**14.4**    **Content and Structure Area**        *ISAD(G) §3.3*

14.4A    *Scope and Content (or Abstract)*     *ISAD(G) §3.3.1*
                Date
                Site, locality or place
                Personal or corporate names
                Events or activities
                Subject keywords

14.4B    *Diplomatic Description*
                Form/type/genre
                Problem features
                Predominant language         *ISAD(G) §3.4.4*
                Script
                Special features
                Secondary characteristics

14.4C    *Physical Description*                 *ISAD(G) §3.4.5*
                Physical condition

14.4D    *Archivist's Note*                       *ISAD(G) §3.6.1*
                Relational complexity and status
                Appraisal principle             *ISAD(G) §3.3.2*
                System of arrangement        *ISAD(G) §3.3.4*

**14.5**    **Access, Publication and Reference Area**   *ISAD(G) §3.4–§3.5*

14.5A    *Access Record*
                Access conditions               *ISAD(G) §3.4.2*
                Copying conditions             *ISAD(G) §3.4.3*
                Copyright information          *ISAD(G) §3.4.3*
                      (See also *Issue for Use Record*)

14.5B    *Publication Record*                    *ISAD(G) §3.5.5*
         Publication and citation references

14.5C    *Allied Materials*                      *ISAD(G) §3.5.3*
         Related materials elsewhere
         Existence of copies
         Availability of finding aids

14.5D    *Exhibition Record*
         Circumstances
                  (See also *Loan Record*)
         Physical condition
                  (See also *Conservation Area*)


## MANAGEMENT INFORMATION SECTOR

**14.7    Administrative Control Information Area**
14.7A    *Accession Record*
                  (See also *Custodial History*)
         Number, code, reference
         Date(s) of accession/custody
         Method of acquisition
         Immediate source
         Conditions of deposit
         Deposit agreement
                  (See also *Location Record*)
         Accruals *ISAD(G)§3.3.3*
         Funding
                  (See also *Accession Record*)

14.7B    *Location Record*
         Place of storage
         Bulk
                  (See also *Physical Description*)


**14.8    Process Control Area**
14.8A    *Arrangement Record*
                  (See also *Archivist's Note*)
         Sorting method
         Person responsible

Funding
Date(s) of completion

14.8B    *Description Record*
Description plan
(See also *Archivist's Note*)
Person responsible
Funding
Date(s) of completion

14.8C    *Indexing Record*
System, controls used
Person responsible
Funding
Date(s) of completion

14.8D    *Issue for Use Record*
User's identity
Access status and policy
(See also *Access Record*)
Time, dates of issue and return

14.8E    *Enquiry Record*
Identity of enquirer
Subject
Date(s)
Method

14.8F    *Loan Record*
Borrower
Location of material whilst on loan
Date(s) of despatch
Date(s) of return/due for return
Insurance or security details
(See also *Exhibition Record*)

14.8G    *Appraisal Review Record*
Procedure used
Action taken/recommended
Action date
Appraiser/person responsible
(See also *Archivist's Note*)

## 14.9 Conservation Area

14.9A    *Administration*
        (See also *Physical Description*)

14.9B    *Conservation Record*
    Conservation history
        (See also *Physical Description*)
    Work required
    Level of priority
    Conservator responsible
    Start and finish dates
    Work carried out
    Recommendations for future conservation
    Materials used
    Funding
        (See also *Accession Record*)

# 13

# General rules for the table of data elements

**13.1**   The identity statement is obligatory in every description. Apart from this, all data elements are optional, and may be left unused in any description.

In the context of international access to descriptive information, *ISAD(G)* makes five elements mandatory for any given description – see *ISAD(G)* §1.5.[1]

**13.2**   Any data element may be selected for use at any level of description.

**13.3**   In many cases there may be a choice between two or more alternative areas or sub-areas, for the entry of particular data into a description. The choice is at the discretion of the archivist, but the nature of the alternatives, and wherever possible the preferred practice, is indicated in the specific rules (Chapter 14).

**13.4**   There is in principle no limit to the length of the entry corresponding to any data element in a finding aid. (Limits may of course be imposed by local requirements.)

---

[1] As part of the International Council on Archives review process of *ISAD(G)*, begun in 1998, the Society of Archivists and the PRO recommended that an additional four elements be made mandatory: viz 3.2.1 Name of creator; 3.2.2 Administrative/biographical history (at fonds level); 3.4.2 Access conditions; 3.6 [additional element for] Date of compilation and subsequent revisions. Although at the time of writing the review is not complete (and in fact looks unlikely to result in substantive alterations), these suggested additional mandatory elements have become a requirement within at least two major UK networking projects.

**13.5**   Apart from the identity statement, areas or sub-areas may, if pre-ferred, be treated as blocks of free text. In this case, data elements belong-ing to those areas or sub-areas would be incorporated within the text without necessarily being delimited in any way. This would be normal in many manually constructed descriptions.

**13.6**   Archivists may choose to construct their descriptions on areas or sub-areas rather than upon sets of individual data elements. It is expected that descriptions will not normally be explicitly analysed into data elements except where a system is being used which employs such an analysis in its data entry forms.

**13.7**   Any area, sub-area or data element may contain a cross-reference to the repository's relevant correspondence files and source references for statements made in the text.

**13.8**   The table of data elements is not intended for use with special for-mats. For each of these there are specific tables of data elements in Part V.

**13.9**   The data elements provided in *MAD3* correspond to data elements provided in *ISAD(G)* and *ISAAR(CPF)*. These correspondences are indi-cated in the rules for each element.

# 14

# Specific rules for the use of data elements

Chapter 13 gave general rules for the use of the data elements. This chapter contains an explanation of the *content* of each data element, and rules for its use.

## 14.1 ARCHIVAL DESCRIPTION SECTOR

The purpose of the Archival Description Sector is to contain information primarily of interest to the general user (including, but not limited to, internal or staff users). The information in this sector should be regarded as being in the public domain.

The sector has four areas:

- the *Identity Statement Area*, which identifies the archival entity being described, and gives broad initial information about it (including the level of the current description, its bulk and form), for labelling purposes;
- the *Administrative and Custodial History Area*, which records the context, background and provenance of the archive;
- the *Content and Structure Area* summarizes the information contained in the archive, and gives further information about its form; this provides the basis of a practical finding aid; and
- the *Access, Publication and Reference Area*, which explains how the archive has been or may be used.

More detail is given on each of these areas and their components in the following sections.

## 14.2   The Identity Statement Area

*ISAD(G) §3.1*
The Identity Statement Area has five sub-areas:

- 14.2A    Reference code
- 14.2B    Title
- 14.2C    Simple span or indicator dates
- 14.2D    Level number
- 14.2E    Extent and physical character.

It is obligatory in any description (at whatever level) to use the identity statement. This must be sufficient to establish the identity of the archival entity being described, and to allow its retrieval. Beyond this, the area serves to allow users a means of rapid or preliminary identification of relevant materials.

**14.2A**   *Reference code*
*ISAD(G) §3.1.1*
**14.2A1**   Rules and recommendations for the form of the reference code are given in Section 9.10, and the following example illustrates the points made there:

| Reference | = | GBR141/DCU/GM1/2, p.3 | | |
|---|---|---|---|---|
| Level Number | 0 | 1  2  2.5  3 4 5 | | |
| Reference | | GBR141/ D 42/GM1/2, p.3 | | |
| | | | | **Level** |
| **GBR141** | Repository | (Liverpool University Special Collections & Archives) | | 0 |
| **D** | Management group | (D: deposited archives) | | 1 |
| **42** | Group/collection | (42: Cunard Steamship Co) | | 2 |
| **GM** | Subgroup | (GM: General Manager's Department) | | 2.5 |
| **1** | Series | (1: Registers) | | 3 |
| **2** | Item | (volume no.2) | | 4 |
| **p.3** | Piece | (page no.3) | | 5 |

**14.2A2**   Ideally, alphabetical characters should be used for subgroup and above, and numerical characters for series (Level 3) and below. This rule may be waived if excessive complexity would result, or where long-established styles cannot be varied.

**14.2A3** Reference codes for series descriptions and below should be numbered serially from 1 in each unit of description. The practice of using a continuous series of numbers throughout a group (although it sometimes appears practical in a small, unstructured deposit) is not recommended, especially where there is the possibility of accrual.

**14.2B** *Title*
*ISAD(G) §3.1.2*
The purpose of the Title Sub-area is:

- to give a label which can be used in ordinary speech, or in a preliminary guide;
- to provide the equivalent of a main heading in a bibliographical finding aid; and
- to direct users to more detailed descriptions.

The title should be brief and should include words which uniquely identify the materials being described.

The Title Sub-area may contain one or both of two data elements:

1. a simple term indicating the form, type or genre of the materials; and
2. a name element.

Further details on the components of these elements follow.

**14.2B1** *A simple term indicating the form, type or genre of the materials*
This data element is often left unused, since it is quite normal for the user to assume the type of material from the context. For example:

At group level (2):

> 'Port of Preston, 1831–1899' implies
> Archives of the Port of Preston, 1831–1899

At item level (4):

> [Minute book of] League of Nations Union 1930–1948
> [Volume entitled] Barnes Parish Church Roll of Honour

At series level (3), the element is normally necessary since series are based upon a type or form of material; for example:

> Bucklow Union salary registers

At any level, where this element is to be used, enter the most specific form of material that is applicable. For group or subgroup, use one of the following general terms (use other terms where appropriate):

'Papers': this means an accumulation of personal papers containing more than one kind of material; for example:

Papers of George, 1st Duke of Clarence

'Records' or 'archives': this means the records or archives of corporate bodies or organizations; for example:

Russian–American Company archives

'Collection', or 'collection of papers': any group of materials formed artificially round a person, subject or activity and which otherwise lacks integrity and unity of provenance; for example:

The William Smith collection of documents on local militias

For the description of entities larger than item, use an appropriate plural or collective form of material designation (for example 'letters', 'correspondence', 'diaries', 'journals', 'legal documents', and so on). For single items such as manuscript volumes (for example a diary, a letter-book, an account book, a ledger, and so on) and for uniform accumulations such as letters, speeches, sermons, lectures, and legal or financial documents, enter the form of the material which is most specific and appropriate.

An authority list is recommended.

**14.2B2**   *The name element*
The name element in a title normally consists of, or at least contains, the name or names of the creator, which may be one or more persons and/or corporate bodies or organizations predominantly associated with or responsible for the entity being described.

**14.2B2i**   Choice of name element

1.   *Where there is no formal or original title*, or if the formal or original title is insufficient or misleading, a supplied title is used for the name element. Since most archival entities do not have a formal title in the bibliographic sense, the name element is usually supplied by the archivist. This element should be brief and descriptive. Where names are intended to provide access points or indexing terms, they should be constructed in accordance with the National Council on Archives'

*Rules for the construction of personal, place and corporate names* (1997) (see Section 9.11J).

There is often no original title for subgroups: these titles may be derived from the name of the functional division, or function, which has been the basis of their creation (for example Legal Department (Records); financial (records) and so on), with date, and other qualifiers as necessary. Where there were no functional divisions in the originating body (as in the case of private papers), distinct functions may be inferred from the content or grouping of the items, or from extraneous sources (for example the papers of a scientist divided into research work, conference papers, personal papers, and so on). A suitable title may then be supplied.

The title of a series should wherever possible be that given to the series while it was still in current administrative use. Where this rule cannot be applied, the title should refer to the series' distinguishing characteristic and be derived from an examination of the archive itself. Since the definition of a series is that it is a set of archives with a unifying physical characteristic, the title should normally contain terms describing the physical form of the materials in the series.

Examples of typical series titles are:

Board Minutes
Register of Adoptions
Directors' Out-letters

The name element of an item-level title is derived in one (or more) of the following ways and may be considered as a brief abstract or statement of content of the item:

- from any title or heading written on the item: 'Birthday cards received, 1893';
- an inferred original title by which it might have been known when in current use: Laundry List;
- the physical character of the item: Black, soft-covered notebook containing survey data;
- the diplomatic character of the item: lease and release of land at Lower Sapey; and
- the informational content of the item: notebook containing calculations in Danish and German.

2. *Where there is a formal title,* that is, one which was assigned by the original creator or by the original users of the material, transcribe it exactly as to wording, order and spelling but not necessarily as to punctuation and capitalization.

70

If appropriate, abridge a long formal title, but only if this can be done without loss of essential information. Where there is a formal title which is misleading or insufficient it should be recorded and noted as such in the Content and Structure Area. Alternatively, a supplied extension or subtitle may be used to complete or explain an insufficient formal title. Data provided editorially in this way should be put into square brackets. For example:

St Jude's Mission [and Benevolent] Committee minutes

Traditional titles or titles allocated in common speech may be included as parallel titles or subtitles.

**14.2B2ii**   It is intended that the name element in a title should be short and convenient to provide a satisfactory general label for, or identification of, the entity; however, there is no limitation as to its length. A title may be expanded, or subtitles or parallel titles (as indicated in Section 14.2B2i) may be added if the main title is not clear and self-explanatory. In general, the name element of the title should be kept short, and additional material placed in the Content and Structure Area.

Choose names which record the persons, families or organizations predominantly associated with or responsible for the creation of the entity being described. If the entity consists of the papers of two or more persons or families, or if it holds the archives of two or more organizations (for example where one body has been taken over or replaced by another), use all of the names primarily associated with the creation of the material in the name element.

Example of a group title:

Archives of the Booth Steamship Co and Booth Iquitos Line

Record names in direct order of natural language. Names may be abbreviated if the full name appears elsewhere (that is, in the Administrative and Custodial History Area or in the Content and Structure Area).

**14.2B2iii**   Parallel titles in another language
*ISAAR(CPF) §1.4*
Where standardized alternative names occur in any other language, these parallel names should be recorded in accordance with NCA *Rules*.

**14.2B2iv**   Alternative or non-preferred names
*ISAAR(CPF) §1.5*
Where there are common alternative names or forms of names these

should be recorded, but the fact that they are alternative or non-preferred terms should be stated.

**14.2C**  *Simple span or indicator dates*
*ISAD(G) §3.1.3*

The purpose of the span dates is to help the other elements in the title to give a clear immediate means of reference to the materials, not to give a precise and detailed description of content. The dates should therefore normally be restricted to simple years or spans of years, delineating broad chronological periods, or helping to identify a particular institution, or broad phases in the life of that institution.

The dates must refer to the actual period when the documents were created. If an item consists of, or includes copies of or extracts from, documents of earlier dates, these dates, if cited, should appear in the Administrative and Custodial History Area or the Content and Structure Area, as appropriate.

If the materials deal with or refer to periods different from the period when they were created, these periods may be included in the name element of the title if they are significant for preliminary identification, or in the Content and Structure Area if they are not significant in this way but are needed to complete a true picture of the contents of the archive. For example:

*Tommy Atkins's reminiscences of 1914*        *1936*

Enter span dates directly following the name element or any other title information that has been added to it. Simple dates in the title may follow the name element directly (with or without a comma) or may be placed in a right-margin date column on the same line as the name element (as in the example above).

For groups, subgroups or series, the year or years alone, singly or as a span, are normally sufficient, provided that full date information appears elsewhere. If the dates within the material are scattered, it may be preferable to give the bulk (effective or operative span) dates in the title, rather than literal extreme span dates, exact dates then appearing in the Content and Structure Area as noted above, or as text in item/piece lists.

For example, span dates given in the series title as '1789–1809' may appear more exactly in the item/piece list as:

/1  3 July 1789 – 3 June 1795
/2  14 June 1797 – 22 Feb 1800
/3  14 Jan 1803 – 12 May 1809

For a single item or piece, give the exact date, expressed as day, month, year: for example 7 May 1742. If the item lacks date information or the information is incomplete and must be completed from internal evidence or an external source, enclose it in square brackets in accordance with the standard listing conventions in Part III (Section 16.6). If the date information is incomplete and the missing components cannot be supplied, use 'n.d.'. If month and day information is missing, it may be omitted if there is no strong reason for giving negative information.

It is recommended that simple year dates should be given in a tabulated column at the right of the page, to facilitate scanning. Complex or lengthy dates should not be provided in the Title Sub-area but should be treated as text within appropriate areas.

For more examples of dates (including approximate and estimated dates) see the standard listing conventions (Section 16.6).

**14.2D**  *Level number*
*ISAD(G) §3.1.4*
It is generally desirable that there should be a level number attached to any description. However, it would not normally be displayed in a finding aid intended for public use. (In this respect it is an exception to the other data elements within the Archival Description Sector. It is placed here because it forms part of the identity statement.) The purpose of the level number is to confirm and record the analysis which lies behind the arrangement of the archives being described, and to facilitate the comparison of, and access to, data.

Examples of titles:

| Level | | | |
|---|---|---|---|
| 2 | DH | Papers of the first Duke of Heswall | 1801–1857 |
| 2 | BO/PS | Borchester petty sessional court | 1835–1850 |
| 2.5 | BO/PS/A | Borchester special sittings | after 1840 |
| 3 | BO/LA/CI | Coronation sub-committee minutes | 1937–1955 |
| 4 | BO/LA/CI/3 | Coronation sub-committee minute book No.3 | 1953 |

**14.2E**  *Extent and physical character*
*ISAD(G) §3.1.5*
Give the quantity, extent, size or bulk (dimensions, number, amount), for example 10 vols, 150 boxes. The measures used should be those standard in the repository. Alternatively, give the metric linear shelf space or metric

cubic storage space of the entity. If the extent is given in linear terms, additional information may be desirable, for example 4m (c 10,200 items).

Give a description of the overall physical character of the materials. Terms such as 'file(s)', 'volume(s)', 'box(es)', 'bundle(s)', 'loose papers', and so on are appropriate.

The extent and physical character are usually taken together. They may also refer back to the Location Record Sub-area (Section 14.7B).

Examples:

> 1 bundle (33 items)
> 2 items in envelope
> 300 boxes (30m)
> 20m (548 files)

## 14.3   Administrative and Custodial History Area
*ISAD(G) §3.2*

This area is intended to allow for the information needed to establish the background, context, provenance and archival history of the entity being described. It is characteristic of (but not exclusive to) higher levels of description, and is required for the moral defence of the archive.

The information in this area may be held as separate or linked authority files (which may be contributed to the National Name Authority File when this becomes available).

The Administrative and Custodial History Area contains two sub-areas:

- 14.3A    Administrative or Biographical History
- 14.3B    Custodial History.

These sub-areas may, if appropriate, be written together as connected text. Generally, information on the history of custody should come at the end of a text which deals first with the origin and then with the transmission of an archival entity.

The most recent events in custodial history (especially the circumstances of *transfer to the repository*) may be omitted here and placed in the Accession Record if repository management considerations require; for example, if there is need for confidentiality. Where there is no strong reason for this choice, however, the Custodial History Sub-area should contain information on final transfer even if a separate Accession Record is kept in the Management Information Sector.

Where factual statements are made in the text of this area, it is a good practice to cite sources for them, whether these are external or internal to the materials. Administrative histories frequently include a bibliography section and/or footnotes.

**14.3A**   *Administrative or Biographical History*
*ISAD(G) §3.2.1–3.2.3*
*ISAAR(CPF) 2.1–2.3*
This sub-area is normally treated as free text without limitations as to length.

Record any significant information on the origin, progress, development and work of the creating organization of the archive or on the life and work of the person mainly responsible. Include all details required to explain the structure, nature or scope of the materials, as they were created and used.

For persons, the information needed usually includes dates of birth and death, place of birth, successive places of domicile, occupations or offices, information on original and maiden names or pseudonyms, significant accomplishments, place of death, and so on. If such details appear in readily available and accurate published sources (for example *The Dictionary of National Biography*) these can be listed and the details given in this area need not be lengthy.

For corporate bodies or organizations, the information may include data on the origin, functions, purpose and development of the body, its administrative hierarchy, and earlier, variant or successor names. It is important to include the successive names and offices of principal movers in the organization, since these names are often the access points for subject searches.

For both personal and corporate histories, name authority records may be either created, using NCA *Rules*, or used (when these are available through the National Name Authority File).

Particularly important information, for which data elements are provided, is likely to be:

- the *source of administrative authority* for the function documented;
- information on *individuals or office-holders* important in the formation and development of the function;
- information on *place of origin*;
- information on *previous administrative systems, identification codes* and the sequence of changes in these; and
- *significant dates* for all events mentioned.

An example of a corporate administrative history:

Houghton le Spring Rural Sanitary Authority was set up under the Public Health Act 1872. The Rural District Council, established under the Local Government Act 1894, inherited the functions of the former Rural Sanitary Authority in 1895 when the Act came into operation. Houghton le Spring Rural District Council was abolished on 1 April 1937 and the area split up among the neighbouring local authorities, namely Hetton Urban District Council (UDC), Hetton UDC, Houghton le Spring UDC, Durham Rural District Council (RDC), Easington RDC and Sunderland RDC.

From 1872 to 1894 the office of Clerk was discharged by a local firm of solicitors, Messrs Smith and Jones [address]. Subsequently, the clerkship was discharged by the officers of the RDC.

Although the Rural Sanitary Authority and the Rural District Council were distinct local authorities, significant breaks in series do not occur at 1894 and therefore the records have been treated as one group rather than as two.

Records inherited by Houghton UDC in 1937 and later deposited at Durham Record Office. Transferred to Tyne and Wear Archives Service on 28 July 1976.

[*Source:* Tyne and Wear Archives Service]

An example of an entry relating to a person:

### HORACE WILLIAM BRINDLEY JOSEPH, 1867–1943

Horace Joseph came to New College as a Winchester Scholar in 1886. He had come first on the roll of scholars elected at Winchester College in 1880. At Oxford University he won the junior Greek Testament prize in 1889 and the Arnold History Essay prize in 1891. He gained a double first in Literae Humaniores in 1888 and 1890 and was elected a fellow of New College in 1891. He became lecturer in philosophy the same year and was senior philosophical tutor from 1895 until 1932. In 1895 he also became junior bursar, a post he held until 1919.

On his retirement in 1932, Joseph became a supernumerary fellow of the college, so that he could continue to teach, retaining this position until his death. He also became a member of Oxford City Council, where in due course he became chairman of the Education Committee. He was elected FBA in 1930 and a Fellow of Winchester College in 1940.

Joseph founded the Margaret Bridges Scholarship in Music at New College in memory of his wife Margaret Bridges, the daughter of Robert Bridges, Poet Laureate. By his will he made the college his residuary legatee. There is an article about him in *The Dictionary of National Biography*.

[*Source:* Archives of New College, Oxford]

## 14.3B   *Custodial History*
*ISAD(G) §3.2.4–3.2.5*

This sub-area is normally free text, without limitation as to length. It may be combined with the Administrative or Biographical History Sub-area, but in this case should normally be placed at or towards the end of the main text.

Make a record of the history of the custody of the materials. Include information on:

- the *sequence of ownership changes*, from the original to the present owners, up to the point of transfer to the archives service;
- the place of owner's custody or the sequence of *places of custody* from origin to transfer;
- the *terms of transfer* of ownership or custody to the archives (for example deposit, bequest, rescue) and any *conditions attached to subsequent access* (unless for specific reasons this is given in the Accession Record);
- in cases of purchase, the *price, and source of funding* (unless this is given in the Accession Record);
- the *date of transfer to the archives* (if it is desired that this should remain confidential, use the Accession Record instead); and
- *references to sources* of information on the entity.

Example:

> The papers came into the custody of the college not long after his death in November 1943. If they came from his home at 33 Northmoor Road they would have been handed over by his brother Eustace, who survived him. After evaluation by H A Prichard, fellow of Trinity College, Oxford, they passed into the personal custody of Warden A H Smith, 1883–1958. Warden Smith's executor was Sir Christopher Cox, 1899–1982, who between 1970 and 1976 extracted them from among his own and Smith's papers. The boxes were then housed in the new library building.

[*Source:* Archives of New College, Oxford]

## 14.4   Content and Structure Area
*ISAD(G) §3.3*

This area is intended to record all the other information required to establish intellectual control over the materials, that is, to enable users to identify the materials they need, and to take measures to retrieve the full information held in the original materials. The precise fullness of detail to be entered depends on the policy of the archives service and the objective of the finding aid being constructed. Rules on depth of description in Part I apply (Chapter 8).

The Content and Structure Area has four sub-areas:

- 14.4A    Scope and Content *or* Abstract
- 14.4B    Diplomatic Description
- 14.4C    Physical Description
- 14.4D    Archivist's Note.

**14.4A**    *Scope and Content/Abstract*
*ISAD(G) §3.3.1*

The purpose of this sub-area is to summarize the content or specific informational character of the materials. The amount of detail or the completeness of this record depends on the purpose of the finding aid and the level of description. Prominent abstracts are characteristic of (but not exclusive to) descriptions at series level and below.

The Scope and Content note, or Abstract, is normally a free text entry, without limitation as to length but a contents analysis may serve to structure the information which would normally occur in the abstract; in this case, appropriate data elements include:

- *date* (single or covering); dates entered here may be full, detailed or complex;
- *site, locality or place* (the specificity of site identification, or the use of uniform names, may be determined by general policy in the archives service: for example authority list of place-names, geographical coordinates);
- *personal or corporate names*;
- *events or activities*; and
- *subject keywords* (these may be provided from an authorized vocabulary, or by reference to an authority list of subject titles).

Include also any information additional to that given in the Title Sub-area. This may include more precise information on the form of the materials, the names of individuals or organizations (which may appear in the title in their simplest form), or dates. If the date of the original event differs from that of the archival materials which deal with it and which is given in the Title Sub-area, then record the relevant dates. If the dates given in the date element of the Title Sub-area (Section 14.2C) are simplified or in some way do not correspond with dates occurring in the body of the materials, the full dates may be given here within the text.

Record any sources or documents which have been used to assemble information in this area.

Example:

> Business correspondence of the Corsini Brothers. During the second half of the sixteenth century the brothers Philip and Bartholomew Corsini operated a considerable import and export business out of their house in Gracechurch Street, fully documented in this correspondence. Agents across Europe corresponded with them in the course of their business activities, occasionally including political or family news along with details of local commercial conditions... It should be noted that from 1582 most of the overseas correspondents used New Style dating while the dates of receipt endorsed on the letters were Old Style.

[*Source:* Guildhall Library Manuscripts Department Corporation of London]

Example:

> **Manorial Documents Register – Definition of manorial documents**
> According to the Manorial Documents Rules, manorial documents are defined as 'court rolls, surveys, maps, terriers, documents and books of every description relating to the boundaries, wastes, customs or courts of a manor' but they exclude 'deeds or other instruments required for evidencing the title to a manor or agreements or draft agreements relating to compensation, or any documents which came into being after 31st December 1925'.

[*Source:* Historical Manuscripts Commission]

Example:

> **QSD/SR Sessions Rolls**
> The sessions rolls comprise the documents accumulated at each meeting of the court. The more common items are
>
> - *Writs of venire facias* ordering the sheriff to summon the juries and officials before the justices
> - *Lists* of grand and petty juries
> - *Indictments* generally by the grand jury, for assault, larceny, felony and other misdemeanours

[*Source:* Denbighshire Record Office]

**14.4B**   *Diplomatic Description*
Diplomatic (diplomatics, *diplomatique*) is the name of the academic study concerned with the interpretation of documents by means of a technical examination of their form.

This sub-area is provided so that there can be a technically accurate record of the diplomatic character of the archive. Care should be taken to distinguish between the Diplomatic and Physical Description Sub-areas, though in many cases there may be little or nothing to record under the former, and the physical description will include all the useful information that is available. The Physical Description Sub-area is preferred where there are no technical considerations in connection with the form of the materials which relate to the study of diplomatic.

A special format is provided in *MAD3* for the detailed description of title deeds (Chapter 18).

This sub-area will normally be treated as free text, and may be given at the end of the Scope and Content/Abstract Sub-area. In some cases, where a wide variety of diplomatic forms is not encountered, full descriptions may be replaced by codes or brief headings.

Give notes on the diplomatic of the archival entity, or an indication of its *form, type or genre*. This entry may refer back to the term of form, type or genre element of the title (Section 14.2B1). In this sub-area more detail may be given.

Terms suitable for use in this sub-area are:

- at series level: 'in-letters', 'registered filing system', 'title deeds', 'court rolls', and so on;
- at item level: 'registered file', and so on; and
- at piece level: 'mortgage'; 'letter', and so on.

The following additional data elements may be used:

- *problem features*, such as missing information, difficulty of inter- pretation, and so on;
- *predominant language* of the material (for example Latin) *(ISAD(G) §3.4.4)*;
- characteristic *script* used (for example secretary hand);
- *special features* (seals, watermarks, and so on); and
- *secondary characteristics* (for example that the materials are copies, or drafts; *n.b.* if these materials are microform or photographic copies, indicate this here, unless it is preferred to make this entry under the Access, Publication and Reference Area (Section 14.5), which is preferred unless there is diplomatic relevance).

Example:

Later additions are in a seventeenth century hand.

Example:

Printed English translation of orders recovered from ships scuttled at Scapa Flow in 1918, including manuscript notes, apparently by Jellicoe.

[*Source:* British Library Manuscript Collections]

Example:

> Signed:    A White ('Quhyte').
> Seal and notarial sign.
> Marginal note: 'ultimo Maij 1490'.

[*Source:* National Archives of Scotland, Crown Copyright]

Example:

> Endorsed: "Received from my father, 1802".
> Seal, said to be affixed, now missing.

### 14.4C   *Physical Description*
*ISAD(G) §3.4.5*

This sub-area provides for information on the physical shape, size, character and condition of the materials. This information relates to that in the Identity Statement Area and in the Location Record Sub-area (Section 14.7B). Physical Description is the preferred sub-area when user information, rather than process control, is the principal objective.

### 14.4C1   Physical condition

Note the physical condition of the entity. Where this in broad terms affects access, a possible area is the Access, Publication and Reference Area (Section 14.5); however, access restrictions based purely on considerations of physical condition are often better placed here: for example, where ultraviolet light would be necessary to read the materials.

Examples:

> At level 2:
> Extensive water damage caused by poor storage especially affects series which were kept at floor level: even numbers below *50*
>
> At level 3:
> Parchment volumes sewn with leather thongs; many pages affected by creasing
>
> At level 4:
> Loose binding repaired by local craftsman binder in about 1870
>
> At level 5:
> Bottom right corner torn off, obscuring some lines of text

Cross-reference to the Conservation Area (Section 14.9) will normally be useful.

**14.4D**  *Archivist's Note*
*ISAD(G) §3.6.1*

The purpose of the Archivist's Note Sub-area is to record important facts about the nature of the entity and how it has been treated by the repository.

There are three data elements which note, respectively, the relationships between parts of the entity, how appraisal decisions have been approached and carried out, and how the parts of the entity have been arranged within the repository.

**14.4D1**  Relational complexity and status

If the archive is related by provenance, hierarchy or function to a larger unit or to other materials or is part of or an addition to an existing archival entity at a higher level, give the identity statement for that entity. In addition indicate the relationship of the material to the other entity using such phrases as 'forms part of . . .' , 'in . . .', 'addition to . . .', and other introductory wording as appropriate.

If the archive is related to other entities for which there are descriptions at a lower level, give a brief explanation of the structure of the group, including the identity statements of entities referred to. Phrases such as 'The group [subgroup, and so on] is divided into series [subgroups, pieces, and so on] as follows . . .' can be used.

Example.

The records have been arranged in the following categories:

1. Deeds of settlement, Acts of Parliament
2. Directors' minutes and other papers
3. General (shareholders') meetings minutes; annual reports and accounts
4. Secretary's papers
5. Accounts
6. Gas and electricity contracts papers:

   Belgium
   France
   Germany
   Netherlands
   Romania

7. Staff records

Example:

> The records comprise minute books, ledgers and other volumes from a racked store room; the contents of metal deed boxes holding deeds and agreements and a variety of other documents, many of them doubtless preserved for their historical interest; and files from a filing cabinet of older files. No records later than 1970 were taken, except for examples of publications. A good series of minute books, many deeds and agreements, and a wide range of ledgers and other financial records have survived.
>
> The headquarters of the Association were in London until 1960 and probably much which survives was consciously selected for transfer to Epsom. Several of the bundles bear numbers which related to a modern brief listing, but there is no evidence of original archival arrangement.

[*Source:* Surrey Record Office]

Example:

> Some other records of the Company are with WM427 'Shipping papers' which are a mixed collection of shipping records from various sources.

[*Source:* Anglesey County Record Office]

Example:

> Documents of exceptional size pre-1931 and any supporting items post-1931 form a supplementary series of papers.

Materials related in non-structural or organic ways (for example by subject matter) should be cross-referred in the Allied Materials Sub-area (Section 14.5C).

**14.4D2**  *Appraisal principle*
*ISAD(G) §3.3.2*
Explain the principle upon which appraisal decisions have been made. Where different principles have been applied to different subgroups or series, give sufficient information on the system of arrangement of the entity to allow users to understand its composition and the relevant finding aids. If the appraisal principle adopted might affect the interpretation of the materials (for example if there has been sampling), this should be explained here.

Specific actions arising from appraisal are better placed in the Appraisal Review Record (Section 14.8G).

Examples:

> Following discussions with the Head of Department in July 1998 it was agreed that the alphabetical sequence dating between 1915 and 1956 should be retained in its entirety, and that thereafter – when the files were arranged chronologically by year – a sample should be taken from each successive decade as follows: all students registering in 1962/3 (and 72/3, 82/3 etc), 1965/6 (and 65/66 etc) and 1968/9 (and 78/9, 88/9). The remainder of the files will be destroyed 10 years after the award is made.

[*Source:* University of Liverpool]

> Correspondence files are only retained where they deal with matters of policy or the planning of specific projects. They should in all cases be used in association with the committee minutes and papers.

**14.4D3**  *System of arrangement*
*ISAD(G) §3.3.4*
Give a brief account of the present and former arrangement of the material in so far as this might affect interpretation.

This is the preferred field for this type of information (in preference to the Arrangement Record (Section 14.8A) or Appraisal Review Record (Section 14.8G) Sub-areas) because it forms part of the moral defence of the archive, and is of direct value to users.

If the system of arrangement finally adopted is not described elsewhere (for example in the Administrative or Biographical History Sub-area

(Section 14.3A) or in the Arrangement Record Sub-area (Section 14.8A)), make a note of it, specifying the principal characteristics of the internal structure and order, and how these have been treated. If there are sub-groups in a group, there may be a list of titles or headings of these. Record the levels of arrangement adopted.

Make a note of the presence and nature of any original finding aid.

Explanation of level numbering used may be appropriately entered here.

Administrative information (for use within the repository) about arrangement should be placed in the Arrangement Record Sub-area.

Examples:

> The First Calendar of Corporation Archives was commissioned by the Borough in 1880 when Richard Sims of the British Museum examined and listed in detail 261 individual documents, mainly deeds, from the earliest grant of William Rufus to the burgesses of Walsall, c1220, to items dating from the late C17. The Calendar was published in 1882 and is widely available. To avoid confusion, Sims's order and numbering was retained when the documents were transferred to the Archives.

[*Source:* Walsall Local History Centre]

> The contents of the box files were listed by the Assistant Librarian who gave some items provisional titles, which he wrote in blue crayon. The archival description which follows this text is based on his typescript.

[*Source:* Archives of New College, Oxford]

## 14.5   Access, Publication and Reference Area
*ISAD(G) §3.4–3.5*

This area has four sub-areas:

- 14.5A   Access Record
- 14.5B   Publication Record
- 14.5C   Allied Materials
- 14.5D   Exhibition Record

The purpose of this area is to supply and draw together several categories of information bearing on the use of the original materials, their production to users individually or collectively, and what those users have done with them.

The area may be regarded as intermediate between the Archival Description Sector and the Management Information Sector, since there are circumstances in which a note of these items of information is required as part of the public finding aids, and there are circumstances in which this data would be needed primarily for the control of the materials within the archives service. However, in general this data is needed to support user access, and is in the public domain.

**14.5A** *Access Record*
**14.5A1**   Access conditions
*ISAD(G) §3.4.2*
This sub-area is the preferred one for general statements on access restrictions affected by physical conditions, except where these are very specific: see Physical Description Sub-area (Section 14.4C). Give information on all restrictions that are in force, including general limitations applicable to all users in connection with this entity, special procedures for permitted groups of user, or conditions of special access. Indicate the extent of the period of closure, and the date at which the materials will become open.

Management data on these points, not intended for the information of users who are members of the public, have their preferred place in the Issue for Use Record Sub-area (Section 14.8D).

Examples:

> No access may be given to this item without the written permission of a director of the firm.
>
> Whole series embargoed 100 years, calculated from the last entry in each item.
>
> The following series of more recent records are open to public inspection by statute or usage ...
>
> Access may be refused to any item which is in need of repair.

> ## WW1 Soldiers' Burnt Documents    Update
> The timetable below lists when the film for each alphabetical letter should be available on microfilm at Kew.
>
> | Surname letter | Approximate date |
> | --- | --- |
> | A | Winter 1998 |
> | B | Summer 1999 |
> | C | Summer 1999 |
> | D | Summer 1999 |
> | E | Available now |
> | F | Spring 1999 |

[*Source:* Public Record Office: Crown Copyright]

### 14.5A2   Copying conditions
*ISAD(G) §3.4.3*
This element is provided to allow the explanation of non-legal restrictions.

Give information on any administrative restrictions on the reproduction of the materials for users or for publication, and indicate the general policy on reproduction as applied to this archive.

### 14.5A3   Copyright information
*ISAD(G) §3.4.3*
This element is appropriate for restrictions of a legal character.

If the copyright situation in respect of these materials is unknown, no statement is necessary. If the rights were dedicated or reserved under a legal instrument, or as a condition of deposit, include a descriptive note. If it is known that the copyright is held by an individual or by a corporate body, details should be given, together with the expiry date, or contingency upon which an expiry date depends.

Cross-reference to the Issue for Use Record Sub-area (Section 14.8D) may be made.

### 14.5B   *Publication Record*
*ISAD(G) §3.5.5*
**14.5B1**   If the archive, or part of it, has been published or cited (including microform or digital publication), give the *publication* details. Include journal articles describing portions of the materials, guides describing the archival entity in terms of a particular subject focus, or other published descriptions, indexes and calendars.

**14.5B2**   Entries in this area are likely to be *citations* or bibliographical references, and should therefore be made in accordance with appropriate bibliographical standards.

**14.5C**   *Allied Materials*
*ISAD(G) §3.5.3–3.5.4*
**14.5C1**   Give references to archival or bibliographic materials (possibly including materials in other repositories) or museum objects, and so on, which have a close relationship with the materials being described. Indicate the whereabouts and nature of the *related materials*. (See also the Archivist's Note (Section 14.4D), which is the preferred sub-area for notes on the relationship between components of the archive itself.)

**14.5C2**   If not given in the Publication Record (Section 14.5B) (which would be the preferred sub-area), or elsewhere, indicate the *existence of copies* (microfilm, photocopy, transcript).

**14.5C3**   Give a reference to any other *finding aids* the repository may have to the organization and contents of the materials being described, including inventories, lists, calendars, series descriptions, card indexes, institutional guides, and so on.

Note whether the list has been deposited with and is available for consultation at any other repository, at the National Register of Archives or electronically.

Examples:

There is correspondence from Vice-Admiral Sir Samuel Hood (1762–1814) in the Keats Papers (KEA/10), the McKinley Papers (MCK/11), the Duckworth Papers (DUC/14) and in the museum's collections of single orders and memoranda (HSR/6/11) and letters (AGC/6/17 and 22).

[*Source:* Manuscripts Department, National Maritime Museum]

The Zurich catalogue describes further letters addressed to merchants in Italy, with some addressed to a merchant in Antwerp; microfilm copies of some of these are at Mss 21,323–21,326.

[*Source:* Guildhall Library, Department of Manuscripts, Corporation of London]

A catalogue of this archive is available in the Centre's searchroom and on its website (at http://www.warwick.ac.uk/services/library/mrc/mrc.html), at the National Register of Archives and on the National Inventory of Documentary Sources.

[*Source:* Modern Records Centre, University Library, University of Warwick]

For earlier minute books in previous accessions consult the list of Local Authority Minute Books held in the Reference Room.

**14.5D**  *Exhibition Record*
The purpose of the Exhibition Record Sub-area is to provide an opportunity for a reference to be made to the publication of an archival document by means of exhibition exposure, including formal publication of text or commentary in an exhibition catalogue. Such information is clearly of value to users, and is in the public domain.

Where the record of the exhibition of an archival item is required chiefly as an administrative control the preferred sub-area would be the Loan Record Sub-area (Section 14.8F). This is especially so if there is need for confidentiality, and no need for public user information.

**14.5D1**  Circumstances
Give details of the circumstances in which the materials were exhibited, including place and date, and a citation for any publications (such as an exhibition catalogue) which referred to them.

The preferred sub-area for administrative information about the loan and return of the materials is the Loan Record (Section 14.8F).

**14.5D2**  Physical condition
Give details of any physical changes which occurred to the materials while on exhibit (if this is not dealt with in the Conservation Area (Section 14.9), which would be the preferred area unless this information was of direct interest to users).

## 14.6   MANAGEMENT INFORMATION SECTOR

The purpose of this sector is to record information needed for controlling the processes carried on within the repository. This includes both information which should be held in a permanent record, and also more ephemeral data. Although in some circumstances users may need some of the information recorded here, it is not regarded as being within the public domain. The Archival Description Sector (Section 14.1) is preferred for any information of direct value to users, even though it might relate to processes within the repository.

As in the Archival Description Sector, only areas, sub-areas and data elements which are immediately relevant need be used, all others being omitted.

It is not possible to link the level of description closely to the use of management information areas, sub-areas or data elements. There is in principle an assumption that data elements which give very specific information about small quantities of material may be regarded as being most natural to descriptions at item or piece level; but against this, there are certainly situations in which procedural information is needed in group, subgroup or series descriptions. The general rule that any data element may be used at any level of description therefore continues to apply in this sector.

The Management Information Sector has three areas:

- the *Administrative Control Information Area* forms the accession record and explains where the material is kept;
- the *Process Control Area* allows the repository to track the archive through the various stages of processing; and
- the *Conservation Area* allows the repository to record conservation needs and track the material through conservation processes.

## 14.7    Administrative Control Information Area

The Administrative Control Information Area has two sub-areas:

- 14.7A    Accession Record
- 14.7B    Location Record.

**14.7A**   *Accession Record*
This sub-area deals with information which may as an alternative be wholly or partly recorded in the Custodial History Sub-area (Section 14.3B). The Accession Record is intended to provide information which is both for immediate administrative use and for permanent record. In general, repositories will wish always to maintain an accession register or record, and this sub-area may be used for it, irrespective of whether the custodial history contains accession information. This remains the

preferred sub-area where internal control is the main objective, or where there is need for confidentiality.

### 14.7A1   Number, code, reference
Allocate or record an accession number, code or reference, which may refer to an accessions register.

The permanent reference code (Section 9.10) of an archival entity, where this is different from the accession number, should be cross-referred to it.

### 14.7A2   Date(s) of accession/custody
Give the date(s) of accession, or the date(s) on which the materials came into custody. A reference to the location of the accession may be given here, or in the Location Record Sub-area (Section 14.7B) (which is preferred).

### 14.7A3   Method of acquisition
Describe the method of acquisition, or terms and conditions (for example purchase, gift, loan, deposit, transfer).

### 14.7A4   Immediate source
Record the immediate provenance or source of the accession, with enough detail to allow cross-reference to the Administrative and Custodial History Area (Section 14.3).

### 14.7A5   Conditions of deposit
If there is an agreement with the owner, depositor or originating body, which involves future action, record this here. Such agreements may provide for future contact, the financing or provision of services, and so on. If there is no agreement, but it is perceived that there is a need for future contact with the originating body, then describe this situation. The date and nature of any future contact should be given.

### 14.7A6   Accruals
*ISAD(G) §3.3.3*
If future accruals (Section 9.3) are to be expected, an estimate of their bulk and character and expected date may be given here. Alternatively, these details may appear in the Location Record (Section 14.7B), especially if space in the repository is to be earmarked. The Accession Record is the preferred sub-area if future action is to be administered on the basis of this data.

**14.7A7**   Funding
Give details of any source of funding received to encourage or support the accession.

Example:

| Acc No | Cross ref | Date |
|---|---|---|
| 04822 | 04710 | 12/01/97 |
| **Depositor** | Sydney Chargemore | **Extent** 0.0400 cubic metres; 3vv, 1 map, |
| **Capacity** | Partner | 4 bundles |
| **Organization** | Daws Chargemore, Solicitors | |
| **Address** | Bow St Chester CH1 | |
| **(Approx) span dates** | C19–C20 | |
| **Terms are** | Deposit | |
| **Restrictions** | None | |
| **Notes** | Bundle of papers *re* Egerton of Gresford Lodge to Clwyd Archives | |
| **Status** | Unlisted | **Archivist**   J Pepler |
| **Receipt sent** | Yes | **Conservation required**   No |

[*Source:* Cheshire RO accessions database report]

**14.7B**   *Location Record*
**14.7B1**   Place of storage
Give the place of storage of the materials. In the case of large or mixed-media entities, this may be a complex record.

**14.7B2**   Bulk
Give the size, bulk, quantity, volume or extent of the materials. Cubic metric measurements are preferred, but if this is not possible, metric linear measure of shelving is the preferred option. There may be a cross-reference to the Physical Description Sub-area (Section 14.4C). The Location Record is the preferred sub-area for storage information needed primarily for repository management.

**14.7B3**   The expected or past rate of accrual may be given here if it does not appear in the Accession Record Sub-area (Section 14.7A). The Location Record is the preferred sub-area for this, where the information is intended primarily for repository management.

## 14.8   Process Control Area

The data elements in this area are intended to provide a record of the completion of the main processing stages which are carried on in the repository. The main aim is repository control, making sure that the various processes are carried out to an agreed schedule, and so on, but generally there may also be a need to record what has been done as part of the permanent record.

The Process Control Area contains seven sub-areas:

- 14.8A    Arrangement Record
- 14.8B    Description Record
- 14.8C    Indexing Record
- 14.8D    Issue for Use Record
- 14.8E    Enquiry Record
- 14.8F    Loan Record
- 14.8G    Appraisal Review Record.

**14.8A**   *Arrangement Record*
This sub-area covers ground which may be dealt with in the Archivist's Note Sub-area (Section 14.4D). This is the preferred sub-area where internal repository management is the main objective, and there is no desire to inform users in general.

**14.8A1**   Sorting method
Give a brief account of the sorting method adopted for the physical arrangement of the materials, unless this appears in the Administrative and Custodial History Area (Section 14.3) or in the Content and Structure Area (Section 14.4), including any special problems or features.

**14.8A2**   Person responsible
Record the identity of the archivist who was responsible.

**14.8A3**   Funding
Record details of any special funding received or allocated for the processing of this archive.

**14.8A4**   Date(s) of completion
Give the date(s) of completion of arrangement of the materials.

**14.8B**   *Description Record*
This sub-area records progress made towards the completion of the description process.

**14.8B1**   Description plan
Give details of the plan adopted in embarking on the description of the archive. This information may as an alternative appear in the Content and Structure Area (Section 14.4).

**14.8B2**   Person responsible
Give the identity of the archivist responsible. This information may as an alternative appear in the Content and Structure Area (Section 14.4).

**14.8B3**   Funding
Record any funding received for the completion of this work.

**14.8B4**   Date(s) of completion
Give the date(s) of completion of the work. Distribution of the descriptions can be added. Record despatch of a copy of the description to the National Register of Archives, if this was not done in the Allied Materials Sub-area (Section 14.5C).

**14.8C**   *Indexing Record*
If local custom is to treat indexing as a separate process, the work done on this may be recorded here.

**14.8C1**   System, controls used
Note the system used, or an indication of indexing rules, authority lists or other vocabulary controls.

**14.8C2**   Person responsible
Give the name of the person responsible.

**14.8C3**   Funding
Give details of any relevant funding received for indexing.

**14.8C4**   Date(s) of completion
Record the date(s) of completion.

**14.8D**   *Issue for Use Record*
A record of the number of times an archival entity has been consulted may be needed in order to assist or to help in managing the repository and its resources. Information in this area is often most appropriate at item level.

**14.8D1**   User's identity
Give the user's identity

**14.8D2**   Access status and policy
Note the fact if there is any special provision covering this transaction.

**14.8D3**   Time, dates of issue and return
Give the issue and return times and dates, following local repository practice. If production of the material is outside the main repository, include the due date for its return.

Example:

| Document request slip<br><br>One slip per item | DOCUMENT REF (IN FULL) | | |
|---|---|---|---|
| Brief description/covering date(s) of document requested. | | | |
| Name (block capitals) & signature | Date document | | Table No |
| Office use only: Location | Use | Return date | By |

[*Source:* Cheshire Record Office]

**4.8E** *Enquiry Record*
This sub-area allows entries which record where there has been reference to the archival entity in answer to enquiries from users.

**14.8E1** Identity of enquirer
Give the identity of the enquirer.

**14.8E2** Subject
Record the subject or purpose of the enquiry.

**14.8E3** Date(s)
Give the date(s) at which the reference was made.

**14.8E4** Method
Record the method of enquiry (for example telephone, e-mail, letter).

**14.8F** *Loan Record*
This sub-area allows for a record where materials have been loaned for exhibitions or reference in another repository. Some of this information may have been recorded in the Access, Publication and Reference Area (Section 14.5). The purpose of the Loan Record Sub-area is to control the administration of the loan. Data held here is not intended for the information of public users.

**14.8F1** Borrower
Give the identity of the person or organization to which the material has been loaned, with contact information.

**14.8F2** Location of material whilst on loan
Give the location where the material is being kept/displayed.

**14.8F3** Date(s) of despatch
Give the date(s) of despatch or issue of the materials.

**14.8F4** Date(s) of return/due for return
Give the date(s) of return, or the date(s) on which return is due or expected.

**14.8F5** Insurance or security details
If relevant, insurance or security details information may be added.

Example:

| Name of borrower | *Mrs Frances Wentworth (Hon Sec, Chadsworth Fine Art Society), 42 High St, Chadsworth* |
|---|---|
| Item(s) borrowed | *D181/17–19 Minute books, 1898–1912* |
| Location of borrowed item(s) | *Chadsworth Manor* |
| Event etc. | *PCC centenary display* |
| Date of issue | *24 Feb 1999* |
| Date for return | *26 Feb 1999* |
| Signature of borrower & contact tel no. | *F W Wentworth (01456 789789)* |
| Signature of archivist receiving loan/date | *H Jenkinson, 26 Feb 1999* |

**14.8G**  *Appraisal Review Record*
This sub-area is intended for recording the operations, past or future, involved in the appraisal of the archival entity. Section 14.4D2 is more appropriate for recording the appraisal principle, or general policy involved.

**14.8G1**   Procedure used
Give the appraisal procedure or house rules which have been used in the case of these materials.

**14.8G2**   Action taken/recommended
Record the action which has been taken or recommended.

**14.8G3**   Action date
Give the action date, that is, the date on which future action is to be taken in order to implement the appraisal decision.

**14.8G4**   Appraiser/person responsible
Give the identity of the person responsible for the appraisal decision.

## 14.9 Conservation Area

The purpose of the Conservation Area is to provide for a permanent record of the conservation (either environmental or remedial) of archival entities, and to contain information which will help control the conservation processes within the repository.

The Conservation Area contains two sub-areas:

- 14.9A     Administration
- 14.9B     Conservation Record.

The Conservation Area may, like the other areas, be used at any level of description. Its mode of operation will therefore be different when working at different levels. Data which relates to groups, for example (especially when the group in question is large), can only deal in very broad terms with the conservation of the group, and will probably be confined to information in support of environmental or preventative conservation.

Example:

Parts of this group have been exposed to damp over long periods and are fragile.

When the data relates to items or pieces, it is likely to be specific and to deal with repair; it can, indeed, be used to monitor the repair process.

Example:

Rebound October 1996, as two volumes.

**14.9A**   *Administration*
This sub-area is intended to contain data relating to the management aspects of conservation, in relation to the archival entity being described.

**14.9A1**   Indicate the general situation of the entity in relation to its physical character; this may include information on the storage conditions under which the entity is or has been kept. Cross-refer to the Physical Description Sub-area (Section 14.4C), and, if necessary, to the administrative records of the repository.

**14.9B**   *Conservation Record*
The sub-area is intended to contain information which will allow for the monitoring of conservation processes and repair.

**14.9B1**   Conservation history

Record the previous conservation history of the entity; however, if public information is intended, these details would be better placed in the Physical Description Sub-area (Section 14.4C).

**14.9B2**   Work required

Indicate details of any repair work required, immediately or in the future.

**14.9B3**   Level of priority

Indicate the level of priority which is to be given to the work.

**14.9B4**   Conservator responsible

Record the name of the conservator responsible.

**14.9B5**   Start and finish dates

When repair is done, record the dates on which repair work started and the dates on which the materials subjected to repair were returned to their storage location.

**14.9B6**   Work carried out

Include a description of the repair carried out.

**14.9B7**   Recommendations for future conservation

Add any recommendations for future conservation. These may refer to special storage conditions, further repair work, periodic examination, and so on.

**14.9B8**   Materials used

This sub-area may also be used to record the type and quantity of new materials used in the work of repair, so as to provide control over stocks.

**14.9B9**   Funding

Record any relevant funding received in respect of the conservation or repair of this archive.

# PART III
# MODELS FOR DESCRIPTION

# 15

# Models for description

**15.1**  Archival descriptions are composed by selecting relevant data elements from the table of data elements (Part II) and arranging them in accordance with the models given here.

Each archive is unique, and presents special features of its own. It is therefore quite usual for archivists to decide that the listing models cannot be used without some modification to suit the job in hand. *MAD* standards have been devised with this qualification in mind. Notwithstanding this, it is quite possible to apply the principles and general rules laid down in *MAD* while at the same time applying any case-specific or relevant local modifications to the actual layout of data on the page.

Finding aids are composed by combining archival descriptions covering different levels in different ways. Section 15.11 gives models for the combination of descriptions.

**15.2**  It is recommended that archivists undertaking description should use the areas and/or sub-areas as wholes, wherever this is suitable (Section 13.6). Individual data elements may be selected without regard to their context in areas or sub-areas, if this suits the work; but this approach will be more suitable where an automated system incorporating the table of data elements is used.

If data capture forms are to be used, it is recommended that areas and sub-areas should be given distinct boxes or locations on the form, with data elements within them being indicated without emphasis.

## 15.3    SUMMARY OF THE STANDARDS

This section summarizes the standards for some applications of important general rules.

### 15.3A    Higher and lower level descriptions

The need for distinct higher and lower level descriptions arises from the multi-level rule, which is explained in Chapter 5.

Descriptions at any of the numbered levels may be treated as being higher or lower level descriptions, depending on their relationship with other descriptions in the same finding aid. Thus, normally, a group description would be a higher level description in relation to its dependent sub-group or series descriptions. However, in other circumstances, a set of group descriptions may be lower level in relation to management group headings (for example in a repository guide to holdings). The same alternatives apply at all levels.

Higher level descriptions give general and contextual information about sets of archives which belong in related groupings. Such higher level descriptions are said to govern the sets of lower level descriptions which deal with the components of the entity. This governing function should be demonstrated in the way in which the two kinds of description are set out. Generally, the higher level description should precede the related lower level descriptions. It can appear separately as a title page or title page section, or it can appear as a headnote (Chapter 6). Headnotes are laid out in a way which shows that they govern the descriptions that come below them.

### 15.3B    Paragraph or list mode

The difference between paragraph and list mode descriptions is explained in Chapter 7. Generally, archivists may choose between variations of one of these modes, following the needs of the entity being described, and the local house rules.


## SUMMARY OF THE MODELS

**15.4**    Models for description at the principal different levels are provided for management group headings (Level 1); group and subgroup descriptions (Level 2); series descriptions (Level 3); item and piece descriptions (Levels 4 and 5), as follows:

*Models for description at specific levels:*

1. Management group headings (Level 1)    See also Fig. 15.1
2. Group descriptions    (Level 2)    See also Fig. 15.2
3. Subgroup descriptions    (Levels 2.nn) See also Fig. 15.3
4. Series descriptions    (Level 3)    See also Figs 15.4 and 15.5
5. Item descriptions    (Level 4)    See also Figs 15.6 and 15.7
6. Piece descriptions    (Level 5)

*Models for the combination of descriptions:*

7. Group and subgroup    (Levels 2,2.nn)
8. Group and series    (Levels 2,3)
9. Group and item    (Levels 2,4)
10. Series and item    (Levels 3,4)
11. Item and piece    (Levels 4,5)
12. Three-level descriptions

## 15.5    Management group headings (Level 1)

**15.5A**    (For an explanation of the term 'management group', see Section 4.6B.) Management groups do not have descriptions in the strict sense, because they are not themselves archival entities. Because of this, the term 'heading' is used in relation to them. In practice, finding aids systems do often require descriptive information to be given at management group level (Level 1), in order to explain the structure of the system, or to give information on background, context and provenance. These descriptions might be drawn from an authority file.

**15.5B**    Although in principle any area, sub-area or data element may be chosen for inclusion in a Level 1 heading, the most characteristic area is the Administrative and Custodial History Area (Section 14.3). The heading therefore consists most typically of the following (Figure 15.1):

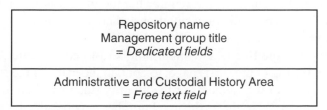

**Figure 15.1    Management group heading (Level 1.5) – general shape**

Example:

GLOUCESTERSHIRE RECORD OFFICE

SMALL BOROUGHS AND TOWN TRUSTS

Many small towns and large villages had anciently acquired some of the attributes of borough status but were not accepted as boroughs under the Municipal Corporations Act 1835. Other settlements had bodies of feoffees who acted for the freeholders as owners of common property, as at Upton St Leonards, where the freeholders had purchased the manor in the 16th century.

The records usually include minutes, accounts and title deeds, and often papers concerning schools and charities.

[*Source:* Gloucestershire Record Office]

**15.5C**  Where Level 1 headings are used, they should if possible contain all the information common to the groups which are contained within them. The group descriptions which follow the heading may then avoid repeating the data given in the heading.

**15.5D**  Although the term 'heading' is used for these descriptions, the relationship between them and the sets of (group) descriptions which are governed by them follows the same rules as for other higher and lower level descriptions (Chapter 5): title pages, title page sections or headnotes may be used (Chapter 6).

## 15.6    Group descriptions (Level 2)

**15.6A**    *General shape*
**15.6A1**    Group descriptions consist essentially of free text, frequently but not always lengthy. Alternatively, where group descriptions are held in authority files, there may be a reference here to the existence and location of that file. This is most likely in situations where the finding aids system is completely automated.

In addition to the free text, a small number of dedicated fields may be provided at the top of the (first) page, to contain the name of the repository, and one or more of the elements of the identity statement (reference code, title) (Section 14.2). To these, the level number may be added, for internal use in the repository (Figure 15.2).

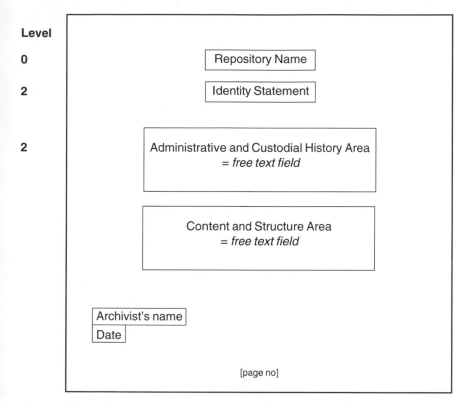

Level

0

2

2

**Figure 15.2   Group description (Level 2) – general shape**

**15.6A2**   The information given in the dedicated fields may if desired be placed on a title page (Chapter 6), together with repository information. In this case local practice may be followed as to layout and the inclusion of additional information, such as the date of the completion of the description, its author, access information, and so on.

**15.6A3**   In accordance with the general style of *MAD3* standards, where there is no separate title page, reference codes should normally appear at the beginning of the description, in the left margin; simple span dates should either follow the name element after a comma, or should appear in a column on the right margin. If level numbers are used, for in-house purposes, they may appear in either margin. It is a recommended practice that these level numbers should be distinguished from reference codes, by using colour codes, distinctive type or bracketing. It is not recommended that they appear on publicly available lists.

**15.6A4**   There may be further dedicated fields if desired, at the head or foot of the free text section. The field for extent and physical character is particularly appropriate here.

**15.6A5**   Within the free text, further structures may be introduced. New paragraphs or headed sections should be used for each area or sub-area. Where the contents of an area are lengthy (as would often be the case in the administrative history), it may be convenient to break the text up into chapters or further headed sections.

**15.6A6**   Chapter or section headings should be underlined, set in capitals or bold characters, in accordance with local practice, and following a hierarchical ranking. Where chapters or a sequence of headed sections are used, the free text field may be preceded by a contents list.

**15.6A7**   It is clear from the above, that group descriptions are normally in paragraph mode (Chapter 7). List mode entries are also possible, where the group descriptions form a set of tabulated headings following a headnote. In this case the central or main text column will contain the title, perhaps followed by a brief entry for the Administrative and Custodial History (Section 14.3) or Content and Structure (Section 14.4) Areas.

**15.6B**   *Data elements*
**15.6B1**   For the structure of data elements, and information on their combination in areas and sub-areas, see Part II. Any of the areas, sub-areas or data elements may be selected for use, but apart from the Identity Statement (Section 14.2), none is compulsory.

**15.6B2**   A typical group description uses the data elements which belong to these areas, in the following order. (An index or other retrieval aid is commonly added.)

| | |
|---|---|
| Identity Statement | (Section 14.2) |
| Administrative and Custodial History Area | (Section 14.3) |
| Content and Structure Area | (Section 14.4) |
| [Index] | |

**15.6B3**   The Identity Statement
The Identity Statement (Section 14.2) consists of reference code, title, dates, extent and level number. The Title Sub-area contains two data elements: these comprise a term for form, type or genre and a name element.
   The recommended style is for the name element in the title to be centred,

with the reference code at the left margin in a column reserved for reference codes; the name element may be followed by the simple span dates after a comma, or these may be placed in a dates column at the right margin, according to house style. Layouts such as these facilitate scanning.

Example:

Level
2
| DV89   Archives of Borchester Town Council  1447–1835 |
| --- |
| (153 boxes) |

*or*
2
| DV89   Borough of Borchester, 1447–1835 |
| --- |

Extent information may appear either here, or after the Administrative and Custodial History or Content and Structure Areas, but it is recommended that it is located on the first page of the description or is otherwise immediately available when scanning the finding aid.

For rules on the choice and construction of titles, see Section 14.2B.

**15.6B4**   The Administrative and Custodial History and Content and Structure Areas
When the description is not drawn from an authority file, both the Administrative and Custodial History Area (Section 14.3) and the Content and Structure Area (Section 14.4) (particularly the Abstract Sub-area (Section 14.4A) within the latter) relating to a group will normally be free text narrative. It is a useful practice to break up long sections of text by subheadings. Cross-references may be written into dedicated fields, placed in the margins or below the paragraph to which they refer, or placed in footnotes at the bottom of the page.

Where groups or subgroups exhibit recurrent characteristics or constantly repeated data, they should be presented in a standard order which allows as much as possible of the repeated information to be given in a headnote. Side headings may be used to signal the start of blocks of specific information.

**15.6C**   *Access points*
**15.6C1**   Group descriptions (like all free text entries) should normally be indexed.

**15.6C2**   In accordance with *MAD* recommendations on depth of description (the rule of information retrieval – Section 8.5), free text entries should be composed with a view to the inclusion of all keywords likely to be needed for a search. If a controlled or structured index vocabulary is being used, some keywords may have to be rewritten as the appropriate preferred term, or cross-references may be necessary. Keywords may be written into dedicated fields to improve their function as access points. Data elements are available to provide for this usage.

**15.6C3**   Page layouts may be established in accordance with *MAD* recommendations (and with existing house styles if necessary). Dedicated fields where used as distinct entities to contain specific data elements may be given pre-formatted positions on the page. Each page after the first should contain the group reference code and the page number in addition to the free text entry.

**15.6C4**   Give the name of the archivist responsible for the description with the date of its completion at the end of the free text. The name of the word processed file or database from which the list is derived should be recorded with these data elements.

## 15.7   Subgroup descriptions (Levels 2.nn)

**15.7A**   *General shape*

**15.7A1**   Subgroups must retain a close connection with their parent group, and their descriptions are framed with this connection in mind. In a context such as this, the group description acts as headnote and contains all common, background or contextual information.

Each subgroup may in consequence consist only of an Identity Statement (Section 14.2), but may additionally have an Administrative and Custodial History Area (Section 14.3) or Content and Structure Area (Section 14.4) of its own.

Subgroup descriptions may be used as headnotes (Chapter 6) to lower level descriptions at series level or below. In this case they take the form of group descriptions, and may repeat or re-use background, contextual or provenance information from the governing group description.

In other circumstances, subgroup descriptions may be treated as distinct and separate entries. Where subgroup descriptions are separated from their covering group descriptions, the text should contain enough common information from the group description to allow the subgroup description to be intelligible by itself.

Sometimes, the description of what *has* been seen as a subgroup appears capable of standing independently in a finding aids system. In this case

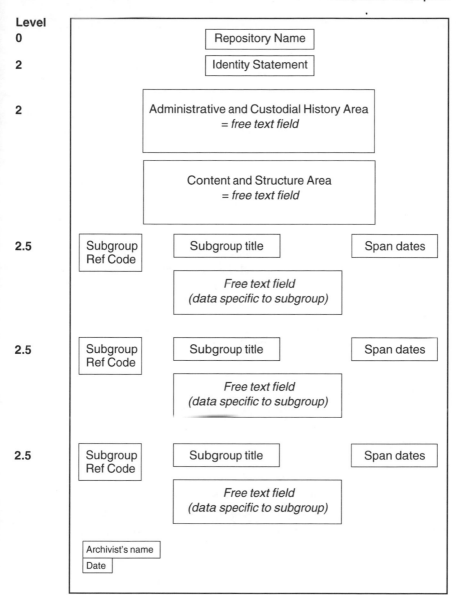

**Figure 15.3    Subgroup descriptions (Levels 2.nn) – general shape**

it is treated as a group and the description may be held in an authority file.

Subgroup descriptions are like group descriptions in their general layout. They should contain the elements of the identity statement in dedicated fields, and all other material (where there is any) in a free text entry without length restriction (Figure 15.3).

**15.7A2**    The identity of a subgroup may be established by a reference code and one or more elements of the title.

It is recommended that subgroup reference codes, where they are used, should contain an element to indicate the relationship to the parent group. This practice may be omitted if the result would be unduly complex.

For rules on the choice of titles, see Section 14.2B. Subgroups are normally named from the functional divisions of the group which they represent.

**15.7A3**    In paragraph mode descriptions (Chapter 7), subgroups are best treated as free text narrative paragraphs appended to the group description and following their own identity statement.

**15.7A4**    In list mode descriptions, or where the structure of the group is particularly complex, it may be useful to list subgroup titles as a list of contents immediately after the group description.

**15.7B**    *Data elements*
A minimum content for subgroup descriptions contains data elements from the following areas:

| | |
|---|---|
| Identity Statement | (Section 14.2) |
| Administrative and Custodial History Area | (Section 14.3) |
| Content and Structure Area | (Section 14.4) |
| [Index] | |

Since subgroup descriptions are normally lower level descriptions governed by a group, all common, background or contextual information will appear in the latter. Where subgroup descriptions are used as headnotes to series descriptions or below, such information may be repeated if necessary.

**15.7C**    *Retrieval aids*
An index is commonly created. In normal circumstances the index would relate to the whole group.

## 15.8    Series descriptions (Level 3)

**15.8A**    *General shape*
**15.8A1**    Series descriptions contain both dedicated and free text fields. At the beginning, dedicated field(s) should contain the Identity Statement. The main free text field contains the Administrative and Custodial History

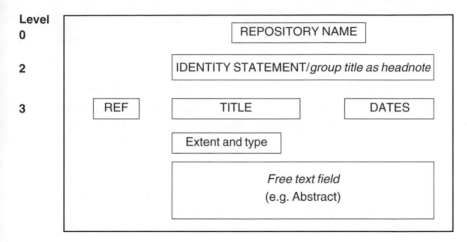

**Figure 15.4   Series descriptions (Level 3) in paragraph mode –
general shape**

Area (if relevant) and the Content and Structure Area. Other dedicated fields
may come before or after the free text field, containing extent and physical
character information. This model constitutes a paragraph mode finding aid,
which is therefore regarded as the norm at this level (Figure 15.4).

**15.8A2**   List mode is available as an alternative (Figure 15.5). In this case

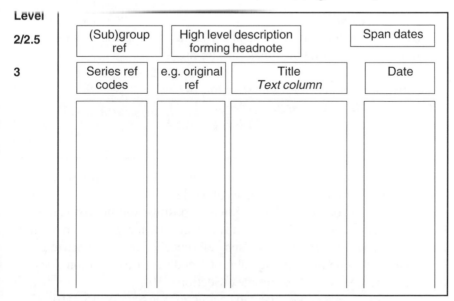

**Figure 15.5   Series descriptions (Level 3) in list mode – general
shape**

the title information should appear on the first line. The reference code should occupy the left margin; the simple date or simple span dates should occupy the right margin. The other elements appear in the central (textual) column: it is recommended that the wording here should be underlined or presented in bold type, in order to mark out the title from any other text. This recommendation may be disregarded where a confused page would result. Textual fields containing Administrative and Custodial History and/or Content and Structure Areas appear below the title elements in the central column.

**15.8A3**   Series descriptions in either mode may serve as headnotes. Layout should follow the rules for composite finding aids: see Section 15.11F.

**15.8A4**   Series descriptions may also be lower level descriptions following a group or subgroup description. Rules for these are in Section 15.11C. In these circumstances underline, or italicize, the name section of the Identity Statement, in order to distinguish the beginning of a new series in the list.

**15.8A5**   Paragraph and list modes are equally common at this level. Further rules and recommendations are given in the section on composite finding aids (Section 15.11).

**15.8B**   *Data elements*
**15.8B1**   A commonly used content for series descriptions contains data elements from the following areas and sub-areas:

| | |
|---|---|
| Identity Statement | (Section 14.2) |
| Content and Structure Area | (Section 14.4) |
| Access Record | (Section 14.5A) |
| [Index] | |

**15.8B2**   The identity of a series may be established by a reference code and/or by one or more of the elements of a title.

The reference code occupies a dedicated position on the first and every subsequent page, preferably at the head of the left margin. A series reference code generally appears as a 'sub-reference' of the appropriate group code. There may be intervening subgroup codes, if this addition does not make the reference code too complex (Section 9.10).

For series reference codes used in headnotes, see Section 15.11F1.

The title of a series should be given as described in the rules for data elements (Section 14.2B).

114

The level number, for use in-house, should (where used) be given in one of the margins, level with the reference code or with the first line of text, but distinguished from reference codes by colour code, distinctive type or bracketing. It is not recommended that level numbers appear on publicly available lists.

If there is to be an Administrative and Custodial History Area, it should appear before the Content and Structure Area.

**15.8B3**   The Content and Structure Area of a series may contain any or all of the data elements for this area, which is the one most characteristic of series descriptions. Elements which are common to all or many series in a group are best included in the higher level description covering them, or otherwise in a headnote.

**15.8B4**   Descriptions at series level are the main instruments for both administrative and intellectual control of archives. Group/subgroup descriptions do not usually give direct retrieval information about specific physical entities of archive material. Series descriptions are usually the highest level at which this is done, though to retrieve particular items a further, more detailed, level of description is usually needed.

Physical descriptions should cover the whole series. Physical descriptions which refer only to particular items or pieces should appear at that level.

In accordance with the rules on depth of description (Chapter 8), textual fields in series descriptions should, if possible, contain all keywords required for searches or for index construction. The Administrative/ Biographical History Sub-area or Abstract Sub-area may be structured to promote this, using the appropriate data elements, and making allowance for permitted vocabularies.

## 15.9   Item descriptions (Level 4)

**15.9A**   *General shape*
The minimum content of an item description contains one or more elements from the following areas:

Identity Statement                 (Section 14.2)
Content and Structure Area      (Section 14.4)
[Index]

In the Identity Statement, an item reference code usually refers back to the group/subgroup and series. It would be normal for each item to have a unique subnumber within the series, since this is usually the call number by which the item is retrieved and produced for readers.

The name element of an item title is derived as described in the rules for data elements (Section 14.2B2). In the absence of a name element, it is quite usual for items not to have titles but instead to have a brief abstract or summary of content.

### 15.9B  *List mode descriptions*

**15.9B1**   Higher level descriptions governing item lists are normally provided as headnotes, though title page sections are possible, especially where there is extensive text.

**15.9B2**   List mode item descriptions are typically set out in tabulated columns (Figure 15.6). A full reference code should appear on each page, preferably at the top left margin. Reference code subnumbers which relate to items should appear against each entry, in the left-hand column. If the full reference code is abbreviated, the item subnumber should appear in the character space directly below the subnumber in the main code (see examples in Part IV); however, where users might find this difficult to interpret, it may be best to repeat the full reference code against each item.

**15.9B3**   Simple span dates, or simple year dates, should normally appear in a dedicated column at the right of the page. Complex dates are better

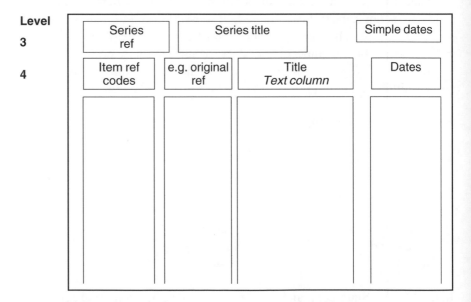

**Figure 15.6    Item descriptions (Level 4) in list mode – general shape**

treated as text, and written into the main text column. Where the governing higher level description contains intelligible and relevant span dates above the item description, it may be preferable to write item dates into the text of the Content and Structure Area, in order to avoid multiple date columns.

**15.9B4**  Other columns may be chosen as required, but may often include columns for size/bulk and form/type/genre. Additional columns may be included as needed, subject to space being available across the page.

**15.9B5**  If the Diplomatic or Physical Description Sub-areas are used, their entries should appear under the main text column which contains the Content and Structure Area.

**15.9B6**  Where page layout permits, tabulated item lists which appear below headnotes should be contained within wider margins, both left and right, than the headnote, in order to emphasize the relationship between higher and lower level descriptions.

**15.9C**  *Paragraph mode descriptions*
**15.9C1**  Where item descriptions contain textual fields longer than six lines, or when the item descriptions are used singly, or are grouped separately from the main finding aids (for example where they are published as a distinct set of descriptions), the paragraph mode is preferred (Figure 15.7).

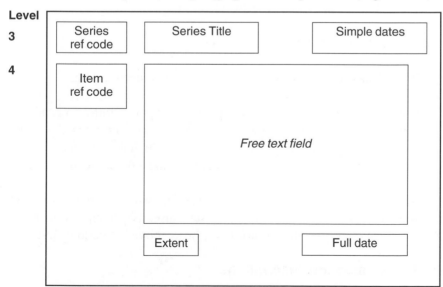

**Figure 15.7    Item descriptions (Level 4) in paragraph mode – general shape**

**15.9C2**   In the Identity Statement, the reference code should appear in the left margin, or as the first element in the paragraph.

**15.9C3**   All other areas may follow in the order established by the table of data elements. The Administrative and Custodial History and the Content and Structure Areas are normally free text, and should be in consecutive sentences arranged in paragraphs as necessary.

**15.9C4**   Elements within the Diplomatic Description Sub-area may be entered in limited-length fields if this is desirable. Such fields may constitute short paragraphs.

**15.9C5**   Related sets of item descriptions will normally be indexed.

For examples, see Part IV.

**15.9D**   For both modes, successive pages of a list should preferably include the repository title (or identifier) and the group/subgroup/series reference code at the top, and a page number at the bottom.
   Where an item list contains a reference to a special format, see Part V.
   Item descriptions within a series and containing textual entries should generally be indexed. Free text fields, such as item titles, should contain all the keywords necessary for searches or index construction. Alternatively, keywords may be provided in a separate field or column.

## 15.10   Piece descriptions (Level 5)

**15.10A**   The rules for piece descriptions follow those for items.

**15.10B**   A list mode is usual where piece descriptions follow a headnote. Governing higher level descriptions in the headnote are normally of the related item, but there may also be cases where linked item and piece descriptions appear together. For composite finding aids see Section 15.11G.

**15.10C**   A paragraph mode is most appropriate where there will be more than six lines of text, or where the distant user is principally in mind. Governing higher level descriptions may be as above in Section 15.9.

## 15.11   Composite descriptions

**15.11A**   *Combining description at different levels*
**15.11A1**   Descriptions at two or more levels may be combined to create a

118

single finding aid. There are always at least two levels of description in any finding aid. Three or more levels of description may commonly be found within a finding aid, and there is no restriction on the number of levels which may be so combined, subject to the following rule:

**15.11A2** Where two levels of description are provided, covering the same set of related original materials, the higher level should be treated as a description governing the lower, in accordance with the multi-level rule (Chapter 5). This rule also applies where the lower level description itself comprises two levels. Higher level descriptions within composite finding aids are displayed as headnotes within the text. Wherever possible, such headnotes should be given a wider text block with its narrower margins, left and right, than the lower level descriptions they govern, in order that the progression of the levels, and the hierarchical relationships these express, should be demonstrated.

**15.11B** *Finding aids containing group and subgroup descriptions (Level 2)*
**15.11B1** The simplest appropriate method of combining these levels should be adopted.

**15.11B2** Subgroups are intimately linked to groups (of which they are organic parts) and the group description will normally include an explanation of the subgroup structure. This explanation should be situated in the Administrative and Custodial History Area (where it arises from an analysis of the original system) and/or the Content and Structure Area (where it is an aspect of the description of the content and meaning of the archive). It may contain a specific reference to the subgroups, identifying them by their reference codes and one or more elements of their titles.

If subgroup references are not embedded in the text in this way, they may be distinguished by adding a list of subgroup references and titles at the end of the main text of the group description.

Alternatively, subgroup descriptions may appear in full, in structural, logical or alphabetical sequence, after the group description.

**15.11B3** If there is an overall title page, it may include a list of subgroup titles immediately following the title of the group they belong to.

**15.11C** *Group (subgroup) and series descriptions (Levels 2,3)*
**15.11C1** The simplest appropriate method of linking group, subgroup and series descriptions should be adopted.

**15.11C2**   A choice may be made between list and paragraph mode. Where the group or subgroup description acts as headnote to the series description, paragraph mode may be appropriate for the higher level description, and list mode for the lower level description.

**15.11D**   *Paragraph mode*
**15.11D1**   Paragraph mode is appropriate where textual fields contain more than one to six lines of text.

**15.11D2**   The group/subgroup description which covers the series description set may appear as title page section or as headnote. Alternatively a special headnote may be used, which contains a reference to the full group/subgroup description.

**15.11D3**   Paragraph mode series descriptions are entered in structural, logical or alphabetical sequence without indentation.

**15.11D4**   The full reference code should appear on each page, preferably in the top left-hand corner. Page numbers should be given, preferably at the bottom of the page.

**15.11E**   *List mode*
**15.11E1**   List mode finding aids are made up of headnote (or title page) and tabulated columns.

**15.11E2**   The left-most column on the page should be dedicated to reference codes. The full code should appear at the head of each page. Codes appropriate to each series should appear on the first line of the series description, and may be limited to that part of the code specific to the series. If this is done, the series number should be printed in the character column below the series reference element in the full reference code at the top of the page. However, user convenience may suggest that the full reference code should be given against each series heading.

**15.11E3**   Write the series title in the main tabulated column, which should be as broad as possible in order to contain free text. The name element of series titles should be underlined, in bold type or italicized, in order to mark the individuality of the series. This rule may be ignored if it would result in an excessively complex page layout. Additional text comprising entries in the Administrative and Custodial History and/or Content and Structure Areas may appear in the central column immediately below the title.

**15.11E4**   The simple span date element of the title (see Section 14.2C) should normally appear in a right-hand tabulated column, in order to assist scanning by users. Simple span dates consist of four figure year numbers, for example 1594–1807.

**15.11E5**   After the last series description, the list should be completed by an end marker. This may take the form of a brief entry identifying the archivist responsible, date of completion, and the name of the file from which the printed list was generated. For example:

H. Jenkinson, 15 May 1995
<o:\winword\lists\D670

**15.11F**   *Series and item descriptions (Levels 3,4)*
**15.11F1**   List mode
**15.11F1a**   The normal page or screen layout for list mode entries is for the series description to appear as headnote above the text of the list. Alternatively the headnote may be specially written, and cross-refer to the relevant series description. Headnotes governing list mode descriptions may themselves be in paragraph mode, but in any case should use narrower margins than the descriptions governed by them. It is generally recommended that the name element of series titles used as higher level descriptions should be underlined or italicized.

**15.11F1b**   Item descriptions in list form which are governed by a headnote should be entered immediately below that headnote.

Example:

| XC2O/5/1–90 | *Corn Rolls* | 1919 |
|---|---|---|
| | Gives by parish, names of holdings, occupiers, landowners, statistics of acreages, labour and livestock, notes *re* soil fertility. | |
| 1 | Maenan | |
| 2 | Llanrhychwyn | |
| 3 | Trefriw, Abbey and Llanrhychwyn | |
| 4 | Dolywddelen | |
| 5 | Eidda | |

[Source: Gwynedd Archives Service]

**15.11F1c**  The important consideration in any layout decision is the need to demonstrate visually the dependence of lower level descriptions upon their governing higher level description.

**15.11F1d**  The reference code at series level should contain the item-level subnumbers expressed as a span. Where bulk is not specifically expressed this also gives some indication of the quantities involved. For example:

   XC2O/5/1–90

At the left-hand end of the line, the item number element in the reference code should appear in the character column below the item number element in the full reference code.

Example:

| TB3/13–15 | *Register of admissions* | 1816–1859 |
|---|---|---|
| 13 | 4 Oct 1816 – 9 Dec 1835 | |
| 14 | 14 July 1835 – 12 Aug 1846 | |
| 15 | 2 Mar 1846 – 20 Nov 1859 | |

**15.11F1e**  Individual or span dates of items, if they can be expressed simply, may appear in the right-margin date column. If they are complex, or if the right-margin column is crowded, they may be written into the main text column as Content and Structure Area data elements.

Example:

| TB17/1 | "Health notes" | 1905–1919 |
|---|---|---|
| | Notebook containing brief observations made by Lord Acton between 6 August 1905 and 2 February 1919 detailing his health problems. | |

**15.11F1f**  If user convenience requires, full reference codes may be given for each item.

Example:

| | | |
|---|---|---|
| TB3/13–15 | *Register of admissions* | 1816–1859 |
| TB3/13 | 4 Oct 1816 – 9 Dec 1835 | |
| TB3/14 | 14 July 1835 – 12 Aug 1846 | |
| TB3/15 | 2 Mar 1846 – 20 Nov 1859 | |

**15.11F1g**  There should be one or more blank lines between each set of related series and item descriptions. As in Section 15.11F1c, the intention is to emphasize visually the dependence of lower level descriptions upon their governing higher level descriptions. The overall effect of the page should be to demonstrate that the headnote and list entries belong in a single related section, distinct from the rest of the list.

**15.11F2**  *Paragraph mode*
**15.11F2a**  The rules applicable to group/subgroup and series descriptions apply, except that where series descriptions appear as headnotes to item descriptions, the latter should be indented from the left margin.
   An example is in Part IV.

**15.11G**  *Item and piece descriptions (Levels 4,5)*
**15.11G1**  The rules for series/item descriptions (Section 15.11F) apply, both in list and paragraph modes.

**15.11G2**  In some series, items and pieces must be treated as equivalent. This might be the case, for example, where the series contains a number of items which consist of pieces bound together, but also a number of unbound pieces. In this case, lists may exist in which items and pieces are treated as on the same level (indicated as Level 4/5), and governing higher level descriptions may be composed from related series descriptions.

**15.11H**  *Three-level descriptions*
Sets of descriptions which include three or more levels are frequently met (see Section 15.11A2). Any combination of the main levels may occur. The principle is that related higher/lower descriptions should be kept together and nested within the main finding aid.
   Either list or paragraph mode may be used. Examples are in Part IV.

### 15.11H1 *List mode*

The rules for series/item finding aids apply, except that a further indentation should if possible be provided at the third level. This can only be done if the paper width or on-screen presentation allows this layout without waste or crowding.

### 15.11H2 *Paragraph mode*

The rules for group/series (Section 15.11C) or series/item (Section 15.11F) finding aids apply, except that there should be an indented left margin at each level.

# 16

# Standard listing conventions

Finding aids should use consistent conventions and follow national authorities wherever applicable. In any case standards should always be followed where the data is designed to provide access points to the archives (for example in providing name authority access using NCA *Rules*), but conventions within the text of a finding aid which are not designed to provide such access should nevertheless be consistent. The data listed here has been based, where appropriate, on PRO practice and on *AACR2*.

## 16.1 Spelling
**16.1A** English words should be spelt as in the *Oxford English Dictionary* and its *Supplements*, or the current edition of the *Shorter Oxford English Dictionary*. The following list is of preferred spellings used in record-based work:

> acknowledgement (not acknowledgment)
> appendixes (not appendices)
> chase (not chace)
> dovecote (not dovecot)
> enclosure (not inclosure)
> endorse (not indorse)
> gaol (not jail)
> judgment (not judgement)
> medieval (not mediaeval)
> mottoes (not mottos)
> recognizance (not recognisance).

**16.1B** In passages quoted from foreign language documents, letters should be given the accents used there. Words of foreign origin which appear with accents in the Oxford dictionaries should also be given them. Where alternative spellings without accents are allowed, these should be preferred.

## 16.2 Punctuation

**16.2A** Standard abbreviations should if possible be drawn from a permitted list. Non-standard abbreviations (for example initials of first names) may have full stops. For example:

B. Williams esq

**16.2B** Entries in free text fields, like other natural-language text, should use normal punctuation, and should have a full stop at the end of the field.

**16.2C** Within the Administrative and Custodial History and the Content and Structure Areas, double quotation marks indicate data transcribed from the original. Wording within such quotation marks, including reference codes or titles, should be reproduced exactly as in the original text. For example:

letter headed "3 x 2/4 Mr Jone's"

**16.2D** Information supplied by the editor of a text, or by an archivist compiling a description, as a result of inference or research into other sources, or derived from an investigation of the archival entity being described, should be enclosed in square brackets. A note on the grounds for making the inference may be useful. For example:

[c. 1936: endorsed note refers to the abdication crisis surrounding Edward VIII]

*Note:* the NCA *Rules* (1.6.1) have no mandatory conventions for punctuation.

## 16.3 Capital letters

**16.3A** Capital letters should be used for proper names, titles of honour when referring to a specific individual, and for acronyms according to the predominant usage of the body. For example:

William 2nd Duke of Albany
Unesco, *but* NATO
Department of the Environment, Transport and the Regions
1st Battalion The Grenadier Guards (where an upper case 't' is consistently used in the title).

See NCA *Rules* Chapter 2 for the construction of personal names when these provide access points.

**16.3B**   Lower case should be used for titles used in a general or generic sense, and generally where there is room for choice. For example:

the dukes of Albany
municipal corporations and town councils
quarter sessions
census returns.

**16.3C**   Upper case characters and underlining may be used to emphasize or pick out significant wording in the body of the text of a description. This practice may be an aid to scanning. (Care should be taken that upper case, underlining and other stylistic usages should not clash with typeface differences meant to clarify archival arrangement in a composite list.) For example:

4 acres in the par of WEST KIRBY

**16.4   Numerals**
**16.4A**   Generally, all quantities in archival descriptions should be expressed in arabic numerals, and numerals are preferred to written numbers. For example:

4 messuages, 23 vols (*not* four messuages, twenty-three vols)

**16.4B**   Ranges of numbers (for example as in reference codes, or in free text) should be expressed in full. For example:

D12/132–139 (not D12/132–9)

**16.5   Measurements**
**16.5A**   To express physical dimensions, metric measurements are preferred. Measurements referred to in the archive should be retained in their original form.

**16.5B**   Decimals should be preferred to fractions, particularly small or complex fractions. For example:

66.05 (not 66 1/20, unless in direct quotation)

## 16.6   Dates

**16.6A**   This section covers dates included in the main body of an archival description. The special rules applying to title dates can be found in Section 14.2C. Dates appearing as qualifiers for authority names should follow NCA *Rules* Chapter 2.5.

**16.6B**   In archival description generally, broader date ranges are preferable to narrower ones: use the year alone when month and day are not strictly required in the context.

**16.6C**   Span dates in the text are used if there are no significant chronological gaps in the sequence being described:

1643–1687
15 Aug 1945 – 16 Sept 1948
  4 Nov 1957 – 12 Dec 1961 and 2 Mar 1971
25 Mar – 6 Apr 1782
  4–10 July 1814

**16.6D**   Span dates and single dates entered into the right-hand tabulated column of lists should normally be confined to simple year four-figure numbers. Where fuller or more complex dates are needed, this more detailed date can be entered into a text field such as the Abstract.

**16.6E**   Span dates in right-hand tabulated columns should ignore minor gaps in a chronological sequence. However, significant gaps should be indicated, and the bulk dates separated by semi-colons. For example:

1699;1827–1847;1961

**16.6F**   When year, month and day are required, the (abbreviated) month should be written in letters, and placed between the numeral of the day and the numeral for the year. The orders year/month/day and day/month/year are both permissible. For example:

1660 May 14

*or*

14 May 1660

128

**16.6G**   Automated systems may use the International Standard ISO 8601 *Representation of dates and times*, which recommends the use of eight-figure dates (for example 18820207 or 1882-02-07 = 7 February 1882).[1]

**16.6H**   *Uncertain and inferred dates*
Where no date is available, indicate this by 'undated' or 'no date' (nd); but wherever possible follow this by an approximation in square brackets []. For example:

undated [?1857]
   [183–]      where the decade is certain
   [156?]      where the decade is probable
   [13– –]     where the century is certain
   [17?]       where the century is probable

**16.6I**   Square brackets can also be used to indicate inferred dates. Any or all of the parameters in a date, or parts of them, may be bracketed:

   2 Jan [1842]     2 [Jan] 1842
   [2] Jan 1842     [2 Jan] 1842
   184[2]

**16.6J**   A similar rule operates with questionable inferences, where '?' precedes the doubtful element:

   [?1842] Jan 2      1842 [?Jan 2]
   184[?2]     18[?4]2

**16.6K**   When the date of a document must lie within a specific timespan (for example a particular reign or a directorship, and so on), note this. The format '1156 X 1204' can be used to indicate this (for example 3 X 15 Ric II).

**16.6L**   'Temp' (= *tempore*) should be reserved for dates known only to have been in a particular reign or period. For example:

   temp Jas I
   temp Duke Humphrey

[1] International Standards Organization ISO 8601 *Data Elements and Interchange Formats – Information Interchange – Representation of dates and times*, 1988.

**16.6M** 'Circa' should be used (abbreviated to 'c') before a date which, on the balance of probability, is more likely to be correct than the one before or the one after it:

c 1636
c 13 May 1314
c 3 Ric II
c 1615 – c 1674

**16.6N** *Double year-dating*
Where the date before 1752 is between 1 January and 24 March, give the equivalent modern year with the old year date. For example:

2 Feb 1711/12
14 Mar 1641/2

[NS = new style, and OS = old style, should be reserved for distinguishing between the Julian and Gregorian calendars; for example 2 Sept 1752 OS; 14 Sept 1752 NS.]

**16.6O** For financial or academic years or similar 'overlapping' year-date spans, give both calendar years in full, separated by an oblique stroke. For example:

1636/1637; 1982/1983

**16.6P** *Biographical dates*
Dates of an individual's birth (b) and death (d), when used, are placed in round brackets. Where names with associated dates are providing access points to information, see NCA *Rules* Chapter 2.5A. For example:

Smith, John (1924–) or Smith, John (b 1924)
Smith, John (1837–1896)
Smith, John (1836 *or* 1837–1896)
Smith, John (?1837–1896)
Smith, John (c 1837–1896)
Smith, John (d 1896)
Smyth, John (fl 1456–1490)
Smeth, John (bap 1669)

**16.6Q**   *Regnal years*

| | |
|---|---|
| Wm I (etc) | Phil & Mary |
| Hen I (etc) | Eliz I (etc) |
| Stephen | Jas I (etc) |
| Ric I (etc) | Chas I (etc) |
| John | Wm & Mary |
| Edw I (etc) | Anne |
| Mary | Geo I (etc) |
| | Vict |

For example:

1 & 3 Phil & Mary
3 Ric III

**16.6R**   *Months*

| | |
|---|---|
| Jan | July |
| Feb | Aug |
| Mar | Sep |
| Apr | Oct |
| May | Nov |
| June | Dec |

**16.6S**   *Weekdays*

Mon
Tues
Wed
Thurs
Fri
Sat
Sun

**16.6T**   *Law terms, return days, and so on*

| | |
|---|---|
| Hilary | Hil |
| Easter | Easter |
| Trinity | Trin |
| Michaelmas | Mich |

| | |
|---|---|
| octave | oct |
| quindene | quin |
| morrow | mor |
| vacation | vac |

For example:

oct Trin 1364

**16.6U**   *Quarter Days*

| **English** | **Scottish** |
|---|---|
| Christmas | Candlemas |
| Lady Day | Whitsun |
| Midsummer | Lammas |
| Michaelmas | Martinmas |

## 16.7   British and foreign place-names

Where used as index terms or other access points, names should be constructed and used in accordance with NCA *Rules* Chapter 3.

## 16.8   Abbreviations

This section lists recommended common abbreviations specially applicable to non-specialist general archives. Standard abbreviations are used wherever possible in lists, or in dedicated fields. Where a description calls for the use of specialized abbreviations, these should be explained in a key provided at the highest level of description, in a headnote, or in a list placed before main passages of text.

However, abbreviations of any kind should be avoided in free text fields, on title pages or in headnotes.

| | |
|---|---|
| abg | abutting |
| abp | archbishop |
| arr | arranged, arrangement |
| | |
| b | born |
| bap | baptized |
| bd | board |
| bdl | bundle |

| | |
|---|---|
| betw | between |
| bldg | building |
| bp | bishop |
| bro | brother |
| bt | baronet |
| bur | buried |
| | |
| (C) | copyright |
| c (or c.) | circa |
| cent | century |
| co | company |
| corp | corporation |
| corr | correspondence |
| cte | committee |
| cty | county |
| | |
| d | death, died |
| decd | deceased |
| deforc | deforcinant |
| dept | department |
| dist | district |
| doc | document |
| dupl | duplicated |
| | |
| E | east |
| edn | edition |
| educ | education |
| esq | esquire |
| execx | executrix(ex) |
| exor(s) | executor(s) |
| | |
| f(f) | folio(s) |
| fl | floruit |
| | |
| gen | general |
| geneal | genealogical |
| gent | gentleman |
| gt | great |
| | |
| husb | husband(man) |
| | |
| inc | includes, including |

| | |
|---|---|
| incorp | incorporated |
| jun | junior |
| kt | knight |
| lre(s) | letter(s) |
| m | marriage, married |
| misc | miscellaneous |
| ms(s) | manuscript(s) |
| mtg | meeting |
| N | north |
| nat | national |
| nd | no date |
| nr | near |
| occ | occupation |
| p(p) | page(s) |
| par | parish |
| pr | printed |
| pt | part |
| pub | published |
| r | recto |
| reprod | reproduction, reproduced |
| Rev | reverend (if with surname) |
| S | south |
| sec | secretary |
| sen | senior |
| sig | signature |
| sis | sister |
| soc | society |
| suppl | supplement(ed) |
| ts(s) | typescript(s) |
| v | verso |
| var | various, variant |

| | |
|---|---|
| vol(s) | volume(s) |
| W | west |
| witn | witness |
| yeo | yeoman |

# PART IV
# TYPOLOGY OF ARCHIVAL DESCRIPTIONS

# PART IV

# Typology of archival descriptions

Part IV contains examples of different types of archival description. Each of these has been derived from actual practice in working repositories. The repository which is the origin of the description is acknowledged at the foot of each example, but most descriptions have been edited and in some cases altered (with permission), so as to increase the capacity of the example to illustrate *MAD3* principles and rules.

**Figures**

## LISTS OF TYPICAL MANAGEMENT GROUP TITLES

**Level**

| | | |
|---|---|---|
| 1 | | Court of Quarter Sessions |
| | 1.5 | The court in session |
| | 1.5 | Administration |
| | 1.5 | Enrolment, registration and deposit |
| | 1.5 | Justices of the peace |
| | 1.5 | Clerk of the peace |
| | | |
| 1 | | Other courts |
| | 1.5 | Petty sessions |
| | 1.5 | Coroners |
| | 1.5 | County courts |
| | | |
| 1 | | Statutory authorities |
| | 1.5 | Boards of Guardians |
| | 1.5 | Turnpike trusts |
| | 1.5 | Local boards of health |
| | | |
| 1 | | Medical authorities |
| | 1.5 | Area health authorities |
| | 1.75 | Hospital committees |
| | | |
| 1 | | Ecclesiastical |
| | 1.5 | Roman Catholic |
| | 1.5 | Church of England |
| | | |
| 1 | | Families and estates |
| | | |
| 1 | | Businesses |

**Figure IV.1    List of typical management group titles (Level 1.5): local authority record office**

**Level**

| | | |
|---|---|---|
| 1 | | Atmospheric sciences |
| | | |
| 1 | | Earth sciences |
| | 1.5 | Topographical survey |
| | | |
| 1 | | Life sciences |
| | 1.5 | Biologists' papers |
| | | |
| 1 | | Deposited and donated archives |

[*Source:* British Antarctic Survey Archives]

**Figure IV.2    List of typical management group titles (Level 1.5): specialist repository**

| Level | | |
|---|---|---|
| 0 | | **Nottinghamshire Archives** |
| 1 | PU | **POOR LAW** |
| | | Poor Law Unions were set up by the Poor Law Amendment Act 1834. They were dissolved in 1930 under the terms of the Local Government Act 1929 and their poor law functions were transferred to county and county borough councils. (See CC3/29, CC4/1, 17, CC/SS . . . ) |
| 2 | PUB | Basford |
| 2 | PUD | Bingham |
| 2 | PUE | East Retford |

[*Source:* Nottinghamshire Archives]

**Figure IV.3  A management group heading (Level 1.5)**

## GROUP DESCRIPTIONS

| Level | | |
|---|---|---|
| 2 | **DBHB/5** | **KINGSTON STEAM TRAWLING CO,    1891–1973** |
| | | The company was incorporated in 1891. Hellyer Bros acquired a majority shareholding in 19[?] and the company was absorbed into Associated Fisheries when Hellyer Bros merged with that company in 1961. It ceased trading in 1965 and was dissolved in 1973. |
| | | The group includes records of holdings and transfers of shares and proceedings of the board of directors, with some annual reports and accounts. |

[*Source:* Hull City Archives]

**Figure IV.4   Group level (Level 2) description: corporate archives**

Level
2

> **380J MENDELSON PAPERS**         **1949–1976**
>
> Papers of John Mendelson, MP (1917–1978). John Mendelson was born (as Jakob M.) of Jewish parents at Plock, Poland. He came to England in 1939, after a spell in a refugee camp at Zbaszun, and completed his education at the London School of Economics. He worked for a time as an extra-mural lecturer for Cambridge University prior to his call-up in 1943. After initial service in the Pioneer Corps, he transferred to the Royal Army Education Corps in which he was commissioned in 1947. Most of his post-war experience was at the College of the Rhine Army, Gottingen.
>
> In 1949 he was appointed as a staff tutor in the Department of Extra-Mural Studies, Sheffield University, a post he held until June 1959 when he won the Penistone by-election in the Labour interest. He held the seat until his sudden death in 1978. J. M. was on the left wing of the Labour Party and was an active member of the Tribune Group. He was a member of the Labour Party delegation to the Council of Europe 1973–77 and to the Western European Union 1973–76.
>
> The group includes papers relating to his personal affairs, the conduct of Penistone constituency and elections there, and a number of photographs of overseas visits and lecturing engagements.
>
> Some parts of the group are subject to access restrictions.

[*Source:* Sheffield Record Office]

**Figure IV.5    Group level (Level 2) description: personal papers**

| Level | | | |
|---|---|---|---|
| 1 | | PRIVATE ARCHIVES | |
| 1.5 | | **FAMILY AND ESTATE ARCHIVES** | |
| 2 | **DAL** Aldersey of Aldersey<br>Mainly title deeds of estates in and<br>around Aldersey and Bunbury. | | 13–19 cent |
| 2 | **DAR** Arderne of Alvanley and Harden<br>Title deeds, estate and family papers<br>of the Done, Crewe and Arderne<br>families, estates in and around<br>Utkinton, Delamere Stockport. | | 13–20 cent |
| 2 | **DBN** Brooke of Norton<br>Mainly title deeds of estates in Runcorn. | | 1553–1891 |

[*Source:* Cheshire Record Office]

**Figure IV.6    Group level (Level 2) description: list mode**

## SUBGROUP DESCRIPTIONS

Level
2
2.5

**BOARD OF TRADE**
**601.2.16  Fisheries Departments                    1867–1903**

Sea fisheries were the responsibility of the Commercial Department until 1867, when they were transferred to the Harbour Department. In 1875 the Board
of Trade took over responsibility for shell-fish indus-
tries and in 1886 that for salmon and freshwater fisheries from the Home Office and in the latter year a
Fisheries Department was established to perform
these functions. In 1887 it took over from the Marine
Department questions relating to fishing vessels and
their crews. In 1896 it took over wreck, harbour loans
and quarantine duties from the Harbour Department,
with which it was united in 1898 to form the Fisheries
and Harbour Department. Responsibility for fisheries
was transferred to the Board of Agriculture (501) by
the Board of Agriculture and Fisheries Act 1903. The
Board of Trade's remaining duties relating to fishing
vessels, international regulations and general fishery
questions passed to the Marine Department in the
same year. Correspondence and papers of the
department are in MAF12, MAF41 and MAF71 with a
few others in BT13.

[*Source:* Public Records Office, Crown Copyright]

**Figure IV.7    Subgroup description (Level 2.5): paragraph mode**

| Level | | | |
|---|---|---|---|
| **2** | **387 PEA Papers of Captain George Peacock** | | **1805–1893** |
| 2.5 | P | Papers relating to his career, and biographical notes. | 1820–1892 |
| 2.5 | E | Papers relating to his explorations and surveys. | 1845–1863 |
| 2.5 | I | Papers relating to his inventions and ideas. | 1867; 1886–1891 |
| 2.5 | B | Papers relating to Peacock & Buchan, manufacturers of compositions for ships' bottoms. | 1856–1879 |
| 2.5 | S | Papers relating to the *Swan of the Exe*. | 1820–1890 |
| 2.5 | W | Papers relating to Exmouth Warren. | 1841–1843 |

[*Source:* Liverpool Record Office and Local History Service]

**Figure IV.8    Subgroup description (Level 2.5): list mode**

## SERIES DESCRIPTIONS

Level
3

**POWE 14 Electricity Division, correspondence and papers 1898–1974**

787 files

Files relating to administration and legislation, electric lighting companies, distribution charges, metering, overhead lines, power stations and generating plant. Some earlier files of the Harbour Department of the Board of Trade and the Electricity Branch of the Ministry of Transport and the Electricity Commission are included in this class. The class also includes the papers of the Committee of Inquiry into the Electricity Supply Industry in England and Wales, 1854–1856.

**See also** POWE 11–13.

Some items closed for 50 years.

[*Source:* Public Record Office: Crown Copyright]

**Figure IV.9    Series description (Level 3): paragraph mode**

| Level | | | | |
|---|---|---|---|---|
| 2 | | **DIS  LIVERPOOL SHIPOWNERS' ASSOCIATION  1888–1964**<br>Founded 1810, incorporated 1888. | | |
| | | [*Administrative/custodial history*] | | |
| 2.5 | | ***Liverpool Shipowners Freight, Demurrage<br>and Defence Association*** | | c 1845–1917 |
| | 2.75 | <u>Administration</u> | | |
| 3 | | 1–3 | Minute books<br>(3 vols) | 1895–1917 |
| 3 | | 4–7 | Board agendas register<br>Some damaged by damp<br>(4 vols) | 1902–1903 |
| | 2.75 | <u>Finance</u> | | |
| 3 | | 8–10 | Subscriptions & expenses account<br>books<br>(3 vols) | 1895–1917 |

[*Source:* National Museums and Galleries on Merseyside]

## Figure IV.10    Series description (Level 3): list mode

## ITEM DESCRIPTIONS

| Level | | | |
|---|---|---|---|
| 3 | PS2/2 | Minute books | 1796–1797 |
| 4 | PS2/2/1 | Minute book of sessions held at Chipping Barnet including Special Licensing Session, 19 Sept 1796, of the Liberty of St Albans for the parishes of Chipping Barnet, East Barnet, Ridge, Northaw and Elstree. The business transacted by the justices is partly administrative, namely appointing parish officials, passing accounts and approving rates, and partly criminal. Cases heard include non-payment of rates, vagrancy, use of false weights, riotous assembly and theft.<br>24 Feb 1796 – 10 Aug 1797<br>(1 vol) | |

[*Source:* Hertfordshire Record Office]

## Figure IV.11    Item description (Level 4): paragraph mode

| Level | | | |
|---|---|---|---|
| 3 | AC6/1/3/ | Pickled herring trade in Germany | 1925–1929 |
| 4 | | 1 Report of a visit to the principal importing centres by the Fishing Officer of Imperial Secretary's Department. | |
| 4 | | 2 Herring fishing in Ardglass, Kilkeel and Portavogies – weekly report. | 1925–1929 |
| 4 | | 3 Provision for loan of suction pumps to farmers for use in drawing flax water from dams. | 1926 |

[*Source:* Public Record Office of Northern Ireland, Crown Copyright]

**Figure IV.12    Item description (Level 4): list mode**

## PIECE DESCRIPTIONS

| Level | |
|---|---|
| 2 | Letters to G B Lloyd from Thomas Stewardson    1 Mar – 2 May 1863 |
| 5 | Letter from T S at Philadelphia, referring to G B L's religious beliefs; Russell's 'North and South'; asks for foreign stamps for nephew; marriage of the Prince of Wales; blockade and the North's case in the Civil War; Canadian news; compares attitudes of the British in India and those of people in the South; post-mark on a letter from Lloyd, relates comments on part of it on civil war made by a young Quaker. Restates his opinion on Britain's attitude to the United States and comments on the 'Alabama' incident. Mentions G B L's opinion of the Society of Friends' attitude; holiday walking in Pocomo Mountain; banking law, some family news, English and Irish immigration into the United States and prices there; G B L's belief in omens concerning royalty; revenue from land transfer.<br>Good condition; available. |

[*Source:* Birmingham City Archives]

**Figure IV.13    Piece description (Level 5): paragraph mode**

| Level | | | |
|---|---|---|---|
| 4 | **E/3/90** | **Letter book 7** | **1682–1685** |
| 5 | f1 | President & Council at Surat | 1682 July 5 |
| 5 | ff2–3 | Agent and Council in Persia | |
| 5 | f3 | Fort St George | |
| 5 | ff4–5 | Bay of Bengal | |
| 5 | f7 | Sultan Abul Kahar Abul Nasser, King of Bantam | 1682 July 7 |
| 5 | ff8v–9 | Capt Benjamin Harry of the *Kempthorne* | 1682 June 30 |
| 5 | ff10v–11 | List of goods to be provided at the Coast | [1682 Aug 28] |

[*Source:* British Library, Oriental and India Office Collections]

## Figure IV.14  Piece description (Level 5): list mode

| Level | |
|---|---|
| 2 | **THE ASTAM DESIGN PARTNERSHIP, 1800–1966** |

Records deposited by the ASTAM Design Partnership, Gloucester on 2 December 1970 (Acc 2593), 6 March 1987 (Acc 5428), 12 May 1987 (Acc 5462) and September 1987 (Acc 5548). The records form the archive of the predecessor firms to the ASTAM Design Partnership, and were previously located in the attics of the firm's former premises at 17 College Green, which had been used by the practice since the 19th century.

*History*
The earliest architect to be represented ... and the firm has expanded, but the acronymic name has remained.

*Content and organisation of the records*
All the papers relating to projects were originally stored together, as was common practice in Victorian architects' offices ... This arrangement seems unlikely to be the original order ... The papers listed below are known to be incomplete.

The following abbreviations have been used throughout ...

| Level | | | |
|---|---|---|---|
| 2.5 | | OFFICE PAPERS | 1881–1932 |
| 3 | D2593/1 | "Private ledgers" | |
| | | (4 vols) | |
| 4 | /1 | 1881–1888 | |
| | /2 | 1889–1904 | |
| | /3 | 1905–1923 | |
| | /4 | 1924–1932 | |

| 3 | D2593/2 | Client's rough and summary ledgers 1876–1966 |
|---|---|---|

The rough ledgers record in some detail the expenses with which clients were charged, and the various stage of professional work charged for; the summary ledgers are of value only in bringing together long-running accounts. There is no system of cross reference between the rough and summary ledgers, although both series are comprehensively indexed.
(8 vols)

| **3.5** | | Rough clients' ledgers 1886–1966 |
|---|---|---|

(5 vols)

| **4** | /1 | 1886–1888 |
| | /2 | 1889–1891 |
| | /3 | 1892–1902 |
| | /4 | 1903–1921 |
| | /5 | 1922–1966 |

| **3.5** | | Summary clients' ledgers 1876–1938 |
|---|---|---|

(3 vols)

| **4** | /6 | 1876–1881 |
| | /7 | 1882–1888 |
| | /8 | This volume seems to contain all accounts opened 1889–1894; smaller accounts opened 1904–1921, and a few accounts opened 1936–38; the latter two categories being inserted in blank spaces left when the book was first used. |

| 3 | D2593/3 | Cash books 1882–1942 |
|---|---|---|

The cash books are of value in revealing much of the internal organisation of the firm. They show, for example, the proportions of the work carried out by each of the partners; and the names of the employees in the drawing office.
(3 vols)

| **4** | /1 | 1882–1889 |
| | /2 | 1889–1914 |
| | /3 | 1915–1942 |

[*Source:* Gloucestershire Record Office]

**Figure IV.15    Vertically arranged set of descriptions, including group, series, subseries and item (Levels 2, 3, 3.5 and 4)**

| Level | | | |
|---|---|---|---|
| 3 | **353SCH** | District Education Committee minutes | 1872–1903 |
| | | (14 vols) | |
| | | According to the board minutes 1870–1873 | |
| | | (printed series), p.74, a minute of 12 June | |
| | | 1871 states that a District Education Com- | |
| | | mittee is to be appointed '. . . whose special | |
| | | duty it shall be to see to the attendance of | |
| | | children at the public elementary | |
| | | schools . . .' This committee appears to | |
| | | have met regularly from that date as a | |
| | | board minute of 10 July 1871 (printed | |
| | | series, p.84) records | |
| | | proceedings of the District Education | |
| 4 | | Committee from 12 June 1871 onwards. | |
| | /1 | 5 June 1872 – 2 Dec 1874 | |
| 4 | | (No index) | |
| 4 | /2 | 9 Dec 1874 – 10 Oct 1877 | |
| | /3 | 17 Oct 1877 – 19 Mar 1879 | |
| | | Separate index at 353SCH 2/3a | |

[*Source:* Liverpool Record Office and Local History Service]

**Figure IV.16   Series description (Level 3) as headnote to an item description**

**PART V
SPECIAL FORMATS**

# 17

# Introduction to special formats

The special format section (Part V) completes the general provisions of *MAD3* for setting standards for archival description.

The following general principles apply throughout Part V (Chapters 18–25):

## 17.1 Generalist nature of *MAD3*

*MAD* rules and recommendations are intended primarily to control descriptive practices in general purpose archives services. It is expected that archives services which specialize in the administration of materials in one of the special formats (for example film or sound archives) will continue to develop or use specialized standards, often based upon *AACR2* or the ISBDs, though it is hoped that these standards will not conflict with those of *MAD*.

## 17.2 Finding aids systems

Where groups, series or items which consist of materials in one of the special formats occur within the holdings of an archives service (which is visualized in *MAD3* as the normal situation), the principal finding aids will be framed in the terms of the general *MAD3* rules and recommendations, and will contain a brief reference to the existence of the special format materials. A linked special finding aid will then be prepared to cover these materials at the appropriate depth, conforming to the rules and recommendations for the special format concerned. The special finding aid so produced will form a natural but subordinate part of the repository's finding aids system, all parts of which will be tied together by cross-references.

**17.3** Data elements

Areas, sub-areas and data elements which exist in the main table of data elements are not transcribed into the tables of data elements for the special formats. If the special format does not call specifically for the use of an area, sub-area or element, it is not included. Despite this, any area, sub-area or element from the main table may, if desired, be imported into the structure of a special format description, at the discretion of the archivist.

**17.4** Rules and recommendations given in the special format section apply only to the special format concerned. Each format has a table of data elements proper to itself, followed by models which determine the way in which data elements are selected and arranged to form an appropriate description. In particular *MAD3* standard level numbers do not apply to special formats, unless this is indicated in the relevant section. Similarly *MAD3* general rules and recommendations are not applicable to the special formats unless they are repeated in the relevant section.

## Contents of Part V

*Chapter*

## Acknowledgements

Sincere thanks are due to the many colleagues and institutions who helped with the drafting of the special formats chapters in *MAD2*. There were too many to thank in every case, but we owe a particular debt of gratitude to the following individuals: Michael Bottomley, Graham Cornish, Jacky Cox, Mariann Gomes, Adrian Gregson, Andrew Griffin, Michael Hinman, Steven Hobbs, Ken Howarth, Nicholas Kingsley, David Lee, Barbara Morris, Paul Sargent, Joan Smith, Sara Stevenson, Marcia Taylor, Malcolm Underwood, Alan Ward, Kevin Ward, Christopher Whittick, Margaret Whittick, Bridget Winstanley; and to the following institutions: Bedfordshire Record Office; Berkshire Record Office; British Antarctic Survey; Coventry City Record Office; ESRC Data Archive, University of

Essex; Greater London Record Office; the Guildhall Library; Hampshire Archives Trust; Hereford and Worcester County Record Office; Imperial War Museum; India Office Records; the National Library of Wales; the Committee of the National Photographic Collections; National Sound Archive; North West Film Archive; North West Sound Archive; St John's College, Cambridge; Scottish Film Archive; Scottish National Portrait Gallery; Somerset Record Office; Suffolk Record Office; Tyne and Wear Archives Service; West Yorkshire Archives Service.

In revising the special formats section for *MAD3* we owe additional thanks to Caroline Williams and Sarah Westwood, Liverpool University Centre for Archive Studies; Elizabeth Shepherd, University College London; Audrey Linkman, Documentary Photographic Archives; the Film and Sound Group of the Society of Archivists, especially David Lee and Alan Ward; Peter Garrod, Kevin Ashley and colleagues, UK National Digital Archive of Datasets, University of London Computer Centre; Neal Beagrie, Arts and Humanities Data Service; staff of the Public Record Office, especially Roger Maxwell, Peter Blake and Susan Healy; Francis X Blouin and Nancy Bartlett, Bentley Historical Library, University of Michigan.

# 18

# Title deeds

## 18.1 Introduction
Title deeds are included in the list of special formats because they occur very commonly in the holdings of British (and some other Anglophone) archives services, because they have a very distinctive form which has been the subject of diplomatic study, and because in the past the presence of many title deeds among the materials in groups has tended to cause an imbalance in the depth of treatment within finding aids.

**18.2** The deeds dealt with in this format are those produced within England and Wales.

**18.3** The use of this special format is optional. If it is not used, descriptions of title deeds will form part of the general finding aids, compiled in accordance with the general *MAD* standards. If this option is taken, care is necessary to control the depth of description which is accorded to the deeds within their group. In particular, calendaring is inappropriate within the general finding aid.

**18.4** Title deeds have some characteristics of their own which influence rules for their description. These are as follows:

### 18.4A  *Original bundles*
**18.4A1**  Because in the past the reason for creating and preserving title deeds was the operation of the law of real property and the protection of property rights, it is commonly found that sets of title deeds are held together in bundles which were created by the original owners and which, taken in sequence, demonstrate the ownership history of a property. Such

156

bundles often have original binding tapes, wrappings or containers, and frequently also original numbering or coding which indicates the place of each item in the bundle. Single deeds which have become separated from such bundles may still display some indication of their origin.

**18.4A2** In actual practice, original bundles often contain materials which are not title deeds, though they might have been brought together as a convenience to owners interested in defending title. Typical contents of bundles are:

- abstracts of title;
- documents ancillary to title, such as plans, sale particulars, insurance policies, solicitors' bills and correspondence, contracts for sale, financial papers, bankruptcy papers, valuation and auction sale papers; and
- wills and documents produced in the course of probate.

Where these documents are encountered in any number, this should be recorded in the description in the general finding aid.

**18.4A3** Original bundles may be linked together in an original system of arrangement, especially where larger estates were concerned. In some cases, for example in college archives, original sequences are preserved by using original or ancient methods of storage, pigeonholes, cupboards, and so on.

**18.4B** *Diplomatic character*
**18.4B1** Title deeds, especially those of early date (say before 1300), have long been the subject of the historical auxiliary science of diplomatic. This study developed a technique for the analysis of words, phrases and composition in legal documents (originally 'diplomas') which served to illustrate some features of the society which produced the documents. These features were usually connected with the development of the law of real property, or with the structure of legal administration. Though the study of the diplomatic of early deeds is no longer at the centre of historical investigation, its techniques and findings remain valid, and a descriptive standard must continue to allow for diplomatic features to be displayed to the user.

**18.4B2** A study of the work of diplomaticists, economic historians and archivists suggests that treatment of title deeds is affected by period. The following periods can be distinguished (although existing office practice may play a part in defining divisions in individual cases):

1. *Early deeds (before 1300).* Since these constitute an important part of the surviving documentation of the period, as well as displaying the development of important aspects of society, it remains necessary to recommend as full a description of the individual documents as possible. In particular, there is a strong case for transcribing significant phrases, and including full reference to all names (including names of witnesses) and descriptions of property. These documents are likely to be of interest across national boundaries.

2. *Late medieval to early modern deeds (14th to 17th centuries).* These documents demonstrate important developments in the operation of the land law and the effects of these on the creation of landed estates, and through these on society in general. They may also be important material for the study of the formation or expansion of urban centres. In this period, too, there exist considerable quantities of centrally recorded versions of the deeds, in the form of enrolments. However, the deeds do not form such a large proportion of the surviving documentation as with the earlier material, and the development of particular formulations was in some respects more regular (although examples of local or aberrant formulations occur and should be recorded). References to the diplomatic form of documents therefore remain important, but it is not so necessary to recommend very full treatment of names or property descriptions.

3. *More modern deeds (to 1925).* These become very numerous with the development of estate management practices in the 18th and 19th centuries, and the coming of sustained urban growth. Especially large numbers of deeds, including drafts and estate copies, survive particularly from the period at the end of the 19th century and into the 20th. The evidence they give is increasingly duplicated by alternative sources, some of which are easier to consult. The need for full descriptions of such material is accordingly less than with the earlier periods, and archivists may have appraisal problems where it is very bulky.

**18.4C**   Within local record offices, deeds are often of particular interest as sources for the history of houses. The indexing of local features and topographical coordinates is therefore valuable. Where a detailed treatment of deeds has been possible, much potential value for various fields of research has been revealed.

**18.4D**   Because of these special features, title deeds present difficulties in connection with levels of arrangement and depth of description.

## 18.5 Levels of arrangement

**18.5A** The general rule of multi-level description must apply: sets of title deeds, like other archival materials, are described at more than one level. The complete finding aid should consist of higher level descriptions governing lower level ones.

**18.5B** In accordance with Section 5.11, if two (or more) levels are not required only the higher level descriptions should be given.

**18.5C** The function of a higher level description is to record the provenance and general character of the set of deeds being described, with context and background. Lower level descriptions with detail about smaller entities or single documents should be provided within the coverage of these higher level descriptions.

It would be easy to envisage the higher level description as corresponding to descriptions of the original bundles and sets of bundles as mentioned above. In the rules which follow, this is presented as one option. In other cases, quantities of deeds which have lost their original context, have been rearranged in the past or have no surviving original arrangement must also be dealt with. Higher level descriptions must therefore be allowed as part of finding aids to material of this kind.

**18.5D** Within the context of this title deeds special format, standard *MAD* levels do not apply. In the context of general archives, bundles would be items (Level 4) and the documents within them would be pieces (Level 5). Finding aids which are confined to deeds as a special format may ignore these level settings, and use an independent system of levels based upon group, bundle and document, with intermediate sublevels as necessary. For example:

| | | |
|---|---|---|
| i | Group | Source, context or provenance (for example estate) |
| ii | Subgroup | Original groupings, such as distinct parts of the estate or sets of bundles |
| iii | Bundle | Original bundle or sets of deeds with a common factor |
| iv | Sub-bundle | Sets of related documents within a bundle |
| v | Compound documents | Sets of documents which belong together or are closely related (for example lease and release with final concord) |
| vi | Document | Individual deeds |

**18.5E**    In principle, further levels needed may be inserted.

**18.5F**    These levels of arrangement and description are for use within the special format finding aids. These levels are not numbered, though there is a data element for them (if required) within the Identity Statement Area.

**18.5G**    The general rule that any level of description may be omitted remains applicable.

**18.5H**    Within the special format, group descriptions are essentially higher level descriptions, and therefore aim to give the administrative and custodial history (within the format, termed Context and Provenance) of the archival entities they govern. They should conform to the general *MAD3* standards. It is expected that usually these descriptions will appear in the general finding aids with a cross-reference to the special format. In other cases they may be repeated as a headnote to the special format, or represented by a shortened version.

**18.5I**    Bundle-level descriptions aim to set out an abstract of the story recorded by the documents within the bundle, noting the significance and scope of original bundles or sets of bundles. They may indicate particular documents if these are significant, but in general descriptions at this level do not seek to deal with individual documents in any detail. Significance and scope may refer to legal developments, family or estate history, date range, topography or the development of land use, and/or dealings in the financial or labour markets. Recitals of names or places within deeds, or distinctive types of deed, may provide lists of significant value.

**18.5J**    Descriptions of individual documents or sets of closely related documents aim to set out the diplomatic character of the document(s), together with content.

**18.5J1**    Individual documents may be described in a long (calendar) form, or in a short (list entry) form.

**18.5K**    Descriptions at these different levels may be linked by headnotes or title pages, and the special format finding aid may include retrieval aids such as guides or indexes.

**18.6    Summary table of data elements for title deeds**
**18.6A**    The following table gives data elements which belong to the title

deeds special format. Where the general data elements are relevant, this is indicated.

**18.6B** The general rules relating to data elements apply. In particular:

- any data element may be used at any level; and
- any data element (except one from the Identity Statement) may be left unused.

**18.6C** *Data elements summary*

**Archival Description Sector**
*Identity Statement*
    Reference code
    Title
        Term for level (group, bundle, document)
        Term for diplomatic character
        Name element
        Simple date or span
        Extent

*Context and Provenance Area*
    Estate/property history
        Source of original foundation
        Names of parties
        Places
        Development of estate or property
        Dates of significant events or documents
    Custodial history
    Archivist's note
        Original arrangement and bundles

*Content and Structure Area*
    Diplomatic description
        Technical forms
        Individual or problem features
        Language
        Script
        Authentication
            Seals
            Signatures
            Enrolment or endorsement

Notarial authentication
Original annotations
Abstract
Full date
~~Site, place, estate, parish~~
Parties: personal, corporate, family names
Recitals
Considerations, covenants, conditions, rents
Effect of deed
Property descriptions
Boundaries
Field names
Other names in the main text (neighbouring owners/tenants;
previous owners/tenants)
Warranty clause
Subject keywords
Witnesses and witness endorsement
Executed; not executed
Counterpart; part of indenture
Enclosures; plans, schedules

*Conservation Area*
Seal conservation


**18.7    Rules for the use of data elements in title deed description**
**18.7A**    *Identity Statement*
**18.7A1**    Term for diplomatic character
The *term for diplomatic character* (applicable at compound or single document level) can be chosen from one of the terms in the following authority list. In other cases a term can be composed which summarizes the diplomatic features of the document(s).

admission
articles of agreement
assignment
award of arbitrators
bargain and sale (enrolled)
bond
common recovery
contract for sale
copy of court roll

counterpart
covenant to produce deeds
covenant to stand seized
declaration of trust
deed of gift (gift)
deed to declare uses (of...)
deed to lead uses (of...)
defeasance
demise (in trust, etc)
exchange
exemplification (of...)
extract of court proceedings
feoffment
final concord
grant
grant of probate
inspeximus (of...)
lease (for lives, years, lives and years)
lease and release
letters of administration
letters of attorney
letters of confraternity
letters patent (close, royal etc)
licence to alienate
marriage settlement
mortgage (in fee, by demise etc)
partition
quitclaim
recognizance (of...)
release
surrender
will

### 18.7A2   Name element

The *name element* is applicable at group or bundle level. It should be chosen to identify the entity by using the principal associated name as a title. The name will generally be that of the estate, the family connected with the estate or with the parish in which the property mainly lies, or the property itself.

### 18.7A3   Dates

*Simple dates or simple span dates* appear in the right margin as part of the Identity Statement. These should as far as possible be restricted to four-figure year numbers, but at individual deed level should be restricted to day/month/year.

*Complex or non-standard dates* should be given within the free text fields, preferably the diplomatic description (individual features). These dates may include regnal years, feast days, uncertain cases and the supporting argument for inference in undated documents.

**18.7A4**   Extent

At group level this may be the number of bundles.

At bundle level this may be the number of documents within the bundle.

**18.7B**   *Context and Provenance Area*

**18.7B1**   This area is provided for higher level descriptions, and should be linked to the relevant entries in the general finding aids.

**18.7B2**   Estate/property history

The data for this will normally be entered as free text, observing the rule of information retrieval (see Section 8.5). Alternatively, dedicated fields may be provided for names of parties, places and other keywords. The story of the development of the estate or property, like the administrative history in the general standards, is generally only suitable to unstructured text.

If free text is not used, a data structure may be built on these elements: source of original foundation, names of parties, places, development of estate or property, dates of significant events or documents.

**18.7B3**   Custodial history

The custodial history may consist only of a reference to the entry in the general finding aids or in the accessions register.

**18.7B4**   Archivist's note

The archivist's note follows the general standard but should include a description of the sequence of original bundles, which may require a description of the order and place in which they were originally stored.

**18.7C**   *Content and Structure Area*

**18.7C1**   Diplomatic description

This sub-area is provided to contain the special elements required for the study of diplomatic. It holds the following data elements:

**18.7C1i**   *Technical forms.* This refers back to the term for diplomatic character in the title. Although the title entry will normally be only a simple term of one or two words, in most cases this will be sufficient, and the technical forms entry can be left unused. In complicated or unusual cases a free text entry can be made, to allow supporting or explanatory argument, with appropriate citations.

**18.7C1ii** *Individual or problem features* allows an extension of the technical description to cover additional features relating to the form of the document. A particular instance is the possibility of variants in the technical form introduced by way of copy; or the case where copies have replaced the original in unusual circumstances. If the materials are actually or possibly forgeries, this may be explained here.

**18.7C1iii** The *language* entry should be made in the higher level description where it is standard through a group or bundle. Variations can then be indicated in the lower level descriptions of pieces.

**18.7C1iv** The *script* entry may use standard terms such as Carolingian minuscule, chancery hand, secretary hand, and so on.

**18.7C1v** The *authentication* set of data elements is intended to cover all the technical items which originated in the need to authenticate documents in early times. Technical terms can be used to cover:

- *Seals* A full seal description can occupy a special format of its own, for which there are national and international models.[1] *MAD* does not include a standard for this. The seals element of this format, however, can be made to contain any descriptive items which are required: size, shape, composition and colour; method of attachment; recto and verso images, and attribution; motto or inscription; skippets or containers; state of preservation.

- *Signatures* is intended for data on the authenticating signatures. Where the deed is an indenture, the identity of the signature is an indication of provenance; there may be other points of interest.

- *Enrolment or endorsement* is intended for data on endorsements which have a bearing on the content and effect of the document. Enrolment indicates if an official copy has been made and kept centrally. Endorsements of witnesses' names may preferably be entered in the Abstract Sub-area unless there is a special reason for indicating them here.

---

[1] Paul Harvey: 'Computer catalogue of seals in the Public Record Office, London' (*Janus* 1996.2) includes (pp. 32–36) a descriptive list of data elements used to describe seals and the documents to which they are attached).

- *Notarial authentication* (names and/or marks) should be included if present.

**18.7C1vi** *Original annotations* may be noted.

**18.7C2** Abstract

The purpose of the Abstract Sub-area is to give a summary of the information contained in the entity being described. It is normally a free text field, but it is possible to structure it into dedicated fields to contain the elements which follow, if required. The list of data elements can in any case be used as a checklist, to ensure a complete entry.

**18.7C2i** Date

Give the full version, including editorial comment and interpretative information (for example Old or New Style dates).

**18.7C2ii** Site, place, estate, parish

Give a simple heading only. Fuller description of topographical data appears in Section 18.7C2vi. Follow an authority list.

**18.7C2iii** Parties

Normally the parties are numbered by roman characters within round brackets. For example:

(i)   Robert Herwarde, clerk
(ii)  William Hole of Crownley, esq
(iii) Leonard Yeo, Citizen & Mercer and Armynell, widow and executrix of John Broke.

These numbers may be used later in the description to identify the parties referred to.

It is normal for names to follow the sequence: forename(s), surname, domicile, rank or profession. Names should be transcribed as in the original, abbreviating terms which are common form. Family or legal relationships should be transcribed. Square brackets can be used for editorial inferences, and '?' for questionable inferences and doubtful readings. (See Section 16.6H–M.)

**18.7C2iv** Recitals

Recitals (lists of previous transactions set out in the text) can be of value in that they can indicate transactions not recorded in original surviving deeds, or in parallel dealings. From this point of view they are valuable data. On

166

the other hand, they may duplicate the information given in surviving deeds, or otherwise available. They can sometimes be very lengthy. Recitals are very valuable for the construction of bundle descriptions. In single deed descriptions, they should be transcribed in summary form if the data is otherwise not recorded; in other cases, their presence and scope should be indicated.

**18.7C2v**   Considerations, covenants, conditions, rents
Legal considerations, covenants, conditions and rents mentioned in the text of the document should be transcribed, but this can be done in the form of a summary. Note special or unusual covenants.

**18.7C2vi**   Property descriptions
In early deeds especially, all information about places should be recorded. In general the data in the original can be summarized, especially avoiding the repetition of common form phrases. Place names should be transcribed as in the original, but where their interpretation has been established editorially this may be added in square brackets immediately after. For example:

> messuage and lands in Nytheragabwyll [?Lower Gabwell, par Stokein-teignhead]

**18.7C2vii**   Boundaries, field names, other names
Boundaries, including field boundaries, and the names of abutting tenants are of value in early deeds especially. The names of previous tenants and neighbouring holdings are equally valuable. Field names should be carefully recorded, as they are the subject of specialist study.

**18.7C2viii**   Warranty clause
The presence of a warranty clause should be indicated in deeds prior to 1300. In early deeds variations of the standard form should be transcribed as in the original.

**18.7C2ix**   Subject keywords
In free text entries the information retrieval rule of the general standard (Section 8.5) should be observed, that is, all subject keywords should be included in the text.

**18.7C2x**   Witnesses and witness endorsement
Witnesses' names should be recorded exactly as in the original in deeds earlier than 1300, if necessary with editorial explanation. For example:

Tedbaldo dapifero [Theobald the steward]

In deeds later than 1300 the recording of witnesses' names should follow local practice, but if given should preferably be translated into English forms. Endorsements of witnesses should be recorded or not, following the same practice.

**18.7C2xi**   Executions, counterparts, enclosures
Other notes could include any outstanding information not already covered: whether the deed was executed, or was aborted before execution; whether the deed is the 'original' of an indenture, or a counterpart; any enclosures, added documents, plans or schedules. This particularly applies to inventories enclosed with copy wills, and plans with exchanges or partitions.

**18.7C3**   *Conservation Area*
This area may be used to record the specialized processes needed for seal repair and conservation.

## 18.8   Models for description
**18.8A**   *Group descriptions (source, context, provenance)*
**18.8A1**   All sets of descriptions of title deeds should begin with a higher level description which gives information on source, context and provenance, and general data valid for the whole set. This description may appear as a headnote or title page, as in the general rules. It may refer to the brief description which appears in the general finding aids.

**18.8A2**   Such higher level descriptions should contain an Identity Statement containing at least one of the elements for that area. Typically entries will be:

Example:

| | | |
|---|---|---|
| Reference code | Title | Simple date or simple span |
| Abstract *(free text field )* | | |
| Extent | | |

**18.8A3**   The title contains an element for level. This is intended to provide for cases where a bundle or several linked bundles are being covered by the description. As in general descriptions, level indicators (group, sub-group, bundle, sub-bundle, compound documents or single deed) may be marked in either left or right margin, level with the reference code, but are not intended for use by readers.

Example:

| Level:<br>group | 371 | **Estate of Summers Cocks family, 1597–1901**<br>including manors of Reigate and Reigate Priory and burgage tenements in Reigate. |
|---|---|---|
| | | [Administrative and Custodial History,] |
| | | 0.75 m shelving in 10 boxes |
| sub-<br>group | 371/1 | *Burgage deeds*<br>These cover most of the burgage tenements recognized in the survey by William Bryant in 1786. For many of them the sequence begins in the late 17th century, but for one in the early 15th. Many original deed bundles were found intact, or could be reconstructed. A register of deed bundle numbers of Lord Somers's properties exists [ref], and these numbers were found on the documents. The order of the numbers appears to be haphazard, bearing no relation to the geographical position of the properties, though adjacent numbers sometimes indicate properties bought in one transaction. There may have been a plan of the borough on which the numbers were shown, but this has not come to light. |

[*Source:* Surrey History Centre]

**18.8B**   *Bundle descriptions*

**18.8B1**   This level may be used for related sets of original bundles, single original bundles, or individual deeds brought together because of some common characteristic.

**18.8B2**   The aim of these descriptions is to summarize the story documented by the bundle. The essential feature here, therefore, is the abstract, a free text field used to contain an account of the sequence of events recorded in the documents: acquisition of property, its passage from one individual or family to another, the administration of the estate, and its dissolution or absorption. The narrative may include reference to diplomatic aspects and note individual documents of interest, but the objective at this level is not to concentrate particularly on single documents, but to give an overall view. Significant names of persons and places, and subject keywords should be given.

Example:

| | | |
|---|---|---|
| Reference code | Title | Simple date(s) |
| Abstract *(free text field )* | | |
| Extent | | |

Example:

**Level: bundle**   DD/EV21 *Stoke St Michael*                1782–1826
13 documents
Paper mill at Stoke Bottom, described in latest deeds as "new erected paper mill and new erected houses in Stoke Bottom". This had been built probably in or soon after 1803 by Henry Fussell of Stoke St Michael, paper maker, on the site of a "late decayed mill with the barton behind of equal breadth and [the site of] an old stable", held originally of the manor of Doulting, together with a mill house and decayed or gutted mill. The earliest deed of 1782 adds that the first part had been leased for years and lives in 1733 to Ralph Stocker and describes the second part as a "new erected mill for grinding dye stuff". This latter had belonged to the Homer estate of the manors of Stoke Lane and Doulting and had been sold, probably earlier in 1782. The mill was gutted between 1782 and 1795.

[*Source:* Somerset Record Office]

170

**18.8B3**   *Individual deeds*

(a)   *Short form*

Example:

| Level: document | Reference code    Diplomatic term    Simple date |
|---|---|
| | Abstract |
| | Diplomatic features and Authentication (if used) |

Example:

| Level: document | DVA/1/1 Agden estate                              30 Jan 1401/2 |
|---|---|
| | (i)  William le Spencer and John de Norley, chaplains |
| | (ii) Ellen, formerly wife of Thomas of Warburton of Agden |
| | Feoffment from (i) to (ii) of all lands, tenements, rents, services, in Agden, with reversion of lands etc of William le Walker in Agden for her life; and after her death to Ellen, wife of William le Venables and their heirs. |
| | Witnesses: John le Masty esq, Roger de Merynton, Robert de Werberton,  Hugh de Molynton, William de Werberton. |

[*Source:* Cheshire Record Office]

(b)   *Long form (calendar)*

Example:

| Level: document | Reference code    Diplomatic term    Simple date |
|---|---|
| | Abstract: *(contains all information held in the document which is not in common form)* |

Example:

| Level: document | |
|---|---|
| | (i) Thomas Christian of Bexhill, tailor & shopkeeper, and Arthur Brook of Bexhill, gent (his trustee for (1) below). |
| | (ii) William Lucas Shadwell, and William Bishop of Hastings, attorneys at law and copartners. |

**Level:
document**

(i) Thomas Christian of Bexhill, tailor & shopkeeper, and Arthur Brook of Bexhill, gent (his trustee for (1) below).

(ii) William Lucas Shadwell, and William Bishop of Hastings, attorneys at law and copartners.
Recites mortgage of (1) for £300 by (i) to George Robinson and John Piper, tailors and copartners, 11 Jan 1806.

(i) mortgages to (ii) for £450:

1. House to which considerable additions have been made by (i), once enclosed with a stone wall with stable buildings and land, once occupied by John Cooper, then Christopher Deval, then John and Edward Prior, but now Thomas Christian and Thomas Bean; in High Street, Bexhill.

2. 26 roods of land, formerly part of Butt Field, with house built on it by Thomas Christian, occupied by Thomas Coveney Markquick; bounded on S by Hastings–Bexhill road; on W by garden occupied by John Crowhurst; on N by part of Butt Field belonging to Arthur Brook; on E by part of Butt Field on which a house, now belonging to William Curteis, is erected.
Dower of Elizabeth wife of TC excluded.

Endorsed in pencil "Osborn House, High Street".
Witnesses, William Thorpe, James Norton.

[*Source:* East Sussex Record Office]

172

Example:

**Level:
document**

312/TY135 Confirmation of grant          [c.1160]
(i)   William Fitz-Stephen
(ii)  to Gaufridus Dagulf de Toton', wife Sarra and
      heirs. Land near Toton' [Totnes] which Stephen de
      Tunstealle gave to Fulco and Basilia [William's
      sister] in jointure: viz, a garden between those of
      Hugh and Mark the younger; 2 acres called Wal-
      crot between the hollow way and the castle; 3
      acres and waste [mora] outside the walls between
      the monks' land and the boundary of Little Totnes;
      1 acre called Dotacar lying across the said acres; 1
      acre called Vineyard, between the garden of
      William Gaidulf and the river bank. These were
      given to Gaufridus de Toton' by William de Mor-
      tona with his sister Sarra [the donor's niece],
      daughter of Stephen de Morton' in jointure.
      2 and a half silver marks in hand, and 2 gold
      besants to his wife, Isabel de Lingeure.
Witnessed by Henr' de Nonant, Roger de Nonant his
brother, Guido de' Britevilla, domina Isabel de
Lingeure, Ric[hard] her son, Guido Croc senescallo
[steward], Henr' de Nonant, Ric' capellano [chaplain],
Joce capellano, Benedict clerico [clerk] of Hurberton,
Ric' de Nonant, Robert son of Herbert, Abbot Roger,
Abbot Rad'[ulfus], William Crispin, Reginald de
Westeton, Baudewin de Baccamora, Reginald de
Harastan, William Crispin junior, Robert Eustachii,
Ric' de Camera, Rad' clerico [clerk], Gaut' Camel,
Philipp' Will' preposito [reeve] of Totnes.

Pendent seal lost.
Printed in H. R. Watkin, *History of Totnes Priory and
Medieval Town* (Vol I, Torquay, 1914), No. XXVIII,
p.97.

[*Source:* Devon Record Office]

# 19

# Letters and correspondence

## 19.1 Introduction

**19.1A** Letters are included in *MAD3* as a special format because groups or collections often contain very large numbers of them, or are entirely composed of them. In these cases, a special format may be the best way to provide a suitable finding aid.

**19.1B** Most groups contain some letters, and where this is so, it may be best to include the description within the general finding aid, and avoid the use of a special format.

Examples:

**Level**
2    Papers of Daniel Crumble          1920–1965
3    Copy letters sent to Lucy Smith, 1789–1813
4    J. Wallace's letter-book, 1850
5    Letter, KBC to William Breakspear on social questions, 3 June 1790

**19.1C** The special format for letters is provided for relatively or very detailed descriptions of letters or correspondence at item or piece level (Levels 4 or 5 of the general standard).

**19.1D** The *MAD* concept of levels of description does not apply to the special format. Natural groupings of letters, such as subgroups, bundles, volumes of letter-books, or files, may be described in the general finding aids system without using a special format.

**19.1E** The multi-level rule (Chapter 5) operates in that contextual and background information should be supplied, usually in a headnote but alternatively in one of the forms indicated in the main sections.

## 19.2 Terminology

**19.2A** Although these terms are not insisted upon in any standard of general applicability, it is recommended that:

- the term 'letters' should be used where the letters emanate from one originator (individual or corporate);
- the term 'correspondence' should be used where the letters are between two or more correspondents, whether or not there are copies of outgoing letters; and
- where the letters constitute the file of a recipient, containing letters from several correspondents, the term 'in-letters' may be used, but 'correspondence' may also be used if there are a number of correspondents.

## 19.3 Arrangement

**19.3A** Arrangement of letters is difficult if there is no original order. It may be necessary to choose an arbitrary arrangement. Indexes and other access points, for correspondent or for subjects, or both, are likely to be an important part of the finding aid.

**19.3B** Arrangement may be chronological by date of origination, sending or receipt; or it may be alphabetical by correspondent, or arranged by function or subject. Examples are also available where there is a dual arrangement: a main text section in which documents are listed in chronological order of origination, and a second section in which summary descriptions are arranged in subject groupings.

**19.3C** Subgroups may be established within the general arrangement, where sets of letters arise from a particular function, or deal with a particular topic. Such subgroups should be marked only as headings, or brief headnotes, which break up what otherwise would be a continuous series of item descriptions.

### 19.4   Depth of description

There is a general presumption that groups or collections of letters call for considerable depth of description. The model for this is provided by editions of the letters or correspondence of statesmen or artists: for example the letters of the first Duke of Wellington, or of Rudyard Kipling. Where individuals of this stature are concerned, full calendars for distant use are the ideal. Descriptions which are less full than these may be required, but very summary descriptions will be confined to higher level descriptions which are covered in the general sections of *MAD3*.

### 19.5   Summary table of data elements for letters and correspondence

*Identity Statement*
   Reference code
   Title
      Name element
      Term for general description
      Simple date
   Extent and character

*Archivist's Note*
   Arrangement adopted
   Depth of description
   Particular problems

*Origination Area*
   Sender
   Place of origin or despatch (address)
   Signature

*Recipient Area*
   Recipient or addressee
   Recipient's address

*Date Area*

*Subject Area*
   Abstract

*Diplomatic Area*
   Form/type/genre
   Status

Authority
Philatelic details

*Physical Description Area*
Condition

*Access, Reference and Publication Area*
Access conditions
Citations and references in publications
Publication of text, extracts or summary


## 19.6  Rules for the use of data elements in letters and correspondence description
**19.6A**  *Identity Statement*
**19.6A1**  Reference code
As for general format.


**19.6A2**  Title
1. *Name element*: use either sender, recipient or subject heading as appropriate.
2. *Term for general description*: use one of the following terms:

   – correspondence
   – letter
   – postcard
   – note
   – card
   – telegram
   – letter-book entry
   – letterpress copy
   – draft/unsent.

3. *Simple date.* Complex dates are entered in free text in the date area. See Date Area and/or Archivist's Note for details of which date is being used.

**19.6A3**  Extent and character
At Level 4 or 5 this element may be used to record the number of sheets or sides of paper.

**19.6B**  *Archivist's Note*

**19.6B1**  Principle of arrangement adopted
See Section 19.3.

**19.6B2**  Policy on depth of description (calendar or summary)
See Section 19.4.

**19.6B3**  Particular problems
Record any other particular problems encountered.

**19.6C**  *Origination Area*

**19.6C1**  Sender
Enter uniform name if possible; otherwise use a local authority file or
name list.

**19.6C2**  Place of origin or despatch (address)
Use an authority term where possible.
   The address given at the head of the letter is not necessarily the place
from which the letter was actually written. Letters may be written on paper
with a printed heading, perhaps of a hotel, club or business which may be
some years old, or out of date. It is not always safe to accept data provided
in the document itself. However, where accurate, the correspondent's
address may provide important evidence not otherwise available (cf.
place-dating for early medieval deeds).

**19.6C3**  Signature
Note the form of this, together with the signing off phrase.

**19.6D**  *Recipient Area*

**19.6D1**  Recipient or addressee
Note any unusual forms of address (such as pet names) which might make
identification in other sources easier.

**19.6D2**  Recipient's address.

**19.6E**  *Date Area*
Complex or uncertain dates may be entered in free text, with notes as
necessary discussing them. For example:

   on the Sunday Laetare Jerusalem 10 Ric II [17 Mar 1387]

The date used should be explained in this section, or if there is discussion, in the Archivist's Note. For example, indicate whether the date is the one given on the letter by the writer, the one endorsed by the recipient on the letter, the date of the postmark, or the time of the postmark.

**19.6F**  *Subject Area*

**19.6F1**  Abstract

Following determination of depth (Section 19.4), include reference to all specific items of information contained in the text of the letter, omitting common form or generalities. Quotations from the original text should be given in double quotation marks. For example:

Describes in detail "... a quite beastly party at the Woolfs".

**19.6G**  *Diplomatic Area*

**19.6G1**  A term for form/type/genre

A term such as 'holograph letter' may be taken as the default. Otherwise use terms such as: letter, copy, draft, notes, enclosure, airmail form. This entry may refer back to the title.

**19.6G2**  Status

This sub-area refers to the relationship between the item being described and the originator's file. Use terms such as: typewritten, carbon copy, letterpress copy, transcript/copy/draft.

Other possible terms are: autograph, postscript, endorsed "Received..."

**19.6G3**  Authority

This sub-area is provided in order to give an opportunity for recording the manner in which the document is authenticated.

Terms might include: autograph signature, proxy signature, signing-off phrase, and so on. If the entry does not specifically refer to authentication, but to the whole document, the preferred sub-area is Status.

**19.6G4**  Philatelic details

Individual office policy on security issues may be a factor in deciding what is entered into this sub-area.

1.  Stamp.
2.  Postmark or other franking mark.
3.  Envelope endorsements or marks.

**19.6H**   *Physical Description Area*

**19.6H1**   Condition
Indicate the general or special condition of the material (and see Section 19.6I).

**19.6I**   *Access, Reference and Publication Area*

**19.6I1**   Access conditions
Give details of any access restriction which may operate on this item. If the access restriction is due to physical condition, the preferred area is Physical Description (Section 19.6H).

**19.6I2**   Citations and references in publications
Enter any relevant citations.

**19.6I3**   Publication of text, extracts or summary
Enter any relevant notes or citations.

**19.7**   **Models for description**

**19.7A**   Either paragraph or list mode may be selected.

**19.7B**   *Example of headnote*
The function of headnotes as a form of higher level description governing a set of lower level descriptions is explained in Chapters 5–6.

The letters format is essentially a lower level description format, operating at piece level (see Section 19.1), and so requires to be governed by a higher level description. This may normally take the form of a headnote, but alternatively any of the forms indicated by *MAD3*.

Higher level descriptions should give, in addition to information on context, background and provenance, as much data as is common to the set of lower level descriptions which are governed. This rule aims to reduce redundancy and improve ease of reference.

The headnote example is given here in the hope that it may be helpful, but it does not form part of the letters format proper.

**XY23/17 [Letters of]** *William Cecil 1st Lord Burghley* **1575**

Holograph letters from William Cecil, 1st Lord Burghley, to Peter Osborne, Lord Treasurer's Remembrancer, concerning foreign exchange, with particular reference to the grant to Burghley by Letters Patent of 9 March 1575 of the office of Keeper of the change, exchange and rechange in England in the Queen's dominions overseas and of the monopoly to appoint and regulate exchange brokers.

They explain the threat to Burghley's patent from one Hunt who has been authorized by certain Aldermen of the City of London to sue to [Christopher] Hatton for a royal grant to appoint brokers, and the need for the Queen's confirmation of Burghley's monopoly.

From Windsor. 21 Oct 1575.
Paper, 10 sheets and 1 double sheet in guard file.

[*Source:* Guildhall Library MSS Dept.]

List mode:

**DHB/1–6  Letters to his mother, Caroline Hibbert,       1854
      at Birtles Hall**

| | | |
|---|---|---|
| 1 | From Hamburg, concerning his continental tour. | 4 April 1854 |
| 2 | From Orinoco (troopship), off Southampton. | 4 April 1854 |
| 3 | From Orinoco, at sea; ship is bound for Gibraltar. | 9 April 1854 |
| 4 | From Constantinople. Lord Raglan's arrival; description of Turkish allies and of Constantinople "squalid beyond belief". | 9 & 10 May 1854 |
| 5 | From Scutari. His fever; visit of Lord Cardigan; character of [Gustavus St John] son of Lord Crofton. | 27 May 1854 |
| 6 | Near Sebastopol. Detailed description of battle of Alma; conditions and losses; realities of battle field after action; his ankle wound. | 2 Oct 1854 |

[*Source:* Cheshire Record Office]

# 20

# Photographs

## 20.1 Introduction

**20.1A**   The special format for photographs, like the other special formats, is provided for the use of general repositories. Specialized photographic archives will continue to use and develop their own practices, though it is hoped that common standards and conventions will emerge.

**20.1B**   General repositories normally hold photographs as part of groups or collections. In many cases these now amount to considerable holdings which require finding aids specially designed for their form.

**20.1C**   The general rule is that information on the background, context and provenance of photographic holdings is given as an entry in the main or central finding aids system, together with a reference to the special finding aid for photographic materials. Entries in the main finding aids system follow the normal rules and recommendations of *MAD3*.

**20.1D**   The special format is not intended to cover microforms.

## 20.2 Levels and background

**20.2A**   The general multi-level rule (Chapter 5) applies to the special format photographic finding aid, in that a higher level description giving background, context and provenance, together with information common to the set of descriptions covered, must be given as a headnote or title page at the beginning of the special format finding aid. This higher level description should also appear as an entry in the general finding aids, or be cross-referred to a relevant entry there.

**20.2B**  Outside the higher level description referred to, the special format finding aid to photographic materials forms a distinct entity linked to but distinct from the central finding aids system of the repository. The special format descriptions are single-level, and correspond to individual pieces.

Example of entry in general finding aids:

> QB16/2  Album of photographs displayed at exhibition        1910
>          (See index of photographs)

**20.2C**  For conservation of the photographs as physical objects, repositories may decide to keep these materials together. Archival order can then be preserved by means of the general finding aid (in structural order) and the reference coding system. It may be convenient to use a separate call number for retrieving particular photographs.

## 20.3  Depth of description

**20.3A**  The distinguishing characteristic of the photograph as a documentary medium is that it is the representation of one particular event occurring at a particular moment. The interpretation of the image so created presents difficulties because background and context must usually be supplied editorially. Essential explanatory information must form part of the finding aid at piece level.

**20.3B**  Descriptions of photographic materials should also give information on the technical process used. The technical processes which have been used to produce photographs in their various forms are complex and have undergone a lengthy development. Specialist advice may be necessary.

## 20.4  Physical shape of the photographic index

**20.4A**  The special format finding aid for photographic materials will normally be termed the index of photographs, or the like. It is expected that it will normally take the form of a formatted card index, or of a computerized database.

## 20.5   Summary table of data elements for photographs

*Identity Statement*
  Reference code
  Title
        Term for form/type/genre
        Name element
        Simple date
  Extent

*Content and Character Area*[1]
  Production
  Caption
  Contents note
  Physical description
        Material designation
        Dimensions
        Process used

*Management Information Area*
  Conservation

## 20.6   Rules for the use of data elements in photograph description

**20.6A**   *Identity Statement*

**20.6A1**   Reference code

Generally, each photographic item should have a unique finding number, which should also (directly or indirectly) indicate its proper position within the archive of which it is a part. This reference number may include the original negative or job number of the photographer, but usually this information is better placed in the Content and Character Area.

Give the call number or reference, if this is different from the archival reference code.

**20.6A2**   Title

1.   A simple term indicating the *form, type or genre* of the materials: photograph; aerial photograph; transparency; negative.

This data element is used to give the user an immediate impression of the kind of object that is being described. For example:

[1]   The term 'Content and Structure' belongs to the general set of data elements. 'Content' and 'Character' is used in the Special Formats which have a smaller (and different) range of elements.

'Photograph of Mrs Jane Rochester, 1867'

Suitable terms include photograph, transparency, [photographic] print, negative, glass plate. The term 'photograph' may be used as the default, and so left unstated. More detailed, technical or explanatory terms appear in the Physical Description Sub-area.

2.  The *name element*. If possible, choose names from the persons, schemes, objects or events represented in the item. Otherwise, take the name of any object, physical feature or topic which may appear, or the name of the person or institution responsible for creating and keeping the photographic record.

3.  *Simple date*. The date to be entered here should wherever possible be a simple year date, and should refer to the date of the event or object depicted, or the date the photograph was originally taken. Complex or deduced dates are better placed in the Content and Character area.

Examples of titles:

> xbl2 Portrait photograph of Queen Elizabeth II, 1954
>
> pr2/1/48 Aerial photograph of RMS Aquitania, 1940
>
> 84112 Party of emigrant children, c1935

**20.6A3**   Extent
This element may be used to clarify information given in the general finding aid. For example:

> 79 images on 7 contact print sheets
> album of 30 pages containing 210 prints
> album of 30 pages containing 2 postcards and 14 cartes de visite

**20.6B**   *Content and Character Area*
**20.6B1**   Production
Give the name of the photographer or photographic studio which produced the photograph, with the address or cross-reference to a description containing the address.
   Transcribe the original negative or studio number.

**20.6B2**   Caption

Transcribe any textual or notational caption within quotation marks. However, original negative reference codes should by preference appear within the Production Sub-area.

**20.6B3**   Contents note

The contents note is normally a free text entry, without limitation as to length. However, a contents analysis may be used to structure the information which would normally occur in this sub-area; in this case, appropriate data elements would include:

- *Full date.* Dates may have to be deduced from the pictorial evidence, from knowledge of the type of process involved or from the appearance of the mount. Some evidence may be available from examination of the location of the photographic studio, and so on, or from the circumstances of the acquisition.

    The reasoning behind the dating should be explained here.

- *Site, locality or place* (specificity may be determined by general policy in the archives service: for example authority list of place-names, geographical coordinates). The appearance of man-made buildings or objects may help date photographs.

- *Personal or corporate names.*

- *Events or activities*, with explanation.

- *Subject keywords* (these may be provided from an authorized vocabulary, or by reference to an established list of subject titles).

- *Cross-reference to information concerning the parent group*, or to correspondence files on it.

**20.6B4**   Physical description

This sub-area provides information on the physical shape, size and character of the materials.

**20.6B4i**   General

Information about the origins and background of the photograph itself might be taken from internal evidence, the wrapping, or the type of process which produced it.

**20.6B4ii**   Material designation

Indicate whether the piece is a print, negative, transparency, or other form. One of the following terms may be used:

Cabinet card
Carte de visite
Ferrotype (Tintype)
Lantern slide
Opalotype
Postcard
Stereograph
Wet collodion positive (Ambrotype)
35mm transparency.

Give the polarity: whether negative or positive. Negatives may be described using one of the following terms:

Calotype paper
Collodion plate
Gelatin dry plate
Gelatin paper
Roll film
Sheet film
Waxed paper.

Indicate if there is evidence of retouching, hand-colouring or any reworking of the image.

**20.6B4iii**   Dimensions
Give the dimensions (height and width) with and without mount, in centimetres or inches.

**20.6B4iv**   Process used
Suitable terms are given in the following lists:

*Positive processes*
Albumen print
Bromoil
Carbon
Cyanotype
Daguerreotype
Gelatin silver print
Gum bichromate
Platinum
Salted paper print.

*Colour processes*
   Agfacolor,
   Autochrome
   Cibachrome
   Dufaycolor
   Ektachrome
   Joly process
   Kodachrome.

*Photomechanical printing processes*
   Collotype
   Halftone
   Photogravure
   Photolithography
   Woodbury type.

**20.6C**   *Management Information Area*
If space is provided for management information, it can be used to control activities needed for the conservation, issue and return or any other operations on the material. Confidential information should not be given on a public finding aid.

   The chief use of the area will be to record conservation work, the present and expected state of the piece, and special requirements for future preservation, for example production of a photographic copy at a predicted date, or the availability of a negative for reproduction.

   The area may also be used to record copyright information.

# 21

# Cartographic archives

## 21.1 Introduction
**21.1A** Maps are often extracted physically in general repositories and kept in a map room or specially designated area, for ease of conservation and access. There are often dedicated lists of maps (or map indexes). (Map indexes are often themselves cartographic; *MAD3* does not contain rules for these.)

**21.1B** Archival maps are nevertheless particularly dependent on the evidence of their provenance and context. Provision must therefore be made for recording these, and preserving links which may exist between the map(s) and their associated papers. Because of this, both the general (group) finding aid and the map index should contain cross-references and background information.

**21.1C** In this text, the term 'maps' applies to all types of archival cartographic material, although the most frequently found type will be maps. Separate rules exist for architectural and other plans (Chapter 22).

## 21.2 General rules for cartographic archives
**21.2A** These rules and table of data elements are intended only for use with cartographic archives held by a general archives repository. Where there is no provision in these special format rules, the general rules of *MAD3* should apply.

**21.2B** Archival map description may need to operate at Level 3 (series) as well as at Levels 4 and 5 (item and piece). Level 3 should be used to provide for series of maps in a group; Level 4 is used for related sets of maps which may occur either within a series or as independent items; Level 5 is used for single maps.

**21.2C** The multi-level rule applies: sets of lower level descriptions must be governed by a higher level description. Higher level descriptions may take the form of headnotes above the text of lower level descriptions, or a title page or title page section in front of them. Such higher level descriptions may be the same as, or may refer to, relevant entries in the main finding aids.

## 21.3   Summary table of data elements for cartographic archives

*Identity statement*
   Reference code
   Title
      Term for form/type/genre
      Name element
      Date
   Level number
   Extent

*Context, Provenance and Production Area*
   Context/provenance
   Production
      Surveyor/cartographer
      Caption/cartouche
   Archivist's note

*Content and Character Area*
   Content
      Date of representation or publication
      Area/place
      Site reference
      Map reference
      Events, activities, purposes
      Reference/text description
      Subject keywords
      Sources
   Physical description
      Type
      Scale

Projection
Dimensions
Support
Medium/technique
Decoration

*Management Information Area*

## 21.4 Rules for the use of data elements in cartographic archives description

This section contains a fuller explanation of the content of each data element used in the description of cartographic archives.

**21.4A** *Identity Statement*
**21.4A1** Reference code
As for general format.

An additional call number or reference may be needed if the cartographic materials are kept separately in specialized storage.

**21.4A2** Title

1. A simple term indicating the *form, type or genre* of the materials. *AACR2* uses nine simple terms (atlas, diagram, globe, map, model, profile, remote-sensing image, section, view) with an extended list available if this is necessary (see Section 21.4C2(1)). The default (which need not be entered in a description which is part of a specialized finding aid) is 'map'.

   If a term is to be entered for this element, enter the most specific term applicable, without going into detail. The term may be qualified by noting the purpose for which the map was drawn up, for example tithe map, cadastral map. Ordnance Survey maps, or other maps which form part of a series, may include their standard reference numbers as part of the title if this number is a sufficient ready identification; otherwise these numbers should appear in the Content Sub-area.

2. *Name element.* If there is a title given by the cartographer or surveyor on the map, this should be used, using quotation marks. If the formal title is inaccurate or insufficient, it should be given only in the Content Sub-area, and a supplied title given as usual.

   In other circumstances, give the name of the geographic area represented. Where the map shows a village, town or city and the surrounding area, the name element should be that of the village, town or city

191

and the details of the surrounding area may be further defined in the Content Sub-area. Where two or more centres are shown, these should be named in the title if they are of equal importance on the map.

3. *Simple date(s)*. Give the simple date of the survey or (if different) of the publication or completion of the map. If the map was drawn up retrospectively this should be noted in the Context and Provenance Sub-area. Other complex dates should be entered in the Content Sub-area.

### 21.4A3   Level numbers
(See Sections 21.2B, C.) Levels of description should generally be indicated, as users will need to know where the specialized index refers to series, sets of related maps, or individual maps. Level markers may be indicated in the margin but are not intended for public use.

### 21.4A4   Extent
At Level 3 note the number of maps.

   At Level 4 the number of sheets may be noted.

### 21.4B   *Context, Provenance and Production Area*
### 21.4B1   Context/provenance
Give information on the origin, background, context and provenance of the map or set of maps, including cross-reference to the general finding aids system.

   If the map was drawn up for a particular reason (for example scientific purposes), the circumstances of its creation should be noted. If it can be simply stated, this purpose may be given in the type/form/genre element of the Identity Statement, but otherwise should appear here.

   Note any dedication which shows under what circumstances the map was created, if this does not appear in the description of the cartouche. These elements may alternatively appear in the Content Sub-area.

### 21.4B2   Production
If it does not appear in the cartouche, transcribe any information on the *cartographer or surveyor*, or engraver if this is available. Individuals should be listed in the order in which they were involved in the map's production, for example surveyor, engraver, printer, publisher. Information supplied by editorial inference should be included in square brackets.

   If there is a *cartouche*, describe this, giving its wording in quotation marks. Local authority lists may be used to encode decorative types. Alternatively this may appear in the Physical Description Sub-area and this is preferable if there are several physical or decorative features.

**21.4B3**   Archivist's note

Include information on the relationship of sets of maps and of their arrangement in relation to the rest of the group or series.

**21.4C**   *Content and Character Area*

The Content and Character Area has two sub-areas: Content and Physical description.

**21.4C1**   Content

Content information may be written into a free text narrative field in paragraph mode, thus forming an abstract.

The abstract can be used to record more details about the place or location shown in the map. The rule of information retrieval applies: that is, the text should contain all keywords required for indexing or searching. For example, townships might be included as well as parishes; the names of mines and the company that owned them.

The abstract is normally a free text entry, without limitation as to length. However, a contents analysis may serve to structure the information which would normally occur in the abstract; in this case, appropriate data elements would include:

1.  *Date of representation or publication.* This date may not be the same as the date of the survey. The reason for this should be explained. Include the circumstances of the survey, if not given in the Context and Provenance Sub-area.

2.  *Area/place, site reference, map reference.* Use local or national authority lists. Where used as index terms or other access points, names should be constructed and used in accordance with NCA *Rules* Chapter 3. Give a current Ordnance Survey map reference, especially if the place-names mentioned on the map are no longer current. Give the territorial limits of the map.

3.  *Events, activities, purposes.* With explanation

4.  *Reference/text description.* Explanation and/or description of any key or reference table or explanatory text or of accompanying material (if not already recorded in the general format description).

5.  *Subject keywords.*

6.  *Sources.* Record any sources or documents from which the entity being described was derived. This may be particularly relevant in the case of cartographic archives which draw on one or more older surveys without acknowledgement.

**21.4C2**   Physical description

This sub-area is intended to provide for information on the physical shape, size and character of the materials. There may be a need for reference to the call number or location record.

1. *Type.* The following terms for specialized kinds of maps, given in *AACR2*, may be used:

   – aerial chart
   – aerial remote-sensing image
   – anamorphic map
   – bird's-eye view (map view)
   – block diagram hydrographic
   – celestial chart/globe
   – chart
   – map profile
   – map section
   – orthophoto
   – photo mosaic (controlled/uncontrolled)
   – photomap
   – relief mode
   – remote-sensing image
   – terrestrial remote-sensing image.

2. *Scale.* Give scale as a representative fraction if possible. If an inch scale is given, quote this, unless it is clearly inaccurate (and note the inaccuracy). If these options are not available, but a scale bar is given, this should be measured in centimetres or inches and calculated in terms of metric or imperial scales; this calculated scale should be placed in square brackets after the measurement.

   If the scale can only be inferred from other evidence, such as degrees of latitude or distances between known places, a calculation should be made and the result noted, for example *n* miles to an inch (calculated).

   Foreign units of measurement should be translated where there is an exact English equivalent, for example pouce = inch. Note the original usage. Where there is no modern equivalent, state the unit of measurement used, for example Scots chains.

   Where the scale is not constant because of projection, this should be noted. *AACR2* (Cartographic materials) Appendix B, which gives 'Guidelines to Determine the Scale (RF) of a Map', should be used for this.

3. *Projection.* Give the projection: for example Mercator, James.

4. *Dimensions.* Give the dimensions: measured vertically (height), then horizontally (width), in centimetres to nearest half-centimetre, or inches to the nearest quarter-inch. Dimensions should be taken from the marked borders, and if there is a margin containing a title, or reference table, and so on, these larger measurements should also be given. The overall size should be given for searchroom management purposes and may also be cross-referenced to the location record.

   For a circular map give the diameter in the same way.

   If the map is made up of several joined sheets, the overall size of the map should be entered, with the number of sheets.

   The existence of inset or overlay maps should be noted.

5. *Support.* Note the support or mounting – for example linen, tracing cloth, parchment. Note whether dissected, back to back/on both sides, whether rolled or flat (if this is different from usual practice in the repository).

6. *Medium/technique.* State the medium used, for example charcoal, ink wash, colour wash, watercolour, black/colour pencil, and so on.

   State the reproduction technique, for example copperplate or wood engraving, lithograph, print, colour highlights, architect's copy, computer assisted, and so on.

7. *Decoration.* The following may be noted:

   – colour used to differentiate parts of the map;
   – decorated title;
   – decorated border;
   – cartouche: if this does not appear in the Production Sub-area, state contents (for example title) and form (for example decorated oval, unrolled scroll, pedestal, and so on); describe or name the style if recognizable;
   – heraldic or genealogical information;
   – pictorial information, for example people, buildings;
   – compass cards/indicators, for example rose, star, rhumb lines, cardinal points, and so on;
   – any explanatory text.

**21.4D** *Management Information Area*

**21.4D1** If space is provided for management information, it can be used to control activities needed for the conservation, issue and return or any other operations on the material. Confidential information should not be given on a public finding aid.

**21.4D2**    The chief use of the area will be to record conservation work, the present and expected state of the piece, and special requirements for future preservation, for example production of a photographic copy at a predicted date. The size of tables needed for consultation of the materials may be a useful data element.

# 22

# Architectural and other plans

## 22.1 Introduction
**22.1A** This chapter is intended to cover the archival description of plans which are to be found in a general repository. The most usual types are architectural, constructional and technical plans, including engineering drawings.

**22.1B** Like cartographic archives, these plans are often taken out of their physical context, and are kept and used in separate areas of the repository. Their physical similarity to cartographic archives often means that they are kept with the maps, but the differences between them and maps are sufficient to merit a separate table of data elements.

**22.1C** Plans are nevertheless particularly dependent on the evidence of their provenance and context. This is especially the case where they form part of contract documentation. There may also be links with drawing registers or indexes, design manuals, specification books, and so on. Provision must therefore be made for recording these, and preserving links which may exist between the plan(s) and their associated papers. Because of this, both the general (group) finding aid and the plan index should contain cross-references, background and contextual information.

## 22.2 General rules for architectural plans
**22.2A** These rules and table of data elements are intended only for use with archival plans held by a general archives repository. Where there is no provision in these special format rules, the general rules of *MAD3* should apply.

**22.2B**    Archival plan description may need to operate at Level 3 as well as at Levels 4 and 5. Level 3 should be used to provide for series of plans in a group; Level 4 is used for related sets of plans which may occur either within a series or as independent items; Level 5 is used for single plans.

**22.2C**    The multi-level rule applies: sets of lower level descriptions must be governed by a higher level description. Higher level descriptions may take the form of headnotes above the text of lower level descriptions, or a title page or title page section in front of them. Such higher level descriptions may be the same as, or may refer to, relevant entries in the main finding aids.

## 22.3    Summary table of data elements for architectural plans

*Identity statement*
   Reference code
   Title
      Term for form/type/genre
      Name element
      Dates
   Level number
   Extent

*Context, Provenance and Production Area*
   Context/provenance
   Production
      Personnel responsible
      Project sponsor/controller
   Archivist's note

*Content and Character Area*
   Content
      Date of representation, drawing or publication
      Subject or purpose of representation
      Site or place
      Personal or corporate names
      Events, activities, technical operations
      Accompanying material
      Other subject keywords
      Sources
   Physical description
      Type
      Scale

Dimensions
Support
Medium
Technique
Decoration
Special features

*Management Information Area*

## 22.4   Rules for the use of data elements in plan description
This section contains a fuller explanation of the content of each data element used in the description of archival plans.

### 22.4A   *Identity Statement*
### 22.4A1   Reference code
As for general format.

An additional call number or reference may be needed if the cartographic materials are kept separately in specialized storage.

### 22.4A2   Title

1. *A simple term indicating the form, type or genre of the materials.* If a term is to be entered for this element, enter the most specific term applicable, without going into detail. The term may be qualified by noting the purpose for which the plan was drawn up, for example contract drawings. If the plans are part of a related series, include their series reference numbers or codes as part of the title if this is sufficient ready identification; otherwise this information should appear in the Content Sub-area. Use terms such as sketch, working drawings, structural detail, elevation, block plan, cross-section, drawing. The default is 'plan'.

2. *Name element.* Give the name or title indicated on the plan, where this is accurate and useful. If there is no such indication, give the name and type of the structure or operation represented, for example Church of St Mary the Virgin, Merton; Ambridge Church Hall, roof beams; Garrett locomotive, boiler tubing.

3. *Span or indicator dates.* Give the simple date of the drawing or (if different) of the publication or completion of the plan. If the plan was drawn up retrospectively this should be noted in the Context and

Provenance Sub-area. Other complex dates or successive dates should be entered in the Content Sub-area.

### 22.4A3   Level number

Levels should generally be indicated in one of the margins, since they will help in the analysis of the set of plans being described and in laying out finding aids. Users will need to know where the specialized index refers to series, sets of related plans or papers (items), or to individual plans (pieces).

### 22.4A4   Extent

Note number of plan series (Level 3) or number of plans in related sets (Level 4).

### 22.4B   *Context, Provenance and Production Area*
### 22.4B1   Context/provenance

Give information on the origin, background, context and provenance of the plan or set of plans, including cross-reference to the general finding aids system.

If the plan was drawn up for a particular reason (for example a construction project, a planning development), the circumstances of its creation should be noted. If it can be simply stated, this purpose may be given in the type/form/genre element of the Identity Statement, but otherwise should appear here.

Note any titling or title block on the original which shows under what circumstances the plan was created, if this does not appear in the name element of the Identity Statement.

### 22.4B2   Production

If it does not appear in the title block, transcribe any information on the *architect or engineer, or engraver* if this is available. It should be noted that the originator of a plan may be more important than the project or structure involved. Individuals should be listed in the order in which they were involved in the plan's production, for example originator, draughtsman, engraver, printer, publisher. Include information on the *sponsorship or control of the project*, for example the name of the client or firm.

### 22.4B3   Archivist's note

Include information on the relationship of sets of plans, associated documents, and of their arrangement in relation to the rest of the group or series.

**22.4C** *Content and Character Area*
The Content and Character Area has two sub-areas: Content and Physical description.

**22.4C1** Content
Content information may be written into a free text narrative field in paragraph mode, thus forming an abstract.

This abstract can be used to record more details about the place, site or structure shown in the plan(s). A term to indicate status, for example 'proposed' or 'suggested', may be included. The rule of information retrieval applies: that is, the text should contain all keywords required for indexing or searching.

The abstract is normally a free text entry, without limitation as to length. However, a contents analysis may serve to structure the information which would normally occur in the abstract; in this case, appropriate data elements would include:

1. *Date of representation, drawing or publication*, which may not be the same as the date of the structure or project which gave rise to the plan(s). The reason for this should be explained. Include the circumstances surrounding the structure or project, if not given in the Context and Provenance Sub-area.

2. *Subject or purpose of representation*: give details of the scheme, structure or project which gave rise to the plan(s). Use the original project title if this is suitable. Indicate the present state of the structure or site, or the effect of the project.

3. *Site or place*: use local or national authority lists if available. Give Ordnance Survey map reference if appropriate. Give the spatial or subject limits of the plan.

4. *Personal or corporate names*: include the names of sponsoring, financing, commissioning or controlling agencies, if these do not appear in the Identity Statement. Include the names of architects, engineers or designers connected with the project, if these do not appear elsewhere.

5. *Events, activities*, notable characteristics of the structure or project, or the specific *technical operations* which the plan(s) deal with.

6. *Accompanying material*: give an explanation/description of any key or reference table or explanatory text or of accompanying material (if not already recorded in the general format description).

7. *Subject keywords.*

8. *Sources*: record any sources or documents from which the entity being described was derived. This may be particularly relevant in the case of plans which draw on one or more older drawings without acknowledgement.

**22.4C2**  Physical description

This sub-area is intended to provide for information on the physical shape, size and character of the materials. There may be a need for reference to the call number or location record.

1. *Type.* An authority list should be used if possible. Terms may be drawn from the following list:

    – axonometric drawing
    – bird's-eye view
    – block diagram
    – block plan
    – blueline drawing
    – blueprint
    – CAD (computer-assisted design) drawing
    – competition drawing
    – construction design
    – contract drawing
    – cross-section
    – dyeline
    – elevation
    – ground plan
    – landscaping plan
    – ornamental detail
    – perspective view
    – presentation drawing
    – publicity drawing
    – reverse blueline
    – room scheme
    – section
    – site plan
    – sketch
    – structural detail
    – tracing
    – view
    – working drawings
    – worm's-eye view.

2. *Scale.* Give the scale as a representative fraction if possible. If an inch scale is given, quote this, unless it is clearly inaccurate (and note the inaccuracy). If these options are not available, but a scale bar is given, this should be measured in centimetres or inches and calculated in terms of metric or imperial scales; this calculated scale should be placed in square brackets after the measurement.

   If the scale can only be inferred from other evidence, such as existing structures or distances between known places, a calculation may be made and the result noted, for example *n* metres to a centimetre (calculated).

3. *Dimensions.* Measure horizontally, then vertically, in centimetres to nearest half-centimetre. Dimensions should be taken from the marked borders, and if there is a margin containing a title or reference table, and so on, these larger measurements should also be given. The overall size should be given for searchroom management purposes and there may also be a cross-reference to the location record.

   If the plan is made up of several joined sheets, the overall size of the plan should be entered, with the number of sheets. Indicate any revision or appendix sheets attached on the plan to show arrangement of a different option than that of the main structure or project. The existence of inset or overlay plans should be noted.

4. *Support.* Note the support or mounting – for example linen, tracing cloth, parchment. Note whether dissected, back to back, on both sides, whether rolled or flat (if this is different from usual practice in the repository).

5. *Medium.* State the medium used, for example charcoal, ink wash, colour wash, watercolour, black/colour pencil, and so on.

6. *Technique.* For example copperplate or wood engraving, lithograph, print, colour highlights, architect's copy, computer assisted, and so on.

7. *Decoration.* The following may be noted:

   – colour used to differentiate parts of the plan;
   – decorated title;
   – decorated border;
   – title block: if this does not appear in the Production Sub-area;
   – pictorial information, for example people, planning views; and
   – any explanatory text.

8. *Special features.*

**22.4D** *Management Information Area*

If space is provided for management information, it can be used to control activities needed for the conservation, issue and return or any other operations on the material. Confidential information should not be given on a public finding aid.

The chief use of the area will be to record conservation work, the present and expected state of the piece, and special requirements for future preservation, for example production of a photographic copy at a predicted date.

# 23

# Sound archives

## 23.1   Introduction
**23.1A**   This descriptive format, like the other special formats, has been designed for use in a general repository, and is concerned with descriptions of sound materials which are to be included in general finding aids.

**23.1B**   It is probable that no administrative system is based on sound recordings alone. Therefore, in a general repository, sound material will be found enclosed with or dependent on paper based archive material. Some of this sound material will be archival (that is, produced in the course of business and retained for business reference by an individual or organization); some will be collected material.

**23.1C**   An example of clearly archival material might be that produced by radio stations and record companies in the course of their work; these emanate from administrative systems and are consequently transactional in character. On the other hand, interview recordings resulting from oral history projects are a common form of collected material and they have more in common with collections of private papers, correspondence or research notes conventionally held by record offices.

**23.1D**   Commercially published recordings may be received in general repositories as part of an archival accumulation. These too may be described using the format, although the archivist may decide, as an alternative, to use an appropriate form of bibliographic description. Where commercial or published recordings with no archival context are concerned, standard *AACR2* bibliographic descriptions should be used, following the practice of the repository or the data provided by the publishers.

**23.1E** The *MAD3* format is suitable for use in the description of, among others, the following forms of sound recording which may be found among archival materials in a general repository:

- radio broadcasts
- interviews, for example oral history recordings
- recordings of events such as concerts, plays, conferences, panel discussions, meetings, debates, and so on
- 'actuality' recordings (live recordings of, for example, demonstrations, riots, and so on)
- recordings emanating from (scientific) monitoring apparatus
- 'masters' and other material used in the production of published records and tapes.
- 'unpublished' studio and location recordings
- off-air recordings.

## GENERAL RULES

### 23.2 Depth of description
**23.2A** A full range of data elements for technical description has been included in the format, though many data elements will be inapplicable to the requirements of a non-specialist repository. However, sufficient technical information must be included in any description to allow for conservation, retrieval and use.

**23.2B** Because users can only have access to the sound materials by means of an appropriate machine, the accuracy and completeness of the Content and Structure Area of the description is particularly important.

### 23.3 Levels of description
**23.3A** The general multi-level rule (Chapter 5) applies to the special format sound recording finding aid, in that a higher level description giving background, context and provenance, together with information common to the set of descriptions covered, must be given as a headnote or title page at the beginning of the special format finding aid. This higher level description should also appear as an entry in the general finding aids, or be cross-referred to a relevant entry there.

**23.3B** Outside the higher level description referred to, the special format finding aid to sound recordings forms a distinct entity linked to but distinct from the central finding aids system of the repository. We would expect the special format descriptions to represent Level 3 (where sets of recordings are a series), Level 4 (where there may be related recordings in a single complex unit) or Level 5 (individual recordings). Items are series of recordings produced in the course of a project or activity and forming a physical unit. Pieces are single recordings, which may not be physically independent.

**23.3C** Sound recordings are usually extracted physically in general repositories and kept in a sound recordings room or specially designated area for ease of conservation and access. There are often dedicated lists of sound recordings (or sound recordings indexes).

**23.3D** Archival sound recordings are not often self-explanatory and may be particularly dependent on the evidence of their provenance and context. Consequently it is important to preserve links which may exist between the sound recording(s) and their associated papers. Because of this, both the general (group/series) finding aid and the sound recordings index should contain cross-references and background information.

### 23.4   Summary table of data elements for sound archives

*Identity Statement*
   Reference code
   Title
      Simple term for form/type/genre
      Name element
   Simple date of recording
   Extent

*Context and Provenance Area*
   Production history
      Date recording made or compiled
      Personnel responsible
      Purposes and aims
      Participation criteria
   Copyright
   Archivist's note

*Content and Structure Area*
   Abstract
      Complex title or genre

Periods covered
Site or place
Personal or corporate names
Events, activities
~~Subject keywords~~
Part description location
Physical and technical description
Carrier
Material/medium
Size
Duration of recording
Playback speed
Playback mode
Other technical data
(Cross reference to Conservation Sub-area)

*Management Information Area*
Process control
Copies record
Number and format of copies made
Original recording retained/destroyed
Processing carried out
(Cross-reference to Conservation Sub-area)
Copyright
Conservation
Previous history
Repairs required
Level of priority
Routine processes required
Other conservation data
(Cross-reference to Administrative Record)

## 23.5  Rules for the use of data elements in sound archive description
This section contains a fuller explanation of the content of each data element used in the description of sound archives.

**23.5A**  *Identity statement*
**23.5A1**  Reference code
As for general format.

An additional call number or reference may be needed if the sound materials are kept separately in specialized storage and/or where listening copies are used in preference to the original.

**23.5A2** Title

The Title Sub-area may contain two data elements:

1. A *simple term indicating the form, type or genre* of the materials; generally 'sound recording'. A more detailed descriptive term, necessary for technical management, should be entered in the Physical and Technical Description Sub-area.

2. A *name element*, briefly identifying the principal subject, participants or project.

**23.5A3** Date of recording

A simple recording date. The purpose of the simple date in this element is to help give a clear immediate means of reference. It will usually be a simple year date, but day or month may be added if these are significant. More complex dates appear in the abstract.

The simple date refers to the date of the recording. A date which is part of the subject description should appear either in the name element of the title, or in the Content Sub-area. For example:

> Sound recording of Peggy Archer's recollections of the Second World War, 1985

The simple date should be omitted if it is not significant.

Examples:

> Sound Recordings of House of Commons Debates, 1981–1985
> Bolton Sands Oral History Project recordings
> Recorded dialects of South Yorkshire, 1969
> Sussex Bird Song recordings, 1937–1939
> Recording of 'The World at One' (Radio 4), 17 June 1987
> 'Week Ending' (Radio 4) 1983–1986
> Cassettes of 'Aida' rehearsals, 1937–1955
> Cassette of 'Aida' rehearsal at Royal Festival Hall, 7 June 1951

**23.5A4** Extent

This data element refers to the total extent of the entity, which may extend over more than one carrier unit or form part of a compilation within that unit. Use terms such as tracks, number of sides, cassettes, reels.

**23.5B**  *Context and Provenance Area*

This area is provided in order to record the context of the sound recording
and its relationship with other recordings or documents which were associated with it because of the circumstances of their origination.

The provenance of the sound recording includes not only the circumstances of its creation but also its subsequent custodial history and its
transfer to the repository (though if preferred, this may be recorded in the
Management Information Area).

**23.5B1**  Production history

1.  *Date recording made or compiled.* Give the full date of the recording
    if this is not provided in the Identity Statement.

2.  *Personnel responsible.* Give the identity of the creator or originator of
    the material or project, of the recordist and other associated personnel.

3.  *Purposes and aims.* The purposes and aims of the recording are given
    in a series of linked data elements.

    Record the authority, project or scheme responsible for the work:
    title, statement of aims and purposes. Note important features: for
    example, if the recording was made for a specific reason not necessar-
    ily connected with the material recorded in the content summary (for
    example recording of language or dialect, musical forms, and so on);
    where research use may be related to the sound, nature or style of the
    recording rather than, or as well as, the information content. Include
    information on the intended audience of the recording.

4.  *Participation criteria.* Record the criteria which were laid down for
    participation in the creation of the work or in the project.

**23.5B2**  Copyright

Record copyright information; if this is not to be public, enter it in the
Process Control Sub-area.

**23.5B3**  Archivist's note

Include information on the relationship of sets of sound recordings and of
their arrangement in relation to the rest of the group or series, including
special arrangements made by the repository.

Note the existence of any transcripts and their length in pages.

Note the existence of other finding aids to the recordings, for example
indexes or lists of broadcast material compiled by radio stations.

## 23.5C Content and Structure Area
The Content and Structure Area has two sub-areas: Abstract, and Physical and technical description.

### 23.5C1 Abstract
The Abstract Sub-area is an abstract which contains data on the subject matter of the recording.

The sub-area is normally a free text entry, without limitation as to length. However, a contents analysis may serve to structure the information which would normally be given. The following structure demonstrates the use of the data elements supplied for this format:

1. *Complex title or genre.* If the title element of the Identity Statement Area is not sufficient to indicate the scope of the contents, a fuller or more complex caption or title should be given at the head of the abstract. This may be a derived title, with a note to explain the circumstances. Genre types may be drawn from the list in Section 23.1E.

   The subject coverage of the recording is summarized in a series of linked data elements, as follows. The rule of information retrieval applies: that is, the text should contain all keywords required for indexing or searching. Authority files should be used if available.

2. *Chronological periods* covered by the information. Full or complex dates may be used, or a general term for period, such as 'the Depression', 'the Cold War period', and so on.

3. *Site, locality or place* dealt with or mentioned in the recording. Authority lists should be used if possible. (The place where the recording was made should appear in the Context and Provenance Area.)

4. *Personal or corporate names* mentioned in the recording; if not recorded with the contextual information, give the identity of the performer(s), the circumstances under which he, she or they were working, and/or the name of the occasion or project.

5. *Events or activities* mentioned in the recording.

6. Other *subject keywords* for retrieval or indexing.

7. *Part description location.* Where the description is of a part only, indicate where on the carrier the subject of the description is to be found. Use terms such as:

   - disc: side, band,
   - cut tape: reel, track, cut.

Express a fractional extent in forms such as:

– 'on side 3 of 2 sound discs', 'on reel 3 of 4 sound reels'

Express the duration of the part as noted above, for example 'on 1 side of 1 disc (13min.)'.

**23.5C2**  Physical and technical description

This sub-area is intended to provide for information on the physical shape, size and character of the medium carrying the original sound recording (not copies). The general rule that any data element, sub-area or area may be left unused still applies. Much of this information can be cross-referenced to the Conservation Sub-area. The technical part of the description should be precise enough to allow the materials to be played on suitable equipment.

1.  *Carrier.* Describe the material or object which contains, supports or presents the sound recording. Use terms such as:

    – cartridge
    – cassette
    – cylinder
    – disc (compact, direct-cut, optical)
    – tape (magnetic, video [used for sound])
    – wire.

    Other carriers should be specified, with detail if rare (for example Tefitape and Amertape (sound on film); early magnetic discs; direct-cut metal discs; early non-Philips cassettes; also encountered are tapes of greater width than standard quarter-inch, and recordings with individual specifications produced by dictating equipment). The adjective 'sound' should be inserted before the type of carrier if this is not obvious from the context.

2.  *Material/medium.* Indicate the substance from which the carrier (or that part of it which actually holds the message) is manufactured. Use terms such as:

    – Cassette: ferric oxide; chrome dioxide; metal particle coated
    – Cylinder: brown wax; black wax; celluloid
    – Disc: shellac; vinyl; aluminium; polythene
    – Tape: paper; cellulose acetate/PVC; polyester
    – Wire and steel band.

    Cross-refer to Conservation Sub-area.

3.  *Size.* Give the size, capacity or length of the carrier (not the length of the recorded sound).

    In the case of a cassette, indicate the total possible playing time; for a cylinder, give physical length and diameter, and (if known) total possible playing time; for a disc, give the diameter in centimetres; for a tape, physical length, spool diameter or total possible playing time.

    Cross-refer to the location record.

4.  *Duration of recording.* If readily available, give the exact total playing time of the recording in hours, minutes and seconds. Give an approximate duration in hours and minutes if the precise duration is unknown.

5.  *Playback speed.*
    – Disc: rpm (revolutions per minute).
    – Open reel tape (and wire): ips (inches or centimetres per second according to in-house practice).
    – (Compact cassettes play at a standard speed.)

6.  *Playback mode.* Give the information needed to identify the appropriate machine or method. Use terms such as:

    – monaural ('mono')
    – binaural
    – stereophonic ('stereo')
    – quadrophonic.

7.  *Other technical data.* Give any further technical data useful for the preservation or use of the materials. Not all this data is necessarily of interest to lay users. There may be cross-references to the Conservation Sub-area.

    Precise technical details of disc pressings are unlikely to be available or necessary; the headings given below relate mainly to tape recordings, though it may be useful to give technical information on direct-cut discs and other media where available and appropriate.

    Additional technical data elements may include:

    – Method of recording. Use terms such as 'acoustic' or 'electrical analogue' or 'digital'.
    – Quality of recording: note the quality of the original recording before any filtering has taken place.
    – Make and model number of machine used to make recording. Recording equalization standard, for example IEC, NAB.
    – Machine settings, for example Dolby B, DBX, limiter, (on Nagra) music setting, and so on.
    – Recording speed.

- Track configuration and recording mode.
- Other recording equipment used, for example mixer, filtering device, noise reduction system.
- Microphone details: make and model number; accessories (for example windshield, parabolic reflector (for wildlife recordings)); microphone placement (for example tieclip mike, crossed stereo pair, dummy head mounting, suspended overhead).
- Other signal source (for example direct input from house public address system; original recording played on <specification> tape or disc machine).
- Tape details: make, type (for example single play, double play, or give manufacturer's reference number) and date of manufacture.
- Manufacturer's trademark, catalogue number (including prefix and suffix, and, if considered of value to users, matrix number).

**23.5D**   *Management Information Area*

The Management Information Area has two sub-areas – Process control and Conservation.

**23.5D1**   Process control

1.  *Copies record.* The original recording which came into the archivist's custody is not likely to be the one used to provide access. Record details of the archival copying process, including:

    - the *number of reference or conservation copies made*;
    - the *transfer of the original recording into a different format*;
    - whether the *original recording* has been *retained or destroyed*; and
    - any *processing* (for example filtering) carried out.

    Cross-reference to the Conservation Sub-area.

2.  *Copyright.* Indicate as clearly as possible the copyright position; copyright restrictions may appear here if not entered in the Production History Sub-area.

**23.5D2**   Conservation

This sub-area contains further physical and technical details not within the public domain. Cross-reference to the Physical and Technical Description Sub-area may be necessary.

Entries in this sub-area may apply either to the carrier or to the recording, or to both.

1.  *Previous history.* Describe the previous history of the materials, including a note of storage conditions prior to transfer to the repository.

2.  *Repairs required.* Record the current state of carriers and containers, and note any repairs or conservation measures needed.

3.  *Level of priority.* Indicate the level of priority accorded to the group/series or item.

4.  *Routine processes required.* Record routine processes to be carried out, including inspection, rewinding, cleaning, or the creation of conservation copies.

5.  *Other conservation data.*

The Conservation Sub-area may follow that of the general finding aids, including a record of the identity of conservators responsible for work, start and finish dates, the nature of any conservation activity, and recommendations for future action. A record of materials used may be added, and a record of any specific funding.

# 24

# Film and video archives

## 24.1 Introduction

**24.1A**   This section applies to both cinefilm and video recordings except where special features are indicated. In this chapter, the term 'film', where used, should be understood as covering both forms.

**24.1B**   The special format for archival materials with moving images, like the other special formats, is provided for the use of general repositories. Specialized film and video archives will continue to use and develop their own standards, though it is hoped that common conventions will emerge.

**24.1C**   General repositories normally hold film materials as part of groups or collections. In many cases these now amount to considerable holdings which require finding aids specially designed for their form.

**24.1D**   The general rule is that information on the background, context and provenance of film holdings is given as an entry in the main or central finding aids system, together with a reference to the special finding aid for film materials. Entries in the main finding aids system follow the normal rules and recommendations of *MAD3*.

## 24.2 Levels and background

**24.2A**   The general multi-level rule (Chapter 5) applies to the special format film finding aid, in that a higher level description giving background, context and provenance, together with information common to the set of descriptions covered, must be given as a headnote or title page at the beginning of the special format finding aid. This higher level description should also appear as an entry in the general finding aids, or be cross-referred to a relevant entry there.

**24.2B**   Outside the higher level description referred to, the special format finding aid to film materials forms a distinct entity linked to but distinct from the central finding aids system of the repository. The special format descriptions are single-level, and correspond to individual items or pieces. Items are linked cinefilm or video materials belonging to a single title or project; pieces are single units of film or videotape. (If series of films exist, the series description occurs within the general finding aids, without a special format for technical information; the series description may serve as a higher level description governing the special format descriptions.)

Example of entry in general finding aids:

TS9/16 Films of launching ceremonies              1910
(See index of film and video materials for further information)

**24.2C**   For conservation and use of the films as physical objects, repositories may decide to keep these materials together. Archival order can then be preserved by means of the general finding aid (in structural order) and the reference coding system. It may be convenient to use an additional call number for retrieving particular films.

### 24.3   Summary table of data elements for film and video archives
*Identity Statement*
   Reference code
   Title
      Simple term for form
      Name element
   Simple date
   Extent

*Production History Area*
   Personnel
      Producer
      Other key personnel

Context/circumstances of production
Copyright
Related materials

*Content and Structure Area*
Abstract
Date
General character
Site or place
Personal or corporate names
Events, activities
Subject keywords
Information concerning parent group
Physical and technical description
Format dimensions
Carrier
Form of stock
Cinefilm base
Replay or projection
Replay or projection speed
Sound
Colour
Quality
Duration

*Management Information Area*
Process control
Copies record
Number and format of copies made
Original recording retained/destroyed
Processing carried out
(Cross-reference to Conservation Area)
Copyright and access
Loan record
Conservation
Routine processes
Master copy made
Stock destroyed
Repairs required
Level of priority
Other conservation data
(Cross-reference to Administrative Record)

## 24.4  Rules for the use of data elements in film and video description

This section contains a fuller explanation of the content of each data element, and rules for its use. Where no specific explanation is given, refer to the explanation given for the general standard.

**24.4A**  *Identity Statement*
**24.4A1**  Reference code
As for general format.

A separate call number or reference may be needed if the film materials are kept separately in specialized storage and/or where viewing copies are used in preference to the original.

**24.4A2**  Title
The purpose of the Title Sub-area is to provide the equivalent of a main entry in a bibliographical finding aid, and to give a label which can be used in ordinary conversation, or in a preliminary guide, and which will direct users to the more detailed data elements which follow. Film and video archives which have been published will have a title in the bibliographic sense; nevertheless it may be necessary to extend this by reference to one of the data elements contained in the Title Sub-area.

The Title Sub-area may contain two data elements:

1.  *A simple term indicating the form of the materials* A term broadly indicating the form of material is necessary: for example cinefilm, video recording. For example:

    – Cinefilm of royal visit
    – Video recording showing dental operations.

    The term should be as simple as possible, and technical detail or complexity should be left for the Physical and Technical Description Sub-area.

2.  *Name element.* If there is a title given by the original film-maker or producer, this should be used. If the formal title is inaccurate or insufficient, it should be given only in the Content Sub-area, and a supplied title given as usual.

    In other circumstances, the name of the principal subject or event should be used. If there are two or more main subjects or events, these should be named in the title if they are of broadly equal importance.

**24.4A3**  Simple span or indicator dates
Rules for general formats should be followed. If dates have been inferred

from visual evidence within the film, this may be noted in the Production History Area. If footage on one film has been shot at distinct and different times, the two or more dates may be given in simple form, and further explanation given in the Production History Area.

**24.4A4**   Extent
Give the quantity, extent, size or bulk (dimensions, number, amount).

Examples:

'Cine film of WI jam-making, 1963, 1978.'
(One reel )

'Video and film recordings of social and official events at Bolton Town Hall, 1945–1986'
(14 videocassettes and 21 reels)

'Karamazov Bros Co Ltd advertising films, 1923–1978'
(47 items)

**24.4B**   *Production History Area*
The purpose of this area is to record the purpose, nature and circumstances of the project or event which led to the creation of the film materials. It should include information on the background, context and origin of the materials.

**24.4B1**   Personnel
Identify the organization or body responsible for the project and/or the making of the film, and also the person or persons who actually made it. Preface each name or group of names with a statement of their function. Follow local standards and authorities in determining whether to include assistants or associates. Personnel connected with the making of the film may include:

- (on production): director, producer, photographer, animator, writer; and
- (on performance): players, performers, narrator, presenters.

**24.4B2**   Context/circumstances of production
Include enough detail to make the nature or scope of the materials clear, especially if a specific audience or objective was in mind.

Note the location and date(s) of shooting.

Record the occasion of first or principal showing.

**24.4B3**   Copyright

Record copyright information; if this is not to be public, enter it in the Process Control Sub-area.

**24.4B4**   Related materials

Refer to any accompanying documentation (scripts, shot-lists, and so on).

**24.4C**   *Content and Structure Area*

This area is intended to provide an abstract which will contain a description of the content, scene, event, subject or topic of the film or video, together with a physical and technical description which will allow the film to be used on appropriate viewing equipment.

**24.4C1**   Abstract

The abstract is normally a free text entry, without limitation as to length. However, a contents analysis may be used to structure the information which would normally occur in this sub-area; in this case appropriate data elements would include:

1.   *Full date.* Dates may have to be deduced from internal evidence, either from the images (car number-plates or fashions, for example) or from related sound, if any. Evidence may also be available from the container or packaging, from stock marks, from knowledge of the type of process involved, or from any of these. Knowledge of the history and location of the film studios, or of the circumstances of the transfer to the archives, may also help. The reasoning behind the allocation of dates should be explained here.

2.   *General character.* Terms may be selected from the following list:

   – motion picture
   – documentary film
   – film compilation
   – film excerpts or extracts
   – trailer
   – newsreel or newscasts or newsfilms
   – stock shots, rushes or unedited film material
   – film out-takes or unedited film
   – film spot
   – stock footage of film
   – promotional or advertising or propaganda or educational film.

3. *Site, locality or place* (an authority list should be used).

4. *Personal or corporate names.*

5. *Events or activities*, with explanation.

6. *Subject keywords* (these may be provided from an authorized vocabulary, or by reference to an established list of subject titles).

7. *Cross-reference to information concerning the parent group*, or to correspondence files on it.

Distinct subject divisions may occur when the film is made up of different elements, for example a slide presentation, or inserts of still photograph or cinefilm clips. The point at which these subject changes occur should be recorded for ease of access. These reference points should preferably be given in minutes and seconds in preference to footage length.

**24.4C2**  Physical and technical description

This sub-area is intended to provide information on the physical shape, size and character of the materials, extending the brief format description given in the Title Sub-area. Sufficient technical detail to allow access to the materials should always be given. Subject to this provision, any data element may be omitted.

Data given in this sub-area relates to the original materials, not to any copies made in the repository.

1. *Format dimensions.*

   - *Film:* give the gauge (width) in millimetres. Use 8mm, 16mm, 35mm or another width. If 8mm, state whether single, standard, super, or Maurer.
   - *Videotape:* give the gauge. Use ½″ Betamax or VHS, 1″ (25mm), 2″ (50mm), or ¾″ U-Matic.
   - *Videodisc:* give the diameter in inches.

2. *Carrier.* Give a description of the physical carrier of the recording materials. Use terms such as: film cartridge, film cassette, film loop, film reel, videocartridge, videocassette, videodisc, videoreel.

3. *Form of stock.* Use terms such as: negative; positive; reversal; reversal internegative; internegative; interpositive; colour separation; duplicate; fine grain duplicating positive or negative.

4. *Cinefilm base.* Acetate, polyester or nitrate.
   Cross-reference to Conservation Sub-area.

5. *Replay or projection.* Indicate special replay or projection requirements (for example cinerama, Panavision, multiprojector, and so on), and say whether anamorphic, techniscope, stereoscopic, or multiscreen.

6. *Replay or projection speed.* For cinefilm give the speed in frames per second (fps); for a video recording whether standard or long play speed; and for a videodisc revolutions per minute (rpm).

7. *Sound.* Indicate presence or absence of a sound track by *sd* (sound) or *si* (silent).

   Record any special characteristics, for example if optical or magnetic, or whether the soundtrack is physically integrated with the film or separate on a synchronized recording.

8. *Colour.* For black and white use *b&w*. Describe a sepia print as b&w.

   For colour use *col*. If the materials contain a combination of colour and black and white, give this information: for example '1 film reel (30mm), sd, col with b&w sequences'.

   Give the system of colour for film, using terms such as: Technicolor, Kodachrome, Agfacolour, and so on. For videotape use SECAM, PAL, NTSC, and so on.

9. *Quality.* Note the viewing condition of the film: good, poor, badly scratched, and so on. Note if a copy of the original has been 'improved' or changed.

   Note the physical condition of the carrier if this may affect access to it.

10. *Duration.* Give the total playing time in minutes unless the duration is less than five minutes, in which case give the duration in minutes and seconds.

    Give the length of the film in metric linear measure or in feet. Film is measured from first frame to last, and videotape from first programme signal to last.

**24.4D** *Management Information Area*
**24.4D1** Process control
Follow the general rules of the Process Control Area (Section 14.8).

1. *Copies record.* Special features will cover the control of the creation of working or backup copies. Record details of the archival copying process, including:

- the number of reference copies made from the original;
- the transfer of the original recording into a different format;
- whether the original has been destroyed (for example in the case of nitrate stock); and
- any changes, deletions, filterings, or other processes carried out.

Cross-reference to Conservation Sub-area.

2.  *Copyright and access.* Indicate as clearly as possible the copyright position; copyright restrictions may appear here if not entered in the Production History Area.

    Indicate access controls, or restrictions on screening conditions.

3.  *Loan record.* This sub-area allows for a record where materials have been loaned for viewing or reference outside the repository, and the rules for general formats should be followed. When material has left the repository to be copied for conservation purposes, this information should be recorded here and cross-referenced to the Conservation Sub-area.

**24.4D2**   Conservation

1.  *Routine processes, master copy made.* Record any routine conservation work carried out, for example copying of material for reference or backup purposes.

2.  *Repairs required, stock destroyed.* Include details of any repair work required, including transfer of nitrate stock to acetate (destruction or original) or of any material to a different format (for example film to video).

3.  *Current conservation work required.* Record any current conservation work to be carried out and its frequency.

4.  *Level of priority.* Indicate a level of priority accorded to the group/series or item.

5.  *Other conservation data.* Give a cross-reference to the administrative conservation records of the repository.

The record of conservation work may follow that of the general finding aids, including:

- a record of the identity of conservators responsible for work;
- start and finish dates;
- the nature of any conservation activity;

- recommendations for future action;
- materials used; and
- any specific funding.

# 25

# Electronic records

## 25.1 Introduction
**25.1A**    This special format for electronic (also commonly called digital) records[1] is, like the other special formats, provided for the use of general repositories which may accession electronic records as part of their holdings.

Electronic records can be defined as files created by electronic systems, readable by means of those systems, which are created in the course of some business, administration or activity and used to continue that business, administration or activity.

Electronic records deemed to have permanent, archival value are those which have been subjected to a process of appraisal and which have been selected for retention by an archives service, so that their longer-term reference and research values may be exploited. These records, conforming to the classic definition of archives, should therefore be managed as part of an integrated system of records and archives administration.

The format deals with electronic (also called digital) records which are archival, and for which a bibliographic format[2] is not suitable.

The management of electronic records, including their description, is a rapidly developing area of professional concern. At present, practical

---

[1]   The term 'record' in this context derives from the literature and tradition of archives administration. It should not be confused with the same word which, in the context of computer operation, is generally used to mean a set of related data items within a file.

[2]   A format for the description of electronic records as bibliographical entities (for example some datasets) is available through the Data Archive at the University of Essex. See: http://dawww.essex.ac.uk/depositing_data/guidelines_doc.html (viewed 14 April 2000). Metadata for text data is available from the Oxford Text Archives at: http://ota.ahds.ac.uk/ ('An introduction to depositing with the OTA', Sections 9.3 and 9.4) (viewed 14 April 2000).

applications of the theory are not widespread, and the examples illustrating this chapter are drawn from a limited range of available finding aids. Because examples are scarce, it has been thought useful, in contrast to the other special format sections, to include footnotes listing some current reference sources in this area.

**25.1B**   It is likely that general repositories will encounter archival electronic records in two contexts:

1.  The administrative system of an entire organization, particularly where there is an active records management programme.

2.  As individual (physical) items within a larger group of deposited records. Typically these may be found among personal or family papers or the records of small organizations and might include floppy disks, CD-ROMs or digital tape. While the quantity and type of these records may appear to pose fewer problems than those inherent in dealing with a large, active, integrated in-house system (or parts of such a system), they are likely to represent formats whose obsolescent physical character, if not dealt with immediately on receipt, may cause serious data access problems in the future.

**25.1C**   Whatever the provenance of the records, they may be extensive and complex. A complicated administration may create and operate a recording system which consists of interrelated databases and files (and derived datasets), each of which has an individual structure and content. Where this is so, a descriptive system is needed which takes account of the complexity of the system, and does not treat each data file as a distinct entity. This approach is, of course, no different to the traditional approach taken towards paper-based records within a manual record-keeping system.

The records continuum model[3] allows for potential archival value to be recognized and allocated at creation. In this approach, the descriptive information which will later be used to access (intellectually and technically) the electronic records is provided as the record is created and is embedded within the record itself. This information – called metadata – is required for three purposes:

● to record the circumstances in which the data was originally created and used;

[3]   The Australian Standard *Records management* (AS4390.1-1996) defines the continuum as 'The whole extent of a record's existence. Refers to a consistent and coherent regime of management processes from the time of the creation of records (and before creation, in the design of recordkeeping systems), through to the preservation and use of records as archives.'

- to enable the continuing processing and maintenance of the records; and
- to provide means of access to the records.

It remains rare for the whole of this process to be undertaken, but models do exist – the Public Record Office has issued guidelines which set out in great detail issues to be considered in the management and archival retention of electronic records, and these guidelines include examples of the metadata which may be included at creation or during the survey process which precedes archival retention.[4] If the metadata are not embedded at creation, they must of course be collected at a later date to create the description.

However the metadata are arrived at, whether allotted at creation or by the archivist on receipt, they are still vital, required to access the record both physically and intellectually. They may be compiled from the list of data elements provided here (Section 25.3). Other relevant listings and examples of metadata elements (and guidelines relating to their use) are available (for example from the International Council on Archives[5] and the UK National Digital Archive of Datasets[6]).

## 25.2   Level of description

**25.2A**   Like the other special formats providing for the needs of a general repository, it is assumed that higher level descriptions will appear as entries in the general finding aids system, referring users to separate special format descriptions.

**25.2B**   Group and series descriptions are given in the general finding aids system. They contain no detailed technological information, and follow the general rules of *MAD3*. The special format descriptions apply at Levels 3, 4 and 5 only.

Level 3 (analogous to series) is used to describe whole related sets of files; these may be databases but equally may be defined by reference to the character of the object (for example regular snapshots of a system

---

[4] *Management, Appraisal and Preservation of Electronic Records*, Volume 2, Procedures at:
http://www.pro.gov.uk/recordsmanagement/eros/guidelines/default.htm (viewed 14 April 2000) and especially Chapter 2 Creating and capturing records 2.40–2.51 and Chapter 4 Inventory, appraisal and disposal 4.22–4.43.

[5] ICA Committee on Electronic Records. *Electronic Records Management* (ICA Studies 10) available at:
http://www.ica.org/cgi-bin/ica/ica.pl?0508_e (viewed 14 April 2000).

[6] http://ndad.ulcc.ac.uk/help/finding_aids.htm (viewed 14 April 2000).

might form an accruing series). Components of any kind may be regarded as a sublevel analogous to the subseries (Level 3.5).

Level 4 (analogous to item) is used for related sets of materials which form physical units for handling purposes or conceptual units for management purposes (that is, distinct and recognizable files which form the most elementary unit of arrangement and description).

If Level 5 (analogous to piece) is used, it should be employed for parts or components of items (for example individual fields within a record or virtual documents within a virtual folder).

## 25.3   Summary table of data elements for electronic archives

*Identity Statement*
    Reference code
    Title
        Term for form/type
        Name element
        Simple date
    Extent

*Production Area*
    Aim and purpose
    Context
    Statement of responsibility
    Complex dates
    Retirement or closure
    Retention, appraisal and sampling criteria

*Access and Use Area*
    General access conditions
    Legal access conditions
    Network access conditions
    Charges

*Content and Structure Area*
    Scope and content/abstract
        Subject or contents
        Type
    Structure
        Links
        Related material
        Dynamic/closed

*Physical and Technical Description Area*
   Physical carrier
   Other characteristics
   Original application/software dependency
   Original hardware dependency

*Management Information Area*
   Process and validation history
   Archiving
   Updating

## 25.4   Rules for the use of data elements in electronic records description

This section contains a fuller explanation of the content of each data element used in the archival description of electronic records.

**25.4A**   *Identity statement*
**25.4A1**   Reference code

Generally, each electronic file should have a unique finding code, which may also (directly or indirectly) indicate its proper position within the archive of which it is a part.

   Give the call number or reference, if this is different from the archival reference code.

**25.4A2**   Title

1. *Term for form/type.* A simple term indicating the form or type of the materials. Use terms such as:

   – database system
   – database
   – dataset
   – spreadsheet
   – digital document
   – e-mail correspondence.

   This data element is used to give the user an immediate impression of the kind of entity that is being described. More detailed, technical and explanatory terms appear in the Physical and Technical Description Area.

2. *Name element.* Give the name of the administrative or database system which was used to create the materials, together with the name of the

organization responsible, and whose records or archives these are (if this has not been given at a higher level). Indicate parallel or supplementary names.

3.  *Simple date*. A variety of dating is possible. The simple year date may refer to the date at which the materials were compiled, or the date at which they were withdrawn from active use. In span dates, the first date may be the date the file was opened, and the second date the date the last changes were made. The date may be one selected according to predetermined criteria (for example a snapshot). The nature of the date should be made clear to the user. The reasoning behind the date, along with complex or deduced dates, should be placed in the Production Area.

Examples of titles:

| | |
|---|---|
| Level 3 | JN3 Public hearings of the Nolan committee: first and second reports, papers and transcripts of proceedings on disc |
| Level 4 | JN3/1 Agendas 1994–1996 |
| Level 5 | JN3/1/1 Agenda 2, meeting in London, 15 November 1994[7] |
| | |
| Level 3 | Government Direct Initiative Digital Records (CAB 172) |
| Level 5 | CAB 172/3/25 Graphics for inclusion in CD ROM |
| | CAB 172/3/26 Spreadsheet record of green paper suggestions |
| | CAB 172/3/27 Word over for video item on trial of kiosk-based service delivery during 1995 |
| | |
| Level 3 | Coast Protection Survey of England, 1994–1996 (3 datasets) |
| Level 4 | Coast Protection Survey of England, 1994: Length_94 table |
| Level 5 | Coast Protection Survey of England, 1994: Length_94 table <a field name> |
| | |
| Level 3 | Merseyside repositories joint accessions register |
| Level 4 | Merseyside Record Office accessions register |
| | |
| Level 3 | University of Southampton web site, 27 July 1997 |
| Level 4 | Department of Oceanography home page |

---

[7] A Level 5 title is an appropriate place for a hypertext link to the record itself, as in this example.

**25.4A3**   Extent

Enter the extent of the file in kilobytes and give the number of records where applicable (for example within a database). For program files give the number of statements.

Recording the extent is vital to the user where downloading files is an option.

**25.4B**   *Production Area*

This area is provided to record the circumstances in which the materials were produced.

There are six data elements:

- Aim and purpose
- Context
- Statement of responsibility
- Complex dates
- Retirement or closure
- Retention, appraisal and sampling criteria.

**25.4B1**   Aim and purpose

Explain the aim and purpose of the records within the creating institution. This may be a brief statement of the administrative function envisaged, for example 'database system designed for the financial, payroll and personnel administration of Hornblower plc'.

**25.4B2**   Context

Give further contextual information concerning the conditions in which the system was introduced and how it was used (for example the range of permissions in place).

**25.4B3**   Statement of responsibility

Record the names of institutions, departments or individuals who were responsible for system design, data structure, data capture or retrieval, or management.

**25.4B4**   Complex dates

Record the reasoning behind any allocation of complex or deduced dates, or where the simple date of the title requires explanation.

**25.4B5**   Retirement or closure

Record the circumstances in which the materials were brought from current administrative use into record or archive management. This may be obsolescence or replacement of the system by another, or it may be the result of a management decision to take archival copies ('snapshots') from an active system at predetermined moments. In the latter case, reference should be made to other related archival 'snapshots', to the continuing administrative record and to the method used for controlling the extraction of archival data. This data element may be cross-referenced to the Archiving element in the Management Information Area.

**25.4B6**   Retention, appraisal and sampling criteria
Where appropriate, record the criteria used, for example for extracting a snapshot of the data.

**25.4C**   *Access and Use Area*
This area provides information relating to restrictions over use. Technical access requirements appear under the Physical and Technical Description Area.

**25.4C1**   General access conditions
Record general policy on access, including specific closure periods, registration of users, special procedures for permitted classes of user and other specific requirements for providing access once conditions of access are agreed.

**25.4C2**   Legal access conditions
Include details of:

- registration under Data Protection acts
- copyright information
- legal status
- other legislation affecting the records.

Example:

> The Anatomy dataset is a public record under the Public Records Acts, 1958 and 1967. It has been assigned the class reference JA 3.
>
> The Anatomy dataset is subject to Crown Copyright. Copies may be made for private study and research only.
>
> The data is subject to the 1998 Data Protection Act.

[*Source:* UK National Digital Archive of Datasets. Department of Health: Anatomy Office – Anatomy dataset at http://ndad.ulcc.ac.uk/datasets/21/series.htm (viewed on 14 April 2000). Crown Copyright: Public Record Office]

**25.4C3**   Network access conditions

Network system requirements for viewing should be noted:

Example:

How to View Documents
   System Requirements
      Netscape browser version 3.0 or later, Microsoft Internet
      Explorer version 3.0.2 or later for full access to the
      Bentley Library interface.
   Software
      To directly open and view an individual file from the
      Duderstadt digital collection online, users will need the soft-
      ware applications: Microsoft 6.0 or later, PowerPoint 4.0, and
      Excel 4.0 or later installed. If those applications are installed on
      the computer one additional step may be required and that is to
      set the "General Preferences" on the Internet browser applica-
      tion.

[*Source:* Bentley Historical Library, University of Michigan, US
http://www.umich.edu/~bhl/clecrec/d/duderstadt/jjdhtml/view.htm] (viewed 14 April 2000)

**25.4C4**   Charges

Indicate charges applicable for services in giving access, including copying.

**25.4D**   *Content and Structure Area*

This area contains two sub-areas – the Scope and Content/Abstract Sub-
area and the Structure Sub-area. This area is used to describe the subject
matter and type of the data, including more detailed or more complex
information than was possible in the Identity Statement Area.

**25.4D1**   Scope and content/abstract

1.   *Subject or contents.* Describe the subject or contents of the record.

Example:

The Anatomy dataset incorporates data compiled by the Anatomy
Office division of the Department of Health in the process of carrying
out the requirements of the 1984 Anatomy Act and 1988 regulations

which relate to the acceptance and disposal of bodies donated for anatomical research. The dataset is an electronic version of hard copy registers, files and reports similar to those produced by Her Majesty's Inspector of Anatomy since 1832.

[*Source:* UK National Digital Archive of Datasets. Department of Health: Anatomy Office – Anatomy dataset at http://ndad.ulcc.ac.uk/datasets/21/series.htm (viewed 14 April 2000). Crown Copyright: Public Record Office]

At Level 5 describe the contents of each of the fields (within the structure).

Example:

| Name | Description |
|---|---|
| Gridref | The unique national grid reference which locates the centre of the site. |
| Gridsq | Identifies the 1km square area in which the site is located. This is useful in checking on the areas surrounding proposed developments. |
| Proximity | The distance in kilometres to the nearest residential community – typically a group of 3 or more houses. |

[*Source:* UK National Digital Archive of Datasets. Welsh Office: Contaminated Land Survey. Table 1 Conland at http://ndad.ulcc.ac.uk/datasets/15/1988/1.htm (viewed 14 April 2000). Crown Copyright: Public Record Office]

2. *Type.* Give more specific descriptions of data and field types. The following list is not definitive and authority lists should be used.

   *Data type*
   Describes the kind of data being stored or manipulated within the program or system.[8] Includes:

   Alphanumeric data (for example integer data, real type, complex, and so on)

   Character data (for example ASCII, ISO8859, ANSI, and so on)

---

[8] This section is based on British Computer Society *A Glossary of Computing Terms*, 8th edn (The British Computer Society, Longman, 1995) pp. 265–6 and passim where fuller explanations and definitions are given.

String data
Boolean (or logical) data
Sample data (that is, digitally recorded sound data)
Video data
Date data

Within fields, data types may be described[9] as:

Missing
Numeric fields: Integer (Byte); Positive Integer (Byte); Integer
(Short); Positive Integer (Short); Integer; Positive Integer; Single-
Precision Floating Point; Double-Precision Floating Point
Variable and Fixed Length strings
Logical

### *File types*[10]

Description of file type allows identification of the structure of the file
contents. It is often made explicit in the three characters of the file
name extension (.doc, .pdf, and so on). Includes:

RTF (rich text format/revisable text format) files
ASCII *or* text files
Graphic data
Word processed file

### 25.4D2   Structure

1.   *Links.* Indicate the nature of the links between files within the system
or with other files or databases.

Example:

> The Anatomy dataset is divided into two sections, corresponding to
> the tables for bodies donated for anatomical research and their dis-
> posal by the schools of anatomy.

[*Source:* UK National Digital Archive of Datasets. Department of Health: Anatomy
Office – Anatomy dataset at http://ndad.ulcc.ac.uk/datasets/21/series.htm (viewed 14
April 2000). Crown Copyright: Public Record Office]

---

9   The field data types are drawn from the National Digital Archive of Datasets 'Datatype
    Descriptions' help page where fuller explanations are given. See
    http://ndad.ulcc.ac.uk/help/dthelp.htm (viewed 14 April 2000).
10  This section is based on British Computer Society *A Glossary of Computing Terms*, 8th
    edn (The British Computer Society, Longman, 1995) pp. 265–6 and passim where fuller
    explanations and definitions are given.

Indicate the nature of and links between fields (that is, identify key field in a table).

Any attachments linked to e-mail messages should be noted.

2. *Related material.* Note the original electronic or hard copy documentation related to the record: this may include coding schemes, lookup tables, data dictionaries, user manuals, and so on which contain information necessary to interpret the data.

Note whether the record is part of a hybrid file of paper and electronic media, for example part of a filing system where outgoing correspondence is maintained electronically and incoming correspondence preserved in hard copy.

Example:

> For other [hard copy] records of the Committee see classes JN1 and JN2
>
> Some of the responses to the Green Paper were received in electronic form as e-mails and attachments. Others were received in paper form and were then scanned by CITU to obtain tagged image file format (TIFF) images.

[*Source:* Public Record Office. Crown Copyright]

3. *Dynamic/closed.* Indicate whether the original record was dynamic (that is, where data content altered over time) or closed (that is, where records remained static once entered).

Example:

> Each year new data collected is added to the Annual file, i.e. it is a cumulative method of storage giving the results of each year's survey. Data in the Annual file is in effect closed, though it should be noted that where forms are received late, data from the forms is entered into the database. This means that additional data for the years held in the Annual file may be added in subsequent years.
>
> The other files in the DOMUS system are dynamic in that they are continuously updated whenever new information is received (normally as a result of the annual receipt of survey forms). Records are not deleted from the Domus so that information on a museum which

is permanently closed will still be retained on the Domus file, although no further data will be entered in the Annual file.

[*Source:* UK National Digital Archive of Datasets. Digest of Museum Statistics dataset at http://ndad.ulcc.ac.uk/datasets/12/series.htm (viewed 14 April 2000). Crown Copyright: Public Record Office]

This information may cross-refer to the Updating element in the Management Information Area.

### 25.4E   *Physical and Technical Description Area*

Although it is likely that the original physical support for the record will be irrelevant once the information is made available for continuing public access, full and explicit entries in this area are necessary to record details of the history of treatment of the record. Alternatively, where migration is not immediately possible, such information is vital to monitor the possibility of continued access. The information entered here is thus likely to be primarily useful in a management context, but will also be of interest to some external readers. The information may cross-reference to the Management Information Area.

### 25.4E1   Physical carrier

Where the record was received on a physical carrier this should be noted simply. Use, for example:

disk
optical disk
CD-ROM
reel
cartridge
magnetic tape
punched card
cassette tape
ROM chip
ROM cartridge
micro-drive

Give the dimensions of the physical carrier, for example:

disk 5$\frac{1}{4}$″
cartridge 3$\frac{1}{2}$″ (where the measurement is the length of side inserted into the machine).

**25.4E2**   Other characteristics

Give the density, number of tracks, number of sides (disks), number of bits per inch (bpi), number of records per block (magnetic tapes), recording mode (for example double density, single density, and so on).

Details of the type and other characteristics of a physical carrier are primarily relevant to describing older magnetic media.

**25.4E3**   Original application/software dependency

Give the software name, high-level language or code originally used, and indicate subsequent migrations during the active life of the records, or compatibility.

Example:

A GEORGE III operating system running on ICL mainframe computers appears to have been used by the DfEE's Statistics Branch until 1988 when data was converted to a VME operating system. This appears to have been replaced by a UNIX operating system ca.1992. In 1996 the DfEE's Corporate Data Archive utilised a UNIX Solaris operating system, with data being held in ASCII format on optical disks. Magnetic tapes were used for data storage until ca.1992.

[*Source:* UK National Digital Archive of Datasets. Education Departments Schools Census (Form 7) datasets at http://ndad.ulcc.ac.uk/datasets/13/series.htm (viewed 14 April 2000). Crown Copyright: Public Record Office]

**25.4E4**   Original hardware dependency

- *Original input:* record the equipment used for original input or on which the system operated. Terms for peripherals such as microphone, concept keyboard, touch screen, light pen, tracker ball, and so on may be used. Record original settings or calibrations. For example:

    Olivetti M400 (20 Mb RAM) [an IBM compatible PC with Windows].

- *Output dependency:* indicate equipment which was needed in order to achieve output from the materials; terms include graphics facilities (specific terms cover this), plotter, speaker, printer.

**25.4F** *Management Information Area*
This area is provided in order to help control the processing, conservation and use of the materials. Some of the information recorded here may be of use to users.

**25.4F1** Process and validation history
Record the process history of the local file or files, including processing carried out at the point of transfer to the repository, and the processing programme expected for the future.

Examples:

> This class contains records originally created in Word Perfect 5.1 and transferred to the PRO on floppy disks... Upon transfer the Word Perfect files were copied into Word 6 format and verified to confirm the integrity of the data. The Word Perfect files were later copied into Word 7 format and printed to PostScript files for permanent preservation.

[*Source:* PRO. Crown Copyright]

> The documents in this class were transferred to the PRO in either PostScript or TIFF format from which a viewing copy was generated in portable document format (PDF). The documents remain unchanged but an instruction to users appears at the foot of each page together with a header and footer giving the file's class, piece and page number along with notification of copyright. For presentational purposes the final report published on CD ROM is displayed in its original software formats.

[*Source:* PRO. Crown Copyright]

> **Content validation**
> A number of checks on the content of the data set were done. This included checks for missing and non-valid data. The anomalies found include the following:

| Table | Field(s) | Suspect or Missing Values |
|-------|----------|---------------------------|
| Length_94 | Survey Date | 8 records with value before 1993; 1 record with missing value |
| Element_94 | Date Constructed | 2 records with value 1994; 402 records with missing value |

**Transformation validation**

The number of records in each table of the transferred Access database was compared to the number of records in each comma-separated file that was created. These corresponded exactly. The sum, average, maximum and minimum of numeric fields were calculated for the transferred data and transformed data. No discrepancies were found.

### 25.4F2 Archiving

Record the administrative system in force which controls the passage of active records to inactive, or the transfer of databases or files from active administration to the repository. Record also systems in use for security backup. This element may cross-reference to the Retirement or Closure element in the Production Area.

### 25.4F3 Updating

Information is needed in this element where the content of the materials is to be altered as a consequence of subsequent accessions of related material. The information may cross-refer to the 'Dynamic/closed' element in the Structure Sub-area.

# APPENDIXES

# Appendix 1

# Dictionary of technical terms

The dictionary includes only words which are used in a technical sense within *MAD3*, and which therefore are to be regarded as terms of art within the context of archival description. As far as possible, definitions have been based on the forthcoming revision of the International Council on Archives' *Dictionary of Archival Terminology* – where the exact ICA definition has been used, this is noted in this list as (ICA). However, variations have been necessary in a few cases because of the development of underlying concepts.

Words in italic are defined in the dictionary. Additional sources referred to in square brackets are cited at the end of the dictionary.

**Abstract**
In information work generally, "a concise summary of a document" (ICA), without added interpretation or criticism.

In *MAD3*, an alternative name for the Scope and Content *Sub-area* of the *data elements* table.

**Access** *(noun)*
The right, opportunity or means of finding, using or approaching documents and/or information. Access may also be affected by the physical state of the materials, or the need to conserve them.

**Access, to** *(verb)*
The act of obtaining *access* to a document; the act of referring to an *archival entity*.

### Access point
A name, term, keyword, phrase or code that may be used to search, identify or locate a record, file or document. (ICA)

### Accession *(noun)*
An acquisition; an assembly of materials taken into custody at one time.

### Accession, to *(verb)*
To record the formal acceptance into custody of an *accession*.

### Accession number (code, or reference)
The unique number or *code* assigned to permanently identify an *accession* (ICA); in order to identify it for administrative purposes. This number is normally recorded in an accession register and in practice often serves to identify a *group* or *collection* within a *repository*, at least until that group has been fully processed. In some cases accession numbers remain permanently in use as identifiers of groups: in this case the preferred term would be *reference code*.

### Accretion
Use *accrual*.

### Accrual
An acquisition of materials which belong to a *group* already in the custody of a *repository*.

### Analytical inventory
Use *list*.

### Archival entity
In *MAD3*, this term means any unit of an archival accumulation which is under consideration at the time. The term can indicate such a unit at any *level* or size: for example, it can mean a *group*, *subgroup*, *series*, *item* or *piece*, or any temporary grouping of any of these.

### Archival relationships, archival order
The relationships between components of an archival entity arising from the original system under which they were created; the order or sequence of components of an archive which demonstrate this system.

### Archive
A general term which in some contexts can be used in place of *archival*

*entity* to indicate any unit of an archival accumulation which has to be considered separately for management or descriptive action; also used as a synonym for *collection*, for which it is a preferred term.

## Archive group
A synonym for *group*, which is the preferred term.

## Archives
(a)  A *repository*, which is the preferred term for a building or part of a building in which *archives (b)* are preserved and made available for consultation;
(b)  A general term for the materials held within a repository.
See also *papers*, *records*. May be used as an element in the Title *Sub-area*, to indicate the materials which resulted from the business operations of the originating body.
For a fuller definition see Section 1.1A.

## Archives service
In *MAD*, any organization, for example a *record office*, which is responsible for the management and exploitation of archives. The term is broader than *repository*, which refers to an archives service only in its aspect of the holder or custodian of materials.

## Area
In *MAD*, which takes the usage from *AACR2*, a collection of related *data elements* which together provide an aspect of the description of an *archival entity*.

## Arrangement
The intellectual and physical processes and results of analysing and organizing documents in accordance with accepted archival principles, particularly provenance, at as many *levels* as necessary. (ICA)
   Archives are arranged in relation to other related archives, and not in relation to a pre-established *index* of concepts (for example *classification* in librarianship). The physical process is called 'sorting'.

## Authority file
A group of *authority records* searchable by established headings and cross-references. (ICA)

## Authority record
An entry in an *authority file* that contains information about an *access*

*point*. An authority record establishes the form of the heading, determines cross-references and the relationships of the heading to other headings in the authority file, and documents the decisions. (ICA)

## Bibliographic description

The description of a bibliographic item, in conformity with the rules currently in force for this type of description (at present *AACR2*, ISBD, and so on). The term should be avoided for archives, except where (as in entries in on-line databases which refer to archival materials) descriptions are specially written to conform to bibliographical standards.

## Box

A storage and retrieval unit consisting of a rigid container, provided by the *repository*, to contain a number of *items* or *pieces*, whether or not related by content or function.

## Bundle

A storage and retrieval unit consisting of a number of *pieces*, whether or not related by content or function, normally tied together by string, tape, and so on. A bundle may be 'original' or formed by *arrangement*.

## Calendar

A *list*, usually in chronological order, containing very full summaries of individual documents in the same *series* or of a specified kind from a number of sources, giving all content and material information valuable to the user. A calendar differs from a transcript only in that common form phrases are summarized or omitted. Calendars are intended to serve as *surrogates* for the originals they refer to, especially for remote users.

## Call number

See *reference code*; a *code* which identifies an *item* for the purpose of retrieval.

## Catalogue

A set of archival *descriptions (2)* which includes descriptions of all the components of one or more related *management groups*, *groups* or *collections* at all the different *levels* used, and with an index. The concept is explained at Section 6.3.

## Citation

1.  'A note referring to a work, or an archival document, from which a passage is quoted, or to some source of authority for a statement or proposition.' [Evans, 1974]

2.  A brief archival or *bibliographic description* appearing in a secondary work or *list*. There are standards for the form of citations (BS6371/1983).

## Class

Previously used in *MAD2* for Level 3 of archival *arrangement*. The international usage is *series*, which is the preferred term.
    See Section 4.6E.

## Classification

The systematic identification and arrangement of documents in categories according to logically structured conventions, methods and procedural rules represented in a classification plan/scheme. (ICA)

## Classification scheme

A pattern or arrangement of concepts, setting out the relationship of one to another, in any field of knowledge, or, frequently, in the universe of knowledge. In archives administration, there are classification schemes covering *groups* which recur in different places.

## Code

See *reference code*.

## Collection

1.  Equivalent in a manuscript library to a *group*. See Section 4.6C.
2.  An artificial gathering of documents brought together on the basis of some common characteristic (for example means of acquisition, creator, subject, language, medium, form, name of collector) without regard to the provenance of the documents. (ICA)

## Collections

Use *holdings*: all the materials acquired or held by a *repository*.

## Data

1.  Information represented in a formalized manner, suitable for transmission, interpretation, or processing manually or automatically. (ICA)
2.  Loosely used for information, especially in large quantities. (ICA)

## Data element

In *MAD*, the basic unit of information in the structured table of data elements. The elements in the table are structured into sectors, *areas* and *sub-areas*. See Chapters 12–14.

### Dedicated field

A *field* whose function, content and (usually) length are strictly defined by the *file* or *finding aids* system it is part of, as opposed to one (for example *free text*) which has no restriction on its form, content or length.

### Depth of description

In *MAD* this means the amount of detail which is to be included in a description; the fullness of a description. Rules for it are in Chapter 8.

### Description

1. The process of capturing, analysing, organizing and recording information that serves to identify, manage, locate and explain the holdings of repositories and the contexts and records systems which produced them. (ICA)
2. The products of the above process (ICA) – in *MAD* terms a component of a *representation file*.

### Document *(noun)*

1. Recorded information regardless of medium or characteristics. (ICA)
2. A single *archive*, *record* or *manuscript* entity – usually a physically indivisible entity; a *piece*.

### Field

A subdivision of a *record* containing a unit of *data*. [ICA/ADP 1983, p.17.] See also *dedicated field*, *free text field*, *record*.

### File *(noun)*

1. An organized unit (folder, volume, and so on) of documents grouped together either for current use by the creator or in the process of archival *arrangement*, because they relate to the same subject, activity or transaction. A file is usually the basic unit within a *series*. (ICA)

    Often applied to case files or particular instance papers.
2. A set of related *data* items with a common title and purpose. See also *representation file*.
3. In data processing, two or more *records (2)* of identical layout treated as a unit. The unit is larger than a record but smaller than a data system, and may also be known as a dataset (ICA).

### File *(verb)*

To place *documents* or *data* in a predetermined location so that they can be retrieved.

## Finding aid

The broadest term to cover any *description* or means of reference generated by an *archives service* in the course of establishing administrative or intellectual control over its *holdings*.

## Finding aids system

Defined in Chapter 3. The system which results from linking together all the different *finding aids* produced and used by a *repository*.

## Folder

A folded sheet of paper or card serving as a cover for a set of related *documents*.

## Fonds (d'archives)

Use *group*.

## Format *(noun)*

1. A selection of descriptive elements arranged in a prescribed manner and sequence so that the resulting description will be standardized. (ICA)

    Where it refers to the shape of text on a page or screen, the preferred term is *layout*.
2. Also the physical appearance, technical character or size of materials, especially in the context of *special formats*.

## Format *(verb)*

The act of arranging *data* into a specified format, or creating a page *layout*.

## Free text field

*Field* allowing descriptive *data* to be entered in natural language without structural subdivisions.

## Group

The whole of the *documents*, regardless of form or medium, organically created and/or accumulated and used by a particular person, family or corporate body in the course of that creator's activities and functions. (ICA 'fonds')

   The equivalent of *fonds*. Used in *MAD* for Level 2 of archival *arrangement*.

## Guide

1. A *finding aid* giving a general account of all or part of the *holdings* of a *repository*. A guide is usually arranged by *group* and *series*.

2. Also used to mean a *finding aid* describing holdings of one or more *archives* relating to particular subjects, periods or geographical areas or to specified types of documents. This type of guide is usually called a thematic or subject guide. (ICA)

## Heading
1. Title or inscription at the head of a page, chapter or other section of a *document*. (ICA)
2. A name, word or phrase at the beginning of an entry in an *index*, *catalogue* or other *finding aid*, which serves as an *access point* to the materials being described. (ICA)

## Headnote
In *MAD*, a *higher level description* which appears directly above a set of related *lower level descriptions*. See Chapter 6.

## Higher level description
Defined in Chapter 5. A *description* which gives information on the background, context and provenance of a set of related archival entities, the descriptions of which it governs. In *MAD2* the term 'macro description' was used, but because of ambiguities which resulted, higher level description is now the preferred term.

## Holdings
The totality of the material in the custody of an *archives service*, or distinct part of it.

## Index
An ordered list of terms, *keywords* or concepts contained in a set of archival *descriptions*, or in a *file* or *document*, together with pointers to the locations (*reference code*, page number) for those terms, keywords or concepts. See also *vocabulary*, *thesaurus*, *classification scheme*, *access point*.

## Item
In *MAD* the physical unit of handling and retrieval in archives management. Used in *MAD3* for Level 4 of archival *arrangement*.

## Keyword
A word or group of words taken from the title or text of a *document* (or its abstract) characterizing its content and facilitating its retrieval. (ICA)

## Layout
The shape of text on a page: in this sense, preferred term for *format*.

**Levels of arrangement**
See Chapter 4. The hierarchical groupings of archival *holdings* for purposes of physical and intellectual control. (ICA)

**Level of description**
See Chapter 4. The *level of arrangement* that is the basis of a unit of *description* in a *finding aid*. (ICA)

**List**
A one-by-one enumeration of a set of *archives*; the basic *finding aid* for *lower level descriptions*.

**List mode**
See Chapter 7. One of the two principal *modes* or styles of setting out archival *descriptions*, characterized by short *fields*, little connected text, in tabulated columns.

**Location index**
A *finding aid* used to control and locate *holdings*. (ICA)
   Where the *index* format is not a strong characteristic, use *shelf list*.

**Lower level description**
Defined in Chapter 5. *Descriptions* of the individual components of an *archival entity*, which appear below and are governed by a *higher level description*. In *MAD2* the term 'micro description' was used, but because of ambiguities which resulted, lower level description is now the preferred term.

**Management group**
Defined in Section 4.6B.

**Manuscript**
1. Within a manuscripts library, an individual *item* (such as a parchment or volume) without any organic relationship to any other similar item.
2. A handwritten or typed *document*. A typed document is more precisely called a typescript. (ICA)

**Manuscript group**
Use *group* or *collection*.

**Metadata**
*Data* describing data and data systems; [for example] the structure of databases, their characteristics, location and usage. (ICA)

## Modes of listing
Defined in Chapter 7. In *MAD* there are two modes, or general styles, into which *finding aids* can be *formatted*: *list mode* and *paragraph mode*.

## Moral defence
Term coined by Sir Hilary Jenkinson [see his *Manual*, 1965 edn, p. 83] to summarize the professional duties of archivists in safeguarding the integrity and authenticity of the *archives* in their care.

## Papers
A natural accumulation of personal and family materials [Evans p. 426].
  The term may be used as an element in the Title *Sub-area*.

## Paragraph mode
Defined in Chapter 7. One of the two principal *modes* or styles of setting out archival *descriptions*, characterized by blocks of text arranged (in paragraphs) down the page.

## Piece
The smallest physically indivisible archival unit (for example a page in a letter). Pieces can accumulate to form *items* or can be equivalent to an item. (ICA)

## Quality control
Procedures within an *archives service* aimed at ensuring the correctness and *depth of description*.

## Record(s)
1.  *Document(s)* created or received and maintained by an agency, organization or individual in pursuance of legal obligations or in the transaction of business. (ICA)
2.  In data processing, a grouping of interelated *data elements* forming the basic unit of a *file*); by extension, the *description* of one *archival entity* within a set. (ICA)

## Record office
In British usage, an *archives service* or *repository*, which are the preferred terms where the service or the physical custody, respectively, are intended.

## Reference code
The unique symbols, usually alphanumeric, which identify an *archival entity* and which facilitate storage and retrieval.

Reference codes are one of the *data elements* in the Identity Statement Area. See Sections 9.10 and 14.2A.

## Repository
An *archives service*, a manuscript library, or any agency which operates as such, considered as the physical and moral custodian of archival material.

## Representation
In *MAD* a *description* considered as something which stands in place of the original for particular purposes. The concept is discussed in Chapter 3, and is important for the design of *finding aids*.

## Representation file
See Chapter 3. The assembly of *representations*, components of a *finding aids system*.

## Search
The act of a *user* seeking information contained in archival materials, or in *finding aids*. See Section 9.6.

## Series
*Documents* arranged in accordance with a filing system or maintained as a unit because they result from the same accumulation or filing process, the same function, or the same activity; have a particular form; or because of some other relationship arising out of their creation, receipt or use. (ICA)
   Level 3 of archival *arrangement*.

## Shelf list
A list of the *holdings* in a records centre or *archives (a)* arranged in order of the contents of each shelf. (ICA)
   See also *location index*.

## Special formats
In *MAD* types of archival material which call for special treatment in *description*.

## Structural finding aid
A *finding aid* which is arranged in an order which reflects the original system of the creating organization. The concept is discussed at Section 3.6.

## Sub-area
A group of related *data elements*, part of an *area* within an archival *description*.

**Subclass**
Use *subseries*.

**Subgroup**
A body of related *archives* within a *group*, corresponding to administrative subdivisions in the originating agency or organization or, when that is not possible, to geographical, chronological, functional or similar groupings of the material itself. When the creating body has a complex hierarchical structure, each subgroup has as many subordinate subgroups as are necessary to reflect the levels of the hierarchical structure of the primary subordinate administrative unit. (ICA)

Defined in Section 4.6D; Levels 2.5, 2.25, and so on of archival description.

**Subseries**
A body of *records* within a *series*, readily identifiable in terms of filing *arrangement*, type, form or content. (ICA)

**Surrogate**
A *representation* which can be used as an alternative to the original. See *calendar*.

**Thesaurus**
A compilation of words and phrases showing synonymous, hierarchical and other relationships and dependencies, the function of which is to provide a standardized *vocabulary* for information storage and retrieval. (ICA)

**Title page**
A *higher level description* which takes the form of a separate page at the front of a (generally extensive) *finding aid*, carrying introductory information. See also *title page section*.

**Title page section**
A *higher level description* using the *title page* model but which is too extensive to be contained on the title page itself. Where this happens, the title page is followed by one or more further pages of explanatory material, giving the background, context and provenance of the materials the *lower level descriptions* of which follow. See Section 6.7.

**User**
Any person seeking information from archival materials, whether a staff

member, an employee of the archive-creating agency, or a member of the public.

**Vocabulary**
Generally, the terms permitted to be used, or actually used, in a *finding aids system* or an *index*.

## ADDITIONAL SOURCES CITED IN THE DICTIONARY

BS5605/1990 *Recommendations for citing and referencing published material*. London.

BS6371/1983 *Citation of unpublished documents*. London.

Evans, F. B. *et al.* (comps), 'A basic glossary for archivists, manuscript curators and records managers', *The American Archivist* (1974), 415–33.

International Council on Archives, ADP Committee, *Elementary terms in archival automation*, Koblenz, 1983.

Jenkinson, H. *A manual of archive administration*, 2nd edn rev., London, 1965.

# Appendix 2

# Brief bibliography

*Anglo-American Cataloguing Rules*, The Joint Steering Committee Revision of *AACR*, Canadian Library Association, Ottawa. 2nd edn, 1998 revision.

Brunton, P. and Robinson, T., 'Arrangement and Description', in Ellis, J. (ed.), *Keeping Archives*, 2nd edn, Thorpe in association with the Australian Society of Archivists, Inc, Sydney, 1993, pp. 222–47.

Bureau of Canadian Archivists, *Toward Descriptive Standards: report and recommendations of the Canadian working group on archival descriptive standards*, Bureau of Canadian Archivists, Ottawa, 1985.

Bureau of Canadian Archivists, *Rules for Archival Description*, Bureau of Canadian Archivists, Ottawa, 1990.

*Dictionary of Archival Terminology*, ICA Project Group on Terminology, ICA, forthcoming 1999. The *Dictionary* will be available electronically only, through the ICA website at http://www.ica.org and other sites to be announced.

Duff, W.M. and Haworth, K.M., 'Advancing Archival Description: a model for rationalising North American descriptive standards', *Archives and Manuscripts* **25** (1997), pp. 194–217.

Edgecombe, J., 'Finding Aids', in Ellis, J. (ed.), *Keeping Archives*, 2nd edn, Thorpe in association with the Australian Society of Archivists, Inc, Sydney, 1993, pp. 248–72.

Freeth, S., 'Finding Aids', in Turton, A. (ed.), *Managing Business Archives*, Butterworth-Heinemann in association with the Business Archives Council, London, 1991, pp. 266–317.

Hensen, S.L., *Archives, Personal Papers and Manuscripts: a cataloging manual for archival repositories, historical societies and manuscript libraries*, 2nd edn, Society of American Archivists, Chicago, 1989.

Hensen, S.L., 'RAD, MAD and APPM: the search for Anglo-American standards for archival description', *Archives and Museum Informatics* **5.2** (1991), pp. 2–5.

Hildesheimer, F., *Guidelines for preparation of general guides to national archives: a RAMP study*, Unesco, Paris, 1983.

Hurley, C., 'The making and the keeping of records: (1) What are finding aids for?', *Archives and Manuscripts* **26** (1998), pp. 58–77.

*ISAAR(CPF): International Standard Archival Authority Record for Corporate Bodies, Persons and Families*, International Council on Archives, Ottawa, 1996.

ISAD(G): *General International Standard Archival Description*, International Council on Archives, Ottawa, 1994.

Lacasse, J.D. and Lechasseur, A., 'Du record group au fond d'archives: normalisation du classement et de la description d'archives gouverne-mentales aux Archives nationales du Canada', *Archives* (Quebec) **28** (1996–7), pp. 57–79.

Miller, F., *Arranging and Describing Archives and Manuscripts*, Archival Fundamentals Series, Society of American Archivists, Chicago, 1990.

Miller, F., 'Archival description', *Reference Librarian* **56** (1997), pp. 55–66.

National Council on Archives, *Rules for the construction of personal, place and corporate names*, [London], 1997. Also available at http://www.hmc.gov.uk/nca/title.htm [viewed January 2000].

Nougaret, C., 'Classement et description: des principes à la pratique', in Favier, J. and Neirinck, D., *La Pratique archivistique française*, Direction des Archives de France, Paris, 1993, pp. 135–86.

Pepler, J., 'Data elements and types of finding aids', in Society of Archivists, *British archival practice: the Society's archive diploma training manual*, Module 8, Unit 2, Society of Archivists, London, 1996.

Planning Committee on Descriptive Standards, Subject Indexing Working Group, *Subject indexing for archives: report of the Subject Indexing Working Group*, Bureau of Canadian Archivists, Ottawa, 1992.

*Standards for Archival Description: a handbook*, Walch, V.I. (comp.) for the Working Group on Standards for Archival Description, with contributions from Marion Matters, Society of American Archivists, Chicago, 1994.

Stibbe, H., 'Archival descriptive standards and the archival community: a retrospective', *Archivaria* **41** (1997), pp. 259–74.

Taylor, H.A., *The Arrangement and Description of Archival Materials*, ICA Handbooks 2, K.G. Saur, Munich, 1980.

*Toward International Descriptive Standards for Archives: papers presented at the ICA Invitational Meeting of Experts on Descriptive Standards, National Archives of Canada, Ottawa 4–7 October 1988.* K.G. Saur, Munich, 1993.

# Appendix 3

## *General International Standard Archival Description ISAD(G), 1994*

*Adopted by the Ad Hoc Commission on Descriptive Standards, Stockholm, Sweden, 21–23 January 1993 (Final ICA approved version) 1994*

## PREFACE

P.1   A draft set of general rules was developed by a sub-group of the Ad Hoc Commission on Descriptive Standards. The sub-group was established at the first plenary of the Commission during its meeting in Höhr-Grenzhausen, Germany, October, 1990.

P.2   The sub-group consisted of: Wendy Duff (coordinator), Michael Cook, Sharon Thibodeau, Hugo Stibbe (project director and secretary).

P.3   The sub-group met in Liverpool, U.K., in July 1991 to complete the draft which was discussed, amended and extended at the plenary of the Ad Hoc Commission at its meeting in Madrid in January 1992. The draft was formally adopted at that meeting. It is known as the Madrid draft of the 'ISAD(G): General International Standard Archival Description'.

P.4   The Madrid draft of the ISAD(G) was circulated for comment to the international archival community in February 1992, translated into the languages of ICA and distributed as a congress paper for the XIIth International Congress on Archives in Montreal in September 1992 where it was discussed in an open session. The Commission met again in Stockholm in January 1993 to examine and revise the document in response to the comments received from the world wide review and the open session in Montreal. The current document is the result of that process.

P.5   A 5 year revision cycle is proposed for this document and this will be recommended to the ICA when the document is presented for publication.

P.6   The ICA Ad Hoc Commission on Descriptive Standards acknowledges and thanks Unesco for its financial support for this project. It also thanks the National Archives of Canada for its support of the Secretariat and the institutions that have hosted the Commission during the development of this document, the National Archives and the Directorate of the State Archives, Ministry of Culture of Spain and the National Archives of Sweden.

## INTRODUCTION

I.1   This set of general rules for archival description is part of a process that will

  a. ensure the creation of consistent, appropriate, and self explanatory descriptions;
  b. facilitate the retrieval and exchange of information about archival material;
  c. enable the sharing of authority data; and
  d. make possible the integration of descriptions from different repositories into a unified information system.

I.2  As *general* rules, these are intended to be broadly applicable to descriptions of archives regardless of the nature or extent of the unit of description. The rules guide the formulation of information in each of 26 elements that may be combined to constitute the description of an archival entity.

I.3  Each rule consists of:

  a. the name of the element of description governed by the rule;
  b. a statement of the purpose of incorporating the element in a description;
  c. a statement of the general rule (or rules) applicable to the element; and
  d. where applicable, examples illustrating implementation of the rule(s).

I.4  The organization of the rules reflects a preferred structure for any given description incorporating elements governed by the rules. Within this structure the elements are grouped in six information areas:

  1. Identity Statement Area
     (where essential information is conveyed to identify the unit of description)
  2. Context Area
     (where information is conveyed about the origin and custody of the unit of description)
  3. Content and Structure Area
     (where information is conveyed about the subject matter and arrangement of the unit of description)
  4. Conditions of Access and Use Area
     (where information is conveyed about the availability of the unit of description)
  5. Allied Materials Area
     (where information is conveyed about materials having an important relationship to the unit of description)

6. Note Area
> (where specialized information and information that cannot be accommodated in any of the other areas may be conveyed).

I.5 All 26 elements covered by these general rules are available for use, but only a subset need be used in any given description. A very few elements are considered essential for international exchange of descriptive information:

a. reference code;
b. title;
c. date(s) of creation or date(s) of accumulation of the material in the unit of description;
d. extent of the unit of description; and
e. level of description.

If the name of the creator is not included in the title, then the element of description that contains that name is also essential for international exchange.

I.6 The extent to which a given archival description will incorporate more than the essential elements of information will vary depending on the nature of the unit of description and the requirements of the information system (manual or automated) of which it is a part. Some systems may include descriptions of the constituent parts of the fonds (e.g., series, items) as well as the fonds itself. To assure the efficiency and clarity of such systems, preparation of the multilevel descriptions within them should be guided by the rules concerning their linkage and informational content. Multilevel rules designed to accomplish this have been incorporated in these general rules.

I.7 The areas of description covered by these general rules are those thought to have the widest applicability in an international archival context. This is only the beginning of a standardization effort. Further specific rules should be formulated to guide the description of special categories of material (such as cartographic materials, motion pictures, electronic files, or charters, notarial deeds, property titles).

I.8 Access points are based upon the elements of description. The value of access points is enhanced through authority control. Because of the importance of access points for retrieval, international guidelines should be developed for formulating them. The Ad Hoc Commission is developing a standard description for authority records. Vocabularies and conventions to be used with access points should be developed nationally, or separately for each language. The following

ISO standards are useful when developing and maintaining controlled vocabularies: *ISO 5963 Documentation – Methods for examining documents, determining their subject, and selecting indexing terms* and *ISO 2788 Documentation – Guidelines for the establishment and development of monolingual thesauri.*

I.9   In citing a published source in any element of description, follow the latest version of *ISO 690 Documentation – Bibliographic references – Content, form and structure.*

## 0.   GLOSSARY OF TERMS ASSOCIATED WITH THE GENERAL RULES

**0.1**   The following glossary with terms and their definitions forms an integral part of these rules of description. The definitions are to be understood as having been formulated specifically for the purposes of this document.

*Access.* The ability to make use of material from a fonds, usually subject to rules and conditions.

*Access point.* A name, keyword, index term, etc. by which a description may be searched, identified and retrieved.

*Appraisal.* The process of determining the archival value of a set of records.

*Archival description.* The creation of an accurate representation of a unit of description and its component parts, if any, by the process of capturing, collating, analysing, and organizing any information that serves to identify archival material and explain the context and records systems which produced it.

*Arrangement.* The intellectual operations involved in the analysis and organization of archival material.

*Authority control.* The control of standardized forms of terms including names (personal, corporate or geographic) used as access points.

*Corporate body.* An organization or group of persons that is identified by a particular name and that acts, or may act, as an entity.

*Creator. See Provenance.*

*Date of accumulation.* The period over which the material within, or forming part of, the unit of description has been accumulated by the creator.

*Date of creation.* The actual date at which the archival material in a unit of description was created.

*File.* An organized unit of documents grouped together either for current use by the creator or in the process of archival arrangement, because they relate to the same subject, activity, or transaction. A file is usually the basic unit within a record series.

*Finding aid.* The broadest term to cover any description or means of reference made or received by an archives service in the course of establishing administrative or intellectual control over archival material.

*Fonds.* The whole of the documents, regardless of form or medium, organically created and/or accumulated and used by a particular person, family, or corporate body in the course of that creator's activities and functions.

*Form.* The type or kind of material comprising a unit of description, e.g., letters, minute books.

*Formal title.* A title which appears prominently on or in the archival material being described.

*Item.* The smallest intellectually indivisible archival unit, e.g., a letter, memorandum, report, photograph, sound recording.

*Level of description.* The position of the unit of description in the hierarchy of the fonds.

*Location.* The repository, or address of a private owner, at which the archival material is held.

*Provenance.* The organization or individual that created, accumulated and/or maintained and used documents in the conduct of personal or corporate activity.

*Series.* Documents arranged in accordance with a filing system or maintained as a unit because they result from the same accumulation or filing process, or the same activity; have a particular form; or because of some other relationship arising out of their creation, receipt, or use. A series is also known as a records series.

*Sub-fonds.* A subdivision of a fonds containing a body of related documents corresponding to administrative subdivisions in the originating agency or organization or, when that is not possible, to geographical, chronological, functional, or similar groupings of the material itself. When the creating body has a complex hierarchical structure, each subgroup has as many subordinate subgroups as are necessary to reflect the levels of the hierarchical structure of the primary subordinate administrative unit.

*Supplied title.* A title supplied by the archivist for a unit of description which has no formal title.

*Title.* A word, phrase, character, or group of characters that names a unit of description.

> *Unit of description.* A document or set of documents in any physical form, treated as an entity, and as such, forming the basis of a single description.

---

## 1.    MULTILEVEL DESCRIPTION

### 1.1   *INTRODUCTION*

If the fonds as a whole is being described, it should be represented in one description, using the elements of description as outlined below in section 3 of this document. If description of the parts is required, they may be described separately also using the appropriate elements from section 3. The sum total of all descriptions thus obtained, linked in a hierarchy, as outlined in the model in the Appendix, represents the fonds and those parts for which descriptions were made. For the purposes of these rules, this technique of description is called **multi-level description**.

Four fundamental rules apply when establishing a hierarchy of descriptions. They are set out in rules 2.1 to 2.4.

## 2.    MULTILEVEL DESCRIPTION RULES

### 2.1   *DESCRIPTION FROM THE GENERAL TO THE SPECIFIC*

*Purpose:*
To represent the context and the hierarchical structure of the fonds and its parts.
*Rule:*
At the fonds level give information for the fonds as a whole. At the next and subsequent levels give information for the parts being described. Present the resulting descriptions in a hierarchical part-to-whole relationship proceeding from the broadest (fonds) to the more specific.

### 2.2   *INFORMATION RELEVANT TO THE LEVEL OF DESCRIPTION*

*Purpose:*
To represent accurately the context and content of the unit of description.
*Rule:*
Provide only such information as is appropriate to the level being described. For example, do not provide detailed file content infor-

mation if the unit of description is a fonds; do not provide an administrative history for an entire department if the creator of a unit of description is a division or a branch.

## 2.3 *LINKING OF DESCRIPTIONS*

*Purpose:*
To make explicit the position of the unit of description in the hierarchy.
*Rule:*
Link each description to its next higher unit of description, if applicable, and identify the level of description. *(See 3.1.4.)*

## 2.4 *NON-REPETITION OF INFORMATION*

*Purpose:*
To avoid redundancy of information in hierarchically related archival descriptions.
*Rule:*
At the highest appropriate level, give information that is common to the component parts. Do not repeat information at a lower level of description that has already been given at a higher level.

## 3. ELEMENTS OF DESCRIPTION

## 3.1 *IDENTITY STATEMENT AREA*

### 3.1.1 Reference code(s)

*Purpose:*
To identify the repository and to provide a link between the archival material and the description that represents it.
*Rule:*
Record the country code in accordance with the latest version of *ISO 3166 Codes for the representation of names of countries*, followed by the repository code in accordance with the national repository code standard followed by a local repository specific reference code, control number, or other unique identifier.

> *Examples:*
> CA NAC ANC-C2358
> US LC 72-064568
> MY P/AMM Z4
> MY MS ANM P/PESU.H.C.O 410/1915
> FR AD 53/234 J

### 3.1.2 Title

*Purpose:*
To name the unit of description.
*Rules:*
When the unit of description bears a formal title, transcribe it exactly as to wording, order and spelling but not necessarily as to punctuation and capitalization.

> ### Examples:
> Account of occurrences at Peace River 1832
>
> *Hue and cry* and *Police Gazette* 1828–1842
>
> Shipments of rubber for Italy and France
>
> Société ardoisière de l'Anjou. Exploitation de Renazé (Mayenne)
>
> Fonds Perret
>
> Fonds Hennebique

If appropriate, abridge a long formal title, but only if this can be done without loss of essential information.

*Alternatively*, compose a concise title. At the fonds level, include the name of the creator. At lower levels include, for example, the name of the creator and a term indicating the form of the material comprising the unit of description and, where appropriate, a phrase reflecting function, activity, subject, location, or theme.

Distinguish between formal and supplied titles according to national or language conventions.

> ### Examples:
> Minute books of the Women's Christian Temperance Movement
>
> Letters of Presbyterian missionaries serving in Manitoba
>
> Videotapes of Ronald Reagan's campaign speeches
>
> Records of the Coast and Geodetic Survey
> *(Fonds level title)*
> > Records of the Office of the Superintendent
> > *(Sub-fonds level title)*
> > > Letters sent
> > > Letters received
> > > Drafts of Annual Reports to the Congress
> > > *(Series level titles)*

Draft of the First Report
*(File level title)*

Papers of the Rockefeller Family
*(Fonds level title)*
Papers of John D. Rockefeller, Sr.
*(Sub-fonds level title)*
Correspondence relating to business affairs
Correspondence relating to philanthropic activity
Personal correspondence
*(Series level titles)*
Letters to J. Pierpont Morgan
Letter to Theodore Roosevelt
*(Item level titles)*

### 3.1.3 Dates of creation of the material in the unit of description

*Purpose:*
To identify and record the date(s) of creation of the material in the unit of description.

*Rules:*
Give the dates of creation of the material in the unit of description as a single date or a range of dates as appropriate. A range of dates should always be inclusive unless the unit of description is a record-keeping system (or part thereof) in active use

*Examples:*
1900–1919
*(The New York State Joint Legislative Commission to investigate seditious activities operated and accumulated records from 1917 to 1919. The actual dates of the records within the series, however, are 1900–1919, reflecting the creation of the original documents collected as evidence in the commission's investigations)*

*[Compare approach in 3.2.3]*

23 Mar 1927

circa 1930

1858

before 1850

1907–1949

1907

21.2.1915–21.12.1915

*Optionally*, also record

(a) the predominant dates or significant gaps. Never enter predominant dates without inclusive dates.

*Examples:*
1703–1908 (predominant 1780–1835)
1923–1945 (lacking 1933 to 1935)

(b) date(s) for records in custody.

*Examples:*

**Contents:** 1703–1908      **Contents in custody:** 1703–1868
(predominant 1708–1835)

**Contents:** 1907–      **Contents in custody:** 1907–1958
(predominant 1930–  )      (predominant 1930–1958)

### 3.1.4 Level of description

*Purpose:*
To identify the level of arrangement of the unit of description.
*Rule:*
Record the level of this unit of description.

*Examples:*
Fonds

Series

Sub-series

File

Item

### 3.1.5 Extent of the unit of description (quantity, bulk, or size)

*Purpose:*
To identify and record

a. the physical extent and
b. the type of material of the unit of description.

*Rules:*

Record the extent of the unit of description by giving the number of physical units in arabic numerals and the specific unit designation appropriate for the broad class of material to which the unit of description belongs.

*Examples:*
2 film rolls

128 photographs

19 folders

25 volumes

20 enclosures

20 m (548 articles)

*Alternatively*, give the linear shelf space or cubic storage space of the unit of description.

*Example:*
300 boxes (30 m)

If the statement of extent for a unit of description is given in linear terms and additional information is desirable, add the additional information in parentheses.

*Example:*
4 m (ca. 10 200 items)

*Optionally*, where the unit of description is a record-keeping system (or part thereof) in active use, show

the known extent at a given date; and/or
the extent in custody.

*Example:*
128 photographs (at 6 Feb. 1990)    **In custody:** 58 photographs

## 3.2    *CONTEXT AREA*
*[Some of the information in this area, i.e., the name of the creator(s) and the administrative/biographical history, may, in certain applications, be accommodated in linked authority files. See I.8.]*

### 3.2.1  Name of creator
*Purpose:*
To identify the creator (or creators) of the unit of description.
*Rule:*
Name the organization (or organizations) or the individual (or individuals) responsible for the creation of the unit of description provided this information does not appear in the title.

### 3.2.2  Administrative/Biographical history
*Purpose:*
To provide an administrative history of, or biographical details on, the creator (or creators) of the unit of description to place the material in context and make it better understood.

*Rules:*

Record concisely any significant information on the origin, progress, development and work of the organization (or organizations) or on the life and work of the individual (or individuals) responsible for the creation of the unit of description. If additional information is available in a published source, cite the source.

For persons or families record information such as full names and titles, dates of birth and death, place of birth, successive places of domicile, activities, occupation or offices, original and any other names, significant accomplishments, and place of death.

### Example:

Louis Hémon was a French writer born at Brest, France in 1880. He died in Canada at Chapleau (Ont.) in 1913. He studied law at La Sorbonne in Paris. He spent eight years in England before going to Canada in 1911, where he lived in Montréal and on a farm at Péribonka (Lac Saint-Jean). In his short career, he wrote several books and articles. Hémon is famous for: *Maria Chapdelaine: récit du Canada français*, published for the first time in 1916.

For corporate bodies record information such as the official name, the dates of existence, enabling legislation, functions, purpose and development of the body, its administrative hierarchy, and earlier, variant or successive names.

### Examples:

The Freedmen's Bureau was established in the War Department 3 Mar. 1865, to supervise all activities relating to refugees and freedmen and to assume custody of all abandoned or confiscated lands or property. Abolished 10 June 1872, and remaining functions transferred to the Freedmen's Branch, Office of Adjutant General and after 1879, to the Colored Division of the Office of Adjutant General

The Kingston Steam Trawling Company was incorporated in 1891. Hellyer Bros acquired a majority shareholding in 19[?] and the company was absorbed into Associated Fisheries when Hellyer Bros merged with that company in 1961. It ceased trading in 1965 and was dissolved in 1972

La société ardoisière de l'Anjou a été constituée le 16 juillet 1894 par quatre actionnaires dans le but d'acquérir et d'exploiter plusieurs carrières en Maine-et-Loire (Trelazé et

Noyant-la-Gravoyère) et dans la Mayenne. L'acquisition des ardoisières de Renazé s'est étalée sur quatre ans: propriétaire de la carrière d'Ensuzières et actionnaire majoritaire de la Société de Laubinière (1894); propriétaire des ardoisières de la Touche et du Fresne (1895); propriétaire de Laubinière (1897). Victime de la concurrence espagnole vers 1960, la société ardoisière de l'Anjou a fermé son dernier puits à Renazé le 31 décembre 1975

### 3.2.3 Dates of accumulation of the unit of description

*Purpose:*
To supply date(s) of accumulation of the unit of description (e.g., series, file) by its creator.

*Rule:*
Give the date(s) of accumulation of the unit of description by the creator (or creators) as a single date or a range of dates. The date or dates recorded here refer to the record keeping actions of the creator (or creators) and may not antedate the date of establishment of the creating corporate body (or earliest creating corporate body) or the date of birth of the creating individual (or earliest creating individual) These dates may differ from the dates recorded at *3.1.3 Dates of creation of the material in the unit of description* in cases where the unit of description resulted from an activity involving accumulation of documents created prior to filing by the creator (or earliest creator), such as documents accumulated from a variety of sources during an investigation or legal action.

*Examples:*
1917–1919
*(The New York State Joint Legislative Commission to investigate seditious activities operated and accumulated records from 1917 to 1919. The actual dates of the records within the series, however, are 1900–1919, reflecting the creation of the original documents collected as evidence in the commission's investigations.)*
*[See also approach in 3.1.3]*

### 3.2.4 Custodial history

*Purpose:*
To provide information on changes of ownership and custody of the unit of description that is significant for its authenticity, integrity and interpretation.

*Rules:*

Record the successive transfers of ownership and/or custody of the unit of description, along with the dates thereof, insofar as they can be ascertained. If the custodial history is unknown, record that information.

*Optionally*, when the unit of description is acquired directly from the creator, do not record a custodial history but rather, record this information as the ***Immediate source of acquisition***. *(See 3.2.5)*

### Examples:

The Ocean Falls Corporation records remained in the custody of Pacific Mills Ltd., and its successor companies, until the mill and townsite were taken over by the British Columbia provincial government in 1973. In 1976 the records were transferred to the Ocean Falls Public Library, which began the rearrangement of the records in their current form

Originally collected by George Madison and arranged by his nephew, John Ferris, after Madison's death. Purchased by Henry Kapper in 1878 who added to the collection with materials purchased at auctions in Philadelphia and Paris, 1878–1893

Records inherited by Houghton Urban District Council in 1937 and later deposited at Durham Record Office. Transferred to Tyne and Wear Archives Service on 28 July 1976

Le fonds de l'exploitation de Renazé comprend, probablement depuis les années 1895–1897, deux fonds d'entreprises absorbées ceux de la société ardoisière de Laubinière et de l'ardoisière de la Touche, établissement Bourdais et Cie

### 3.2.5 Immediate source of acquisition

*Purpose:*

To record circumstances of the immediate source of acquisition.

*Rule:*

Record the donor or source from which the unit of description was acquired and the date and/or method of acquisition if any or all of this information is not confidential. If the source or donor is unknown, record that information. *Optionally*, add accession numbers or codes.

### Examples:

Transferred from Department of Geography, 16 June 1977

Donated by the sisters of Peter Neve Cotton, Mrs Mary Small of Saltspring Island and Mrs Patricia Jarvis of Bellevue, Washington, March 1983

Purchased at Sotheby's auction, 29 March 1977

The orderly books were transferred from Pension Office, 1909; the letter books were transferred from the State Department. 1915

Received from: Euroc AB, Malmö. Date of acquisition 1978–10–27

Transferred from the Selangor Secretariat, Sultan Abdul Samad Building, Kuala Lumpur, 1967

Don de la Société ardoisière de l'Anjou (exploitation de Renazé) aux Archives départementales de la Mayenne, 1969

## 3.3  CONTENT AND STRUCTURE AREA

### 3.3.1  Scope and content/Abstract
*Purpose:*
To identify the subject matter and the form of the unit of description to enable users to judge its potential relevance.
*Rule:*
Give a brief summary of the subject content (including time period) of the unit of description. Include information on form as appropriate for the particular level of description. Do not repeat here information already given elsewhere in the description.

*Examples:*
General policy files and registers of the Ministry of Health and the Ministry of Housing and Local Government relating to extinguishment of tithe rent charges. The files contain information about grants to local authorities, rates and rate refunds, and evidence submitted to the Royal Commission on Tithe Rent-charge in 1934. The registers contain records of payments of grants to various authorities from 1938 to 1955 under the Tithe Act 1936

High Commissioner's Office file relating to shipments of rubber for Italy and France. The file contains correspondence between the Secretary to F.M.S. and the Secretary to the High Commissioner's Office for the Malay States regarding rubber exports. This includes the name of the vessel, nationality, date of sailing, description of the item, quantity, destination, exporter, and the consignee

Ce fonds unique en Mayenne est susceptible d'intéresser tout à la fois l'histoire sociale, économique et industrielle du département. Il contient des documents très divers, des pièces comptables, de la correspondance, des plans, des papiers relatifs aux grèves, à la sécurité dans les mines, au groupement économique d'achat, à la Société de secours, etc. A titre d'exemple, la longue série constituée par les comptes rendus hebdomadaires de l'ingénieur relatifs à la marche de l'entreprise (1910–1930) constitue une source exceptionelle puisqu'il s'agit d'un véritable "journal de bord" de l'exploitation

### 3.3.2 Appraisal, destruction and scheduling information

*Purpose:*
To provide information on any appraisal, destruction and scheduling action taken.

*Rules:*
Record any appraisal actions taken on the unit of description if that action affects the interpretation of the material.

Where appropriate, record the authority by which the action has been taken.

#### Examples:
Files of every tenth year have been retained

All files are kept permanently under the National Archives of Malaysia ruling: "Permanent retention of records dated before 31.12.1948"

Très peu d'éliminations ont été effectuées au cours du classement de ce fonds: seuls les brouillons informes ou illisibles, les formulaires vierges ou en exemplaires multiples en ont fait l'objet. Globalement, ces éliminations n'ont pas dépassé la valeur d'une liasse

### 3.3.3 Accruals

*Purpose:*
To inform the user of possible changes in the extent of the unit of description.

*Rule:*
Indicate if future accruals, additional transfers or deposits are expected. Where appropriate, give an estimate of their quantity and frequency.

*Examples:*

Records from the Office of the Ceremonials Assistant are transferred to the archives five years following the academic year to
which the records relate. On average, 40 cm of records are
transferred to the archives annually on Aug. 1

Accruals are expected

### 3.3.4 System of arrangement

*Purpose:*

To provide information on the arrangement of the unit of description.

*Rule:*

Give information on the arrangement of the unit of description.
Specify the principal characteristics of the internal structure, the
order of the material and, if appropriate, how these have been treated
by the archivist.

*Examples:*

Records are maintained according to their original provenance,
the direct result of organizational activity of the organizing
body: the High Commissioner's Office

Files arranged alphabetically by file title. A subseries of 17 files
(numbered 163/1–17) depend on file 163, dealing with the
purchase of the Seaford Dock

Chronological/enclosure number within file

Le plan de classement adopté est le suivant: administration,
comptabilité et finances, personnel, fonctionnement, matériel
d'exploitation et outillage, propriétés immobilières, entreprises
absorbées

## 3.4   *CONDITIONS OF ACCESS AND USE AREA*

### 3.4.1 Legal status

*Purpose:*

To provide information on the legal status of the unit of description.

*Rule:*

Record information on the legal status of the unit of description.

*Examples:*

Public records transferred under section 4(1) of the Public
Records Act 1958

Transferred under the National Archives Act, No. 44/1966

Archives publiques consécutivement au don

### 3.4.2 Access conditions

*Purpose:*

To identify any conditions that restrict or affect access to the unit of description.

*Rule:*

Give information on conditions that restrict or affect access to the unit of description. Indicate the extent of the period of closure and the date at which the material will open.

> ### *Examples:*
> No access may be given to the material without the written permission of the director of the firm
>
> Family correspondence closed until 2010
>
> All records subject to Access to Information and Privacy Act
>
> No access until microfilmed
>
> Accessible to all registered researchers
>
> La majorité des documents contenus dans ce fonds est librement consultable. Néanmoins, la communication de certains dossiers relatifs au personnel est soumise à des conditions ou à des délais de consultation particuliers

### 3.4.3 Copyright/Conditions governing reproduction

*Purpose:*

To identify any restrictions on the use or reproduction of the unit of description.

*Rule:*

Give information about conditions governing the use or the reproduction of the unit of description after access has been provided. If conditions governing use, reproduction or publication in respect to the unit of description are unknown or if there are no conditions, no statement is necessary.

> ### *Examples:*
> Rights held by CHYZ-TV
>
> No reproduction without permission of the president of the company
>
> Photographs may be copied for reference purposes only. Use of

photographs in a publication cannot be made without written permission of Kenneth McAllister

Malaysia Copyright Act of 1987 records in public domain, reproduction with permission of the National Archives of Malaysia

### 3.4.4 Language of material

*Purpose:*
To identify the language(s), scripts and symbol systems employed in the unit of description.
*Rule:*
Record the predominant language(s) of the materials comprising the unit of description. Note any distinctive alphabets, scripts, symbol systems or abbreviations employed.

> *Examples:*
> In Portuguese
>
> Main text in Latin; endorsements in Norman French
>
> In English
>
> Français

### 3.4.5 Physical characteristics

*Purpose:*
To provide information about any important physical characteristics that affect use of the unit of description.
*Rule:*
Indicate any important physical details and/or the permanent physical condition of the material that limits use of the unit of description.

> *Examples:*
> Images faded
>
> Legible under ultraviolet light only

### 3.4.6 Finding aids

*Purpose:*
To identify any finding aids to the unit of description.
*Rule:*
Give information about any finding aids that the repository or records creator may have that provide information relating to the contents of the unit of description. If appropriate, include information on where to obtain a copy.

*Examples:*
Box list

Detailed finding aid available; file level control

Finding aid: Records of Parks Canada (RG84) / Gabrielle Blais. – (General inventory series / Federal Archives Division). – Ottawa: Public Archives of Canada, 1985

Geographical index

Correspondence index to 1880

Descriptive Lists, High Commissioner's Office Records

Répertoire numérique du fonds 234 J. Société ardoisière de l'Anjou. Exploitation de Renazé / Isabelle LAS. – (Archives du pays bleu / Archives départementales de la Mayenne). – Laval: Archives départementales de la Mayenne, 1922. Comprend notamment un glossaire des termes techniques de l'industrie ardoisière

## 3.5 ALLIED MATERIALS AREA

### 3.5.1 Location of originals
*Purpose:*
To identify the repository, corporate body or individual which holds the originals if the unit of description is a reproduction.
*Rule:*
If the unit of description is a reproduction, and another repository, corporate body or individual holds the originals, record their name if the information is not confidential. Give also any identifying numbers and other information that mav help in locating the original material. If the originals are known to be no longer extant, give that information.

*Examples:*
Original in National Archives of Canada, C2358

Originals destroyed after microfilming, 1981

Originals retained by the Society of Friends, Newcastle upon Tyne (access by permission from the Secretary)

Originals in Headquarters, National Archives of Malaysia

### 3.5.2 Existence of copies

*Purpose:*

To indicate the existence and availability of copies of the unit of description.

*Rule:*

If the unit of description is available (either in the institution or elsewhere) in another format, record the formats, together with any significant control numbers and the location where they may be consulted.

> *Examples:*
> Diaries and correspondence also available on microfilm
>
> Films also available on videocassette

### 3.5.3 Related units of description

*Purpose:*

To identify related units of description in the same repository.

*Rule:*

If the unit of description consists of material that has a direct and significant connection to another unit of description, indicate the relationship. Use appropriate introductory wording. If the related unit of description is a finding aid, use the *Finding aids* element of description (3.4.6) to make the reference to it.

> *Examples:*
> These include many stray medieval accounts similar to material in E101 and SC6
>
> For further documents concerning the Queen's Jointure see LR5
>
> Related series: In-letters from the Office of the General Manager
>
> Files related to trades, rubber exports, etc., e.g., Export of rubber – S of S 116/15; Export of rubber to Italy and France – H.C.O. 288/15; Shipment of rubber approved by Rubber Export Committee – S of S 388/15; Agriculture Bulletin – Misc. 390/15; Exportation of rubber to Canada – S of S 402/15; Rubber shipment: 7 ton from Harrison and Crossfield to Alcan & Co., Paris, in June – S of S 938/15; Shipment of rubber to New York per SS Indrawadi on 6.9.1915 – H.C.O. 1981/15
>
> Sources complémentaires mentionnées dans l'instrument de recherche imprimé

### 3.5.4 Associated material

*Purpose:*

To indicate the existence in other repositories of material associated by provenance to the unit of description.

*Rule:*

If material in another repository has a relationship by provenance to the unit of description, provide information about the associated material and the repository.

#### Examples:

Ernest Bruckler fonds held by the Public Archives of Nova Scotia

Files relating to trades, customs and excise, rubber exports, estimates, annual reports, etc. at the National Archives of Malaysia Branch Offices

Sources complémentaires mentionnées dans l'instrument de recherche imprimé

### 3.5.5 Publication note

*Purpose:*

To identify any publications that are based on the use, study, or analysis of the unit of description.

*Rule:*

Record a citation to, and/or information about, a publication that is based on the use, study, or analysis of the unit of description.

#### Examples:

Bibliographie dans l'instrument de recherche

Folios 23–24 published in *Chronicon Petriburgense* ed. T Stapleton (1849), pp. 176–182

## 3.6   *NOTE AREA*

### 3.6.1 Note

*Purpose:*

To provide specialized information and information that cannot be accommodated in any of the other areas.

*Rule:*

Record specialized or other important information not accommodated by any of the defined elements of description.

## APPENDIX

A1  The model shows some typical situations and does not include all possible combinations of levels.

A2  Any number of intermediate levels are possible between any shown in the model.

### Model of the levels of arrangement of a fonds

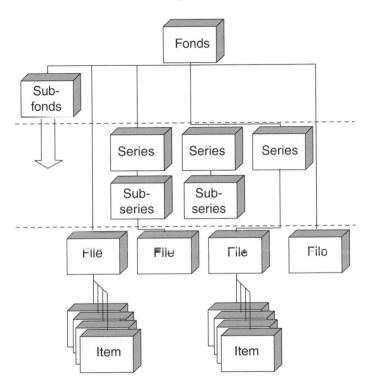

Ad Hoc Commission on Descriptive Standards
(Members shown without service years have been on the Commission from its inception in 1990.)

Christopher J Kitching, *Chair*, United Kingdom
Hugo LP Stibbe, *Project Director*, Canada

Ghislain Brunel (1990–1991), France
Michael Cook, United Kingdom
Jan Dahlin, Sweden
Wendy Duff, Canada

Ana Franqueira, Portugal
Pedro Gonzales (1990–1992), Spain
Chris Hurley (1992–   ), Australia
Christine Nougaret (1992–   ), France
Christine Petillat (1991–1992), France
Sharon G Thibodeau, United States
Habibah Zon Yahaya, Malaysia

Charles Kecskeméti, *Secretary-General ICA*
Wolf Buchmann, *Secretary on Technical Matters, Representative of the ICA Secretariat*
Axel Plathe, *Representative Unesco PGI*

**Secretariat**
c/o National Archives of Canada, Office of Archival Standards, 395 Wellington Street, Ottawa, Ont. K1A 0N3, Canada. Telephone +.1.613.996.7592, Fax: +.1.613.995.2267.
E-Mail: 70550.3371@compuserve.com (Internet).

# Appendix 4

# *ISAD(G)*/EAD/*MAD3* mapping[1]

*ISAD(G)* and *EAD* are described in Sections 9.11A and 9.11E. This table lists all the *ISAD(G)* elements, mapped to the equivalent EAD tags and *MAD3* sub-areas or data elements. The table is included as a reference source to help with preparation for retroconversion, data exchange or other automated network initiatives.

| *ISAD(G)* | EAD | *MAD3 Sub-area*/data element |
|---|---|---|
| 3.1.1 Reference code | \<unitid\> countrycode and repositorycode attributes | *14.2A  Reference code* |
| 3.1.2 Title | \<unittitle\> | *14.2B  Title* |
| 3.1.3 Dates of creation | \<unitdate\> | *14.2C  Simple or span dates* |
| 3.1.4 Level of description | \<archdesc\> and \<c\> level attributes | *14.2D  Level number* |
| 3.1.5 Extent of the unit | \<physdesc\>, \<extent\> | *14.2E  Extent and physical character* |
| 3.2.1 Name of creator | \<origination\> | *14.3A  Admin/biographical history* |

---

[1] The *ISAD(G)*/EAD tag mapping is taken from the *Encoded Archival Description Application Guidelines Version 1.0 Prepared by the EAD Working Group of the Society of American Archivists*, SAA, Chicago, 1999, Appendix B1, and is reproduced with permission of the SAA.

| *ISAD(G)* | EAD | *MAD3, Sub-area*/data element |
|---|---|---|
| 3.2.2  Admin/biographical history | \<bioghist\> | *14.3A  Admin/biographical history* |
| 3.2.3  Dates of accumulation | \<custodhist\>\<date type= ''accumulation''\> | *14.3A  Admin/biographical history* |
| 3.2.4  Custodial history | \<custodhist\> | *14.3B  Custodial history* |
| 3.2.5  Immediate source of acquisition | \<acqinfo\> | *14.3B  Custodial history* |
| 3.3.1  Scope and content | \<scopecontent\> | *14.4A  Scope and content/ Abstract* |
| 3.3.2  Appraisal, destruction and scheduling | \<appraisal\> | *14.4D*  Appraisal principle |
| 3.3.3  Accruals | \<accruals\> | *14.7A*  Accruals |
| 3.3.4  System of arrangement | \<arrangement\> | *14.4D*  System of arrangement |
| 3.4.1  Legal status | \<archdesc\> legalstatus attribute | No *MAD3* analogue[2] |
| 3.4.2  Access conditions | \<accessrestrict\> | *14.5A*  Access conditions |
| 3.4.3  Copyright/ reproduction | \<userestrict\> | *14.5A*  Copying conditions *14.5A*  Copyright information |
| 3.4.4  Language of material | \<archdesc\> langmaterial attribute | *14.4B*  Predominant language |
| 3.4.5  Physical characteristics | \<physdesc\> \<physfacet\> | *14.4C  Physical description* |
| 3.4.6  Finding aids | \<otherfindaid\> | *14.5C*  Finding aids |
| 3.5.1  Location of originals | \<odd\> | *14.5C  Allied materials* |
| 3.5.2  Existence of copies | \<altformavail\> | *14.5C*  Existence of copies |

[2]  In British archival practice, 'Legal status' in the sense used by *ISAD(G)* is usually recorded at management level where a distinction may be made between Public Records and other types of records.

| *ISAD(G)* | **EAD** | *MAD3, Sub-area*/data element |
|---|---|---|
| 3.5.3 Related unit of description | <relatedmaterial> | *14.5C* Related material |
| 3.5.4 Associated material | <separatedmaterial> | *14.5C* Related material |
| 3.5.5 Publication note | | *14.5B Publication record* |
| 3.6.1 Note | <odd> | *14.4D Archivist's note* |

# Index